MacBook® Pro

PORTABLE GENIUS

MacBook® Pro

PORTABLE GENIUS

by Brad Miser

WILEY

Wiley Publishing, Inc.

MacBook® Pro Portable Genius

Published by
Wiley Publishing, Inc.
10475 Crosspoint Blvd.
Indianapolis, IN 46256
www.wiley.com

Copyright © 2009 by Wiley Publishing, Inc., Indianapolis, Indiana

Published simultaneously in Canada

ISBN: 978-0-470-29170-2

Manufactured in the United States of America

10 9 8 7 6 5 4 3 2

For general information on our other products and services or to obtain technical support, please contact our Customer Care Department within the U.S. at (800) 762-2974, outside the U.S. at (317) 572-3993 or fax (317) 572-4002.

Wiley also publishes its books in a variety of electronic formats. Some content that appears in print may not be available in electronic books.

Library of Congress Control Number: 2008929125

WILEY

About the Author

Brad Miser has written more than 25 books, with his favorite topics being anything related to Macintosh computers or starting with "i" such as iTunes, iPhones, and iPods. In addition to *MacBook Portable Genius*, Brad has written *Teach Yourself Visually MacBook*; *MacBook Portable Genius*; *My iPhone*; *Absolute Beginner's Guide to iPod and iTunes*; *Sleeping with the Enemy: Running Windows on a Mac*; and *Special Edition Using Mac OS X Leopard*. He has also been co-author, development editor, or technical editor on more than 50 other titles.

Brad has been a solutions consultant, the director of product and customer services, and the manager of education and support services for several software development companies.

In addition to his passion for silicon-based technology, Brad enjoys his steel-based technology, AKA motorcycles, whenever and wherever possible. Originally from California, Brad now lives in Indiana with his wife Amy; their three daughters, Jill, Emily, and Grace; and a rabbit named Bun-Bun.

Brad would love to hear about your experiences with this book (the good, the bad, and the ugly). You can write to him at bradmacosx@mac.com.

Credits

Senior Acquisitions Editor
Stephanie McComb

Project Editor
Chris Wolfgang

Technical Editor
Griff Partington

Copy Editor
Marylouise Wiack

Editorial Manager
Robyn B. Siesky

Vice President & Group Executive Publisher
Richard Swadley

Vice President & Publisher
Barry Pruett

Business Manager
Amy Knies

Senior Marketing Manager
Sandy Smith

Project Coordinator
Kristie Rees

Graphics and Production Specialists
Stacie Brooks
Ana Carillo
Jennifer Henry
Andrea Hornberger

Quality Control Technician
Laura Albert

Proofreading
Shannon Ramsey

Indexing
Broccoli Information Management

Acknowledgments

Thanks to Stephanie McComb with whom this project had its genesis and who allowed me to be involved. Chris Wolfgang deserves lots of credit for keeping the project on track and on target; I'm sure working with me was a challenge at times. Griff Partington did a great job of keeping me on my toes to make sure this book contains fewer technical gaffs than it would have without his help. Marylouise Wiack transformed my stumbling, bumbling text into something people can read and understand. Thanks also to my agent, Marta Justak, for managing the business of the project and being a support for me during the writing process. Lastly, thanks to all the people on the Wiley team who handle the other, and equally important, parts of the process, such as production, sales, proofreading, and indexing.

On my personal team, I'd like to thank my wife Amy for her tolerance of the author lifestyle, which is both odd and challenging. My delightful daughters Jill, Emily, and Grace are always a source of joy and inspiration for all that I do, and for which I'm ever grateful.

Dedication

The probability that we may fall in the struggle ought not to deter us from the support of a cause we believe to be just; it shall not deter me.

—Abraham Lincoln

Contents

chapter 3

How Can I Connect a MacBook Pro to the Internet? 56

chapter 4

What Can I Do on a Local Network? 78

chapter 5

How Do I Take Advantage of MobileMe? 98

chapter 6

How Can I Manage Contact Information?   118

chapter 7

How Can I Go Beyond E-mail Basics with Mail?   134

Introduction

From its distinctive silver metallic finish to its backlit keyboard, dazzling display, and inviting design, the MacBook Pro is amazing technology that looks as great as it works. Running Mac OS X and including lots of amazing software, MacBook Pros let you do more out of the box more easily than any other computer. In fact, MacBook Pros do so much, it is easy to overlook some of the great things they can do. That's where this book comes in.

While you probably already know how to turn your MacBook Pro on, you might not know how to use Spaces to create virtual working spaces on the desktop so that you can keep many applications and windows open at the same time and move among them easily. While you likely know how to use the trackpad to point to objects on the screen to select them, you might not know how to create your own keyboard shortcuts for just about any command in any application that you use. While you have probably browsed the Web before, you might not have taken advantage of some of Safari's really cool, but not so obvious, features to make your travels on the Web better.

The purpose of this book is to provide a resource for you when you are wondering how to do something better, how to do it more easily, or even how to do it at all. You'll find that each chapter is organized around a question. Within each chapter are answers to its question; these answers are task-focused so you learn by doing rather than by just reading. The steps you'll find are very specific and, hopefully, quite complete; if you start at step 1 and work through each step in sequence, you'll end up someplace you want to go. Thus, the book's title of *Portable Genius*; it is intended to be your companion to guide you on your in-depth exploration of your MacBook Pro. Once you've been through a topic's steps, you'll be prepared to go even further by extending what you've learned to other tasks.

We've designed this book to provide a broad range of topics in which most MacBook Pro users will be interested. There's no particular order to the topics in this book so you can jump to any chapter without having read the proceeding ones. To get started, I recommend that you take a look at the table of contents and decide which question you'd like answered first. Turn the appropriate page and off you go!

How Can I Use My Desktop Space Efficiently?

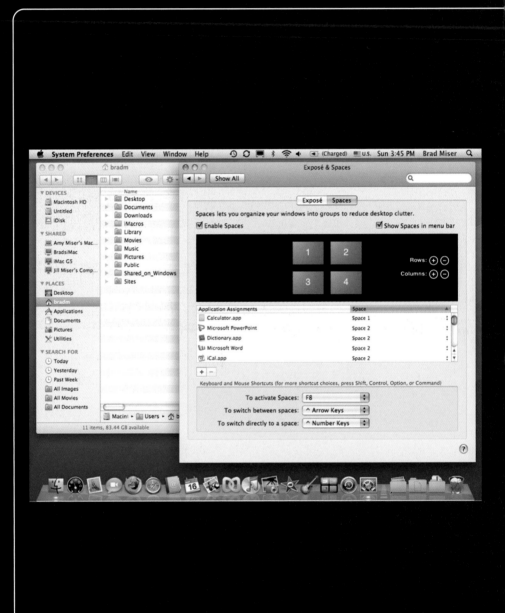

Your MacBook Pro desktop is the area that is displayed on its screen. Like a physical desktop, you place things (in this case, windows) "on top" to focus your attention on them and use their content. As you work, your desktop naturally becomes cluttered with windows for applications, documents, and system tools. Keeping control of all these windows can help you make the most of your MacBook Pro desktop space. The good news is that it's a lot easier to keep your MacBook Pro desktop neat and tidy than it is a real desktop, and you don't even need a dust rag.

Setting Desktop Preferences

You can configure your desktop so it appears the way you want it to. You can control some of the icons that appear on it by default, and you can configure the image that fills your desktop.

Setting Finder desktop icon preferences

By default, icons for your MacBook Pro hard drive, external hard drives, DVDs and CDs, and servers appear on the desktop. This is okay if that is your preference, but they take up space on the desktop that isn't really necessary because you can get to these elements even more easily by opening a Finder window and using the Sidebar. To hide these icons, perform the following steps:

1. **Select Finder ⇨ Preferences.** The Finder Preferences dialog appears.

2. **Click the General tab if it isn't selected already**.

3. **Uncheck each check box if you don't want to see the icon for items of that type on your desktop.** For example, to hide the icon for the MacBook Pro hard disk, uncheck the Hard disks check box (see figure 1.1). As you uncheck the check boxes, the related icons disappear from your desktop.

Setting desktop pictures

I confess that this section has nothing to do with efficiency whatsoever. However, there's more to life than being efficient. Since you stare at your desktop so much, you might as well have something interesting to look at, which is where desktop pictures come in.

You can set any image to be your desktop picture. The images you can use as your desktop

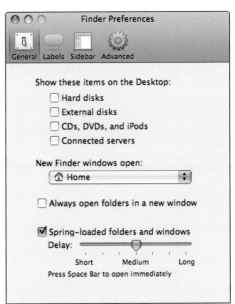

1.1 If you uncheck the four check boxes in the Show these items on the Desktop section, your desktop immediately becomes less cluttered.

include the default images that are included with Mac OS X, image files you create or download from the Internet, and, best of all, photos from your iPhoto Library. You can also configure your MacBook Pro so that the desktop picture changes over time to keep it even more interesting.

To configure your desktop pictures, perform the following steps:

1. **Open the Applications folder and double-click the System Preferences icon.** The System Preferences application opens.

2. **Click the Desktop & Screen Saver icon.** The Desktop & Screen Saver pane appears.

3. **Click the Desktop tab.** The Desktop picture tools appear. On the lower-left side of the pane are the sources of images from which you can select pictures for your desktop, such as black and white images, abstract pictures, or photographs from your iPhoto albums.

Genius

You can use any folder as a source of desktop pictures by clicking the Add (+) button located at the bottom of the source list. Use the resulting dialog to move to and select the folder containing the images you want to use.

4. **Select a source of images in the left pane of the window, such as an iPhoto album.** Thumbnails of the images in that source appear in the right pane of the window.

5. **Click the image that you want to apply to the desktop.** The image fills the desktop and you see it in the image well at the top of the Desktop pane (see figure 1.2).

1.2 Here, I've selected an event called yosemite, and I can see the photos associated with that event.

5

6. **If the selected source is iPhoto Albums, use the pop-up menu at the top of the window to choose how you want photos to be scaled to the screen.**

7. **If the image doesn't fill the screen, click the Color button that appears to the right of the menu when it can be used.**

8. **When it appears, use the Color Picker to choose the background color that appears behind photos when they don't fill the desktop.**

9. **To have the image change automatically, check the Change picture check box.**

10. **On the pop-up menu, choose how often you want the picture to change.**

11. **If you want images to be selected randomly instead of by the order in which they appear in the source, check the Random order check box.** A new image from the selected source is applied to the desktop according to the timing you selected.

12. **To have the menu bar be translucent so you can see the desktop picture behind it, check the Translucent Menu Bar check box.** With this option unchecked, the menu bar becomes a solid color.

13. **Quit the System Preferences application.** Enjoy your desktop!

Working with the Dock

The Dock is an important part of your desktop space. By default, it appears at the bottom of the desktop, but you can control many aspects of its appearance, where it is located, and, to a great degree, how it works. The Dock is organized into two general sections. The area to the left of the application/document separation line (the white, dashed line) contains application icons. On the right side of the line, you see icons for documents, folders, minimized Finder, document, or minimized application windows, and the Trash/Eject icon.

When folders appear on the Dock, they become stacks by default. When you click a stack, it pops up into a fan or appears as a grid (depending on how many items are in the folder) so that you can work with items it contains (see figure 1.3). You can disable this feature for any folder so that it behaves more like a normal folder (more on that shortly).

The Dock performs the following functions:

- **Shows running applications.** Whenever an application is running, you see its icon on the Dock. A small glowing light is located at the bottom of every running application's icon.

- **Enables you to open applications, folders, minimized windows, and documents quickly.**

- **Enables you to quickly switch among open applications and windows.**

Genius

To move between applications quickly, press ⌘+Tab or ⌘+Shift+Tab. The Application Switcher appears. Click an icon to move into the associated application, or keep pressing the keys to cycle through the list; when you release the keys, you move into the selected application.

⊚ **Gets your attention.** When an application needs your attention, its icon bounces on the Dock until you move into that application and handle whatever the issue is.

⊚ **Enables you to customize its appearance and function.** You can store the icon for any item (applications, folders, and documents) on the Dock. You can control how the Dock looks, including its size, whether it is always visible, where it is located, and which applications, folder, and documents appear on it.

Two icons on the Dock are unique and are always on the Dock: the Finder and the Trash. When you click the Finder icon (anchored on the left end of a horizontal Dock or at the top of a vertical one), a Finder window opens if none is currently open. The Trash icon is where all folders and files go when their time is done. When the Trash contains files or folders, its icon includes crumpled paper so that you know the Trash is full (see figure 1.4).

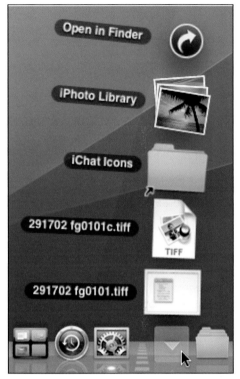

1.3 Clicking a folder's (or stack's) icon on the Dock causes it to fan out.

Unlike open applications, open documents don't automatically appear on the Dock. Document icons appear on the Dock only when you add them to the Dock manually or when you have minimized a document's window. When you minimize a window, by default, the window moves into the Dock using the Genie Effect; it is pulled down into the Dock and becomes an icon that is a thumbnail view of the window. To open (or maximize) a minimized window, click its icon on the Dock, and it is pulled back onto the desktop.

1.4 At least this trash doesn't smell when it is full.

7

Note When you select an ejectable item, such as a DVD, the Trash icon changes to the Eject symbol. You can drag a disc or other ejectable item onto the icon to eject it.

Note When you hide an application, its open windows do not appear on the Dock. The hidden application's icon continues to be marked so that you know that the application is running.

Configuring the Dock's contents

The Dock gets even more useful when you organize it to suit your preferences. You can move icons around the Dock, add more applications to it, remove applications that are currently on it, and add your own folders and documents to it so that they are easily accessible.

Configuring and organizing application icons on the Dock

To add an application's icon to the Dock, simply drag it from a Finder window and drop it onto the location on the Dock where you want it to be stored (see figure 1.5). Application icons must be placed on the left side of the dividing line. When you add an application icon to the Dock, an alias to the application is created; like the default application icons, you can click the icon to open the application and Ctrl+click its icon to open its Dock menu.

1.5 Because I frequently use Firefox, I've added its icon to my Dock.

Genius You can add multiple items to the Dock at the same time by holding down the ⌘ key while you select each item you want to add to the Dock, and then dragging them there.

You can remove an application icon from the Dock by dragging it up onto the desktop and releasing the trackpad button. When you do this, the icon disappears in a puff of digital smoke and no longer appears on the Dock. Because the icons on the Dock are aliases, removing them doesn't affect the applications that those aliases represent.

Note The Dock has two icons that you can't move at all: Finder and Trash/Eject. Other than these two end points, you can change all the other icons on the Dock as much as you like. You can't change the location of the dividing line; it moves to the left or to the right, based on the number of icons on each side of it.

Configuring and organizing stacks on the Dock

When you place a folder's icon on the Dock, it becomes a stack. A stack has some special character-istics, which is why it isn't just called a folder (however, you can configure a stack to behave like a folder). Two stacks are installed on your Dock by default: the Downloads and Documents stacks. You can add any other folders to the Dock just as you add applications to the Dock; simply drag their icons onto the Dock and drop them where you want them to be placed. All folder/stack icons appear to the right of the dividing line. You can also reorganize the stack icons by dragging them around on the Dock.

When you click a stack's icon, its contents fan onto the desktop if there are a few of them, or open into a grid if there are many. You can access an item on the fan or grid by clicking it. You can open the folder's contents in a Finder window by clicking Open in Finder.

You can also configure how an individual stack's icon behaves by using its contextual menu. Ctrl+click the stack icon, and the menu appears (see figure 1.6).

The options you have are:

- **Sort by.** Choose the attribute by which you want the items in the stack to be sorted. For example, choose Date Added to have the most recently added content appear at the bottom of the fan (if the stack is set to fan, of course).

- **Display as.** Select Stack to have the icon look like a stack, or Folder to replace the stack icon with the folder's icon. The only difference is that when you select Folder, you always see the folder's icon on the Dock, as opposed to the icon of the most recently added item, which is what you see when Stack is selected.

- **View content as.** Select Fan to see the default fan layout for the stack (until it contains too many items, at which point it uses the grid instead). Select Grid to have the folder's contents appear in a grid. Select List to display the contents in a list that looks similar

1.6 Stack icons have many configuration options.

9

to a mini-Finder window (see figure 1.7); this is very useful for folders that contain sub-folders because you can select a folder to move into it on another hierarchical menu. Select Automatic to have the Mac OS select the view that is most appropriate, based on the folder's contents.

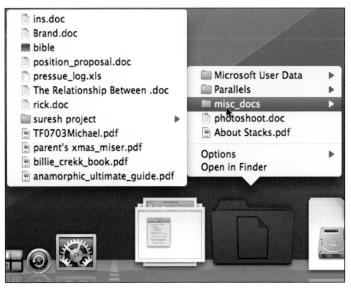

1.7 Setting a stack to be viewed as a list makes sub-folders available through hierarchical menus.

Configuring the Dock's appearance and behavior

The Dock offers several behaviors you can change to suit your preferences. You can also change various aspects of its appearance, as follows:

1. **Choose Apple menu ⇨ System Preferences.**

2. **Click the Dock icon.** The Dock pane appears.

3. **Drag the Size slider to the right to make the default Dock larger, or to the left to make it smaller.** This impacts only the size of the Dock when no applications that aren't installed on it are open and no windows are currently minimized. The Dock changes size automatically as you open applications and minimize windows, but this setting does change its starting size.

4. **Check the Magnification check box if you want to magnify an area of the Dock when you point to it.** This can make identifying items easier, especially when many items are on the Dock or when it is small.

5. **If you use magnification, drag the Magnification slider to the right to increase the level of magnification, or to the left to decrease it.**

6. **Select the position of the Dock on the desktop by clicking Left, Bottom (default), or Right.**

Note

When your MacBook Pro is connected to an external display, the Dock always appears on the primary display (see Chapter 13).

7. **On the Minimize using pop-up menu, select Genie Effect to have windows be pulled down to the Dock when you minimize them, or Scale Effect to have them shrink down into the Dock.**

8. **By default, application icons bounce as the application opens; if you don't want this to happen, uncheck the Animate opening applications check box.**

9. **If you want the Dock to be hidden automatically when you aren't pointing to it, check the Automatically hide and show the Dock check box.** If you set the Dock so that it is hidden except when you point to it, you can use more of your display. When this behavior is enabled and you point to the Dock's location, it pops onto the desktop and you can use it. When you move off the Dock, it is hidden again.

Genius

You can turn Hiding on or off by pressing Option+⌘+D.

10. **Quit the System Preferences application.**

Note

All Dock settings are specific to each user account (see Chapter 2). One user's Dock settings do not affect any other user's Dock.

Working with the Sidebar and Toolbar

Much of the time that you are working on your desktop will involve Finder windows. Two areas of Finder windows that you will use frequently are the Sidebar and the Toolbar. You can use these features as they are, but you can also customize them to make your desktop activities more efficient.

Using and configuring the Sidebar

The Finder's Sidebar makes it easy to get to specific locations; in many ways, the Sidebar is similar to the Dock. It comes with a number of default locations, but you can add items to or remove them from the Sidebar so that it contains the items you use most frequently.

The Sidebar is organized into sections (see figure 1.8). DEVICES includes disks and other devices (including iPods and your iDisk) that are mounted on your MacBook Pro. SHARED items include those you are accessing on a network. PLACES contains folders and files. SEARCH FOR displays saved searches.

1.8 Use the Sidebar to quickly move to items that you want to view in a Finder window.

Using the Sidebar

Using the items on the Sidebar is simple (which is why the Sidebar is so useful). Simply click the icon with which you want to work. What happens when you click depends on the kind of icon you clicked.

You can expand or collapse any of the sections on the Sidebar by clicking the triangle located next to the section title. When expanded, you see all the contents of that section. When collapsed, you only see the section title.

Configuring the Sidebar

You can customize the Sidebar so that it has the content you want. Here's how:

1. **Choose Finder ⇨ Preferences.** The Finder Preferences window appears.

2. **Click the Sidebar tab (see figure 1.9).**

3. **Check the check box for each item that you want to appear on the Sidebar.**

4. **Uncheck the check box for any items that you don't want to appear on the Sidebar.**

5. **Close the Finder Preferences window.**

6. **Open a Finder window.**

7. **To remove an item from the Sidebar, drag it from the Sidebar and release the trackpad button when you've moved the item off the Sidebar.** It disappears in a puff of smoke. Like the Dock, when you remove something from the Sidebar, it's not removed from the computer. The item remains in its current location on your MacBook Pro, but it is no longer accessible from the Sidebar.

8. **To add something to the Sidebar, drag it from a Finder window or desktop onto the Sidebar.**

9. **When you're over the location in which you want to place the item, release the trackpad button.** The item's icon is added to the Sidebar, and you can use it just like the default items.

10. **To change the order of items in the Sidebar, drag them up or down the list.** You can only move items around within their sections.

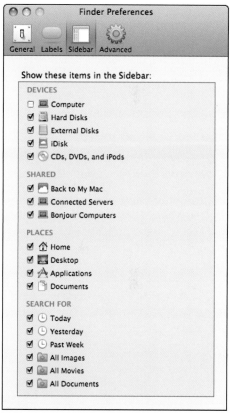

1.9 You can determine the kinds of resources that are available on your Sidebar by setting the appropriate preferences.

Using and configuring the Toolbar

The Toolbar appears at the top of the Finder window and contains buttons and pop-up menus that you can use to access commands quickly and easily. It includes a number of default buttons and pop-up menus, but you can configure the toolbar so that it contains the tools you use most frequently.

Using the Toolbar

When you open a Finder window, the Toolbar appears at the top of the window. The default tools on the Toolbar (as grouped from left to right) are:

- **Back/Forward buttons.** These buttons move you along the hierarchy of Finder windows that you've moved through, just like Back and Forward buttons in a Web browser.

- **View buttons.** You can change the view of the current window by clicking one of the View buttons. For example, to see the window in List view, click the second button in the View group (its icon has horizontal lines).

- **Quick Look/Slideshow button.** When something in the window is selected and you click this button, you see a quick view of the item (such as a thumbnail of an image file) or a slide show if you have selected multiple items.

- **Action pop-up menu.** This menu contains a number of useful contextual commands (meaning the specific commands on the menu depend on the item or items you have selected). These commands are the same as those that appear when you Ctrl+click an item.

- **Search bar.** You can search for items on the desktop by typing text or numbers into the Search bar. As you type, items that match your search term appear in the Finder window.

Genius

You can hide the Sidebar and Toolbar by clicking the Hide Toolbar/Sidebar button located in the upper-right corner of Finder windows. The Sidebar and Toolbar disappear and you only see the "inside" of the Finder window. To restore these elements, click the button again.

Configuring the Toolbar

You can place the tools you prefer on your Toolbar by performing the following steps:

1. **Open a Finder window.**

2. **Choose View ⇨ Customize Toolbar.** The Toolbar Customization sheet appears (see figure 1.10).

Drag your favorite items into the toolbar...

◀ ▶	⩵ ▼	⠿ ≣ ▥ ▥	✱ ▼
Back	Path	View	Action
⏏	⚫	⚒	┆
Eject	Burn	Customize	Separator
☐	◀┈▶	📁	⊘
Space	Flexible Space	New Folder	Delete
ⓦ	ⓘ	▤	Ⓠ
Connect	Get Info	iDisk	Search
◉			
Quick Look			

... or drag the default set into the toolbar.

◀ ▶	⠿ ≣ ▥ ▥	◉	✱ ▼	Ⓠ
Back	View	Quick Look	Action	Search

Show [Icon Only ↕] ☐ Use Small Size   (Done)

1.10 Use the Toolbar Customization sheet to define the tools on your Toolbar and to organize them.

3. **To remove a button from the Toolbar, drag its icon from the Toolbar onto the desktop.**
   When you release the trackpad button, the button disappears in a puff of smoke. The button
   continues to be available on the sheet if you want to add it again later.

4. **To add a button to the Toolbar, drag it from the sheet and drop it on the Toolbar at the
   location in which you want to place it.** When you release the trackpad button, the button
   is added to the Toolbar.

5. **When you're done customizing the Toolbar, click Done.** The Toolbar Customization sheet
   closes and you see your customized Toolbar.

Genius

To return the Toolbar to its default state, open the Toolbar Customization sheet and
drag the default set of buttons onto the Toolbar.

Working with Exposé

As you work on documents, move to Web sites, check your e-mail, choose tunes to listen to, and all
the other things you do while using your MacBook Pro, you can accumulate a lot of open windows
on your desktop. This is a good thing because it makes it easy to multi-task so that you don't have

to stop one activity to start another. The downside is that it's easy to lose track of where a specific window you want might be located, or you might have a hard time getting back to the desktop.

Exposé is the Mac OS X feature that helps you manage screen clutter from open windows. It has three modes:

- Hide all open windows.
- Reduce all open windows to thumbnails.
- Reduce an application's windows to thumbnails.

Each of these options has specific uses, and you access them in slightly different ways.

Using Exposé to hide all open windows

This mode is useful when your desktop is so cluttered that you are having a hard time finding anything. When you activate it, all the open windows are hidden so that you can work on the suddenly uncluttered desktop. To clear away all your windows in one sweep, press F11. All the windows are moved off the MacBook Pro screen, leaving an uncluttered desktop for you to work on. If you look carefully at the now shaded edges of the desktop in figure 1.11, you see the edges of the windows that have been moved off to the side.

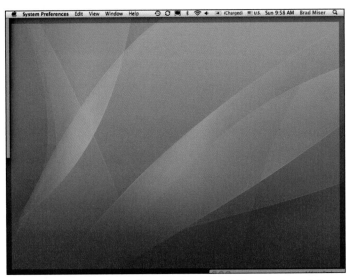

1.11 Where, oh where, have all my windows gone? (If you look carefully at the shaded edges of the screen, you'll see them.)

You can return your desktop to its cluttered condition by pressing F11 or clicking anywhere in the shaded borders of the desktop. The windows slide back onto the visible part of the desktop where you can use them again.

Using Exposé to show thumbnails of open windows

This technique is useful when you have a lot of open windows and you want to move into a specific one. You can reduce all your windows to thumbnails and then move into the window you want to use by clicking it. Press Fn+F9 to shrink all open windows down so that they all fit on the desktop.

When you point to a window, the arrow changes to the pointing finger, the window is highlighted in blue, and the window's name pops up (see figure 1.12).

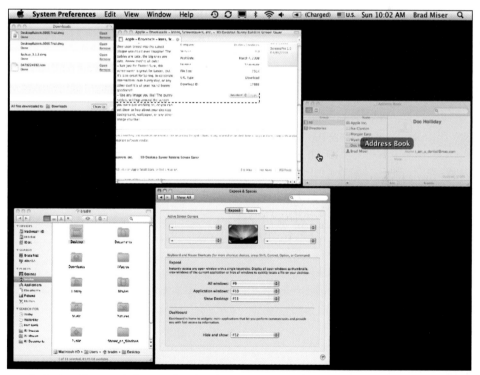

1.12 Reducing all open windows to thumbnails is a great way to find and jump into a specific window (here, I'm pointing to the Address Book window).

17

Using Exposé to show thumbnails of an application's open windows

This mode is similar to the previous one, except that instead of showing all open windows as thumbnails, it shows only the windows in the current application as thumbnails. Use this mode when you are working with multiple windows within the same application and want to jump to a specific one.

Press Fn+F10 to shrink down all windows for one application so that they all fit on the desktop. When you point to a window, the arrow changes to a pointing finger, the window is highlighted in blue, and the window's name pops up. To move into a window, click it. The window becomes active and moves to the front so that you can use it.

Genius

When you have windows showing with Exposé, press the Tab key to quickly move through sets of windows that are associated with specific applications; this makes it easier to find windows that are part of the same application. Press ⌘+Tab to open the Application Switcher bar, showing all open applications. Press ⌘+Tab to move to the application you want to focus on; when you release the ⌘ key, the windows are shown for the application you selected.

Configuring Exposé keyboard shortcuts

You can customize how you activate Exposé by performing the following steps:

1. **Choose Apple menu ⇨ System Preferences.** The System Preferences application appears.

2. **Click the Exposé & Spaces icon.** The Exposé & Spaces pane appears.

3. **Click the Exposé tab.**

4. **To cause an Exposé action when you point to a corner of the desktop, use the pop-up menus located next to each corner of the desktop thumbnail at the top of the pane to select the action you want to happen when you point to that corner (see figure 1.13).**

Genius

To add keyboard modifiers to the function keys, press a key, such as the ⌘ key, while you have a menu open. The symbols for the keys that you press are shown next to the function keys. If you select one of these combinations, you need to hold the same modifier keys down when you click the appropriate function key to activate the command.

| ⇧⌘ All Windows |
| ⇧⌘ Application Windows |
| ⇧⌘ Desktop |
| ⇧⌘ Dashboard |
| ⇧⌘ Start Screen Saver |
| ⇧⌘ Disable Screen Saver |
| ⇧⌘ Sleep Display |

Exposé & Spaces

Show All

Exposé | Spaces

Active Screen Corners

All Windows

Keyboard and Mouse Shortcuts (for more shortcut choices, press Shift, Control, Option, or Command)

Exposé

Instantly access any open window with a single keystroke. Display all open windows as thumbnails, view windows of the current application or hide all windows to quickly locate a file on your desktop.

All windows: F9

Application windows: F10

Show Desktop: F11

Dashboard

Dashboard is home to widgets: mini-applications that let you perform common tasks and provide you with fast access to information.

Hide and show: F12

1.13 You can activate Exposé when you point to a corner of the screen by configuring the pop-up menus located on each corner of the display's thumbnail.

5. **Use the All windows, Application windows, and Show Desktop pop-up menus to configure the keyboard shortcuts for those actions.**

6. **Quit the System Preferences application.** The new keyboard shortcuts for Exposé take effect.

Using Desktop Spaces

As you use your MacBook Pro, it's likely that you'll develop sets of tasks that you work on at the same time. For example, you might use Word to create text and a graphics application to write a book. These kinds of activities invariably involve a lot of windows. While you can use Exposé to manage these windows, it's not so efficient, because you can only focus on one window at a time and it can still take some work to get to the windows you want to use.

With Spaces, you can create collections of applications and their windows so that you can jump between sets easily and quickly. For example, if you have several Internet applications that you use,

19

you can create an Internet space for those applications, such as an e-mail application and Web browser. To use your Internet applications, just open that space and the windows are all in the positions you last left them. You might have another space that contains Address Book, iCal, and your e-mail application. You can use these applications just by switching to their space. Spaces make moving to and using different sets of windows fast and easy, and improve the efficiency with which you work.

You can have as many spaces as you need, so there's really no limit to how you can configure your desktop.

Creating Spaces

To get started with Spaces, first create each space, using the following steps:

1. **Choose Apple menu ⇨ System Preferences.** The System Preferences application appears.

2. **Click the Exposé & Spaces icon.** The Exposé & Spaces pane appears.

3. **Click the Spaces tab.** The Spaces pane appears. At the top of the pane are thumbnails of the spaces you'll be configuring. By default, four spaces are available; you can add more if you need them. Each space is assigned a number that you use to identify that space.

4. **Check the Enable Spaces check box.** Spaces become active.

5. **Check the Show Spaces in menu bar check box.** This puts the Spaces menu on the Finder menu bar, which makes it easier to work with your Spaces without going into the System Preferences application first.

6. **Click the Add button (+) just above the pop-up menus at the bottom of the application list.** The Applications sheet appears. By default, the Applications folder, where most applications are stored, is shown.

7. **Select the application you want to add to the space.**

8. **Click Add.** The sheet closes. On the Spaces pane, you see the applications added to spaces. The applications that are available for spaces are shown on the application list in the Application Assignments column. The space to which the applications are assigned is shown in the Space column. By default, all applications are assigned to space 1.

9. **Open the Space menu for the first application on the list.**

10. **Choose the number of the space in which you want to include that application (see figure 1.14), or choose Every Space to include it in all spaces.** After you make a selection, the space number is shown on the menu for that application, and the selected space's icon at the top of the window is highlighted.

Genius To sort the list of applications by space number, click the Space column heading. This is a more effective view because you see the applications organized by the spaces within which they are contained.

Exposé & Spaces

Show All

Exposé   Spaces

Spaces lets you organize your windows into groups to reduce desktop clutter.

☑ Enable Spaces   ☑ Show Spaces in menu bar

1   2

3   4

Rows: ⊕ ⊖
Columns: ⊕ ⊖

Application Assignments	Space ▲
📖 Address Book.app	Space 2
🖩 Calculator.app	Space 3
📘 Dictionary.app	Space 3
💿 DVD Player.app	Space 4
🌐 Firefox.app	Space 1

+ −

Keyboard and Mouse Shortcuts (for more shortcut choices, press Shift, Control, Option, or Command)

To activate Spaces: F8

To switch between spaces: ^ Arrow Keys

To switch directly to a space: ^ Number Keys

?

1.14 The space shown for each application is the one in which that application will be included.

11. **To add two more spaces in a row, click the Add button (+) next to the word Rows in the thumbnail section of the window; to add two more spaces in a column, click the Add button (+) next to the word Columns in the thumbnail section of the window.** Two new spaces appear in the thumbnail section, and the corresponding spaces are available for application assignment. The numbers of the previous spaces are adjusted according to whether you added new spaces in rows or in columns. Any space assignments are also adjusted so that the applications remain in their current spaces, even if the space number changes.

Genius To delete spaces, click the Remove button (-) next to the Rows or Columns text. The spaces are removed and the applications that were assigned to them remain on the list, but they become assigned to the space adjacent to the ones you deleted.

12. **On the To activate Spaces menu, choose the keyboard shortcut you want to use to activate Spaces.** The default is F8, but you can choose any function key or function key and modifier key, such as ⌘ or Shift.

13. **On the To switch directly between spaces pop-up menu, choose the modifier keys you want to use with the arrow keys to move among your spaces.** The default is Ctrl+arrow key.

14. **To set the modifier key that you use to jump directly to a space by its number, open the To switch directly to a space pop-up menu and choose the modifier key you want to use.** The default is Ctrl+number (of the space you want to jump to).

Using Spaces

After you've configured your spaces, you can start using them. If you might expect that moving to a space causes all of the applications it contains to open, I hate to disappoint you, but spaces only impact running applications. So,

1. **Open the applications associated with your spaces.** As each application opens, the Spaces Manager appears on the screen, and the box associated with the space is highlighted in white.

2. **To move to a different space, press the Spaces activation key (the default is fn+F8).** The desktop is hidden and the Spaces Manager appears (see figure 1.15). Here, you see thumbnails of each of the spaces you have configured. Within each space, you see the windows that are open in that space.

3. **To move into a space, click it.** The open applications associated with that space appear, and you can work with them.

4. **To jump directly to a space, press the keyboard shortcut for switching directly to a space, which, by default, is Ctrl+*number*, where *number* is the number of the space you want to move into.** The open applications associated with that space appear, and you can work with them.

5. **To move between spaces without using a space's number or clicking a space's thumbnail, press the keyboard shortcut for switching between spaces, which, by default, is Ctrl+*arrow*, where *arrow* is one of the arrow keys on the keyboard.** The Spaces Manager palette appears. Each box on the palette represents one of your spaces.

6. **While holding the Ctrl key down, press an arrow key to move to the space you want to enter.** As you press an arrow key, an arrow appears in the palette to show you which direction you're moving in.

7. **When the appropriate space is highlighted with the white box, release the trackpad button.** The open applications associated with that space appear.

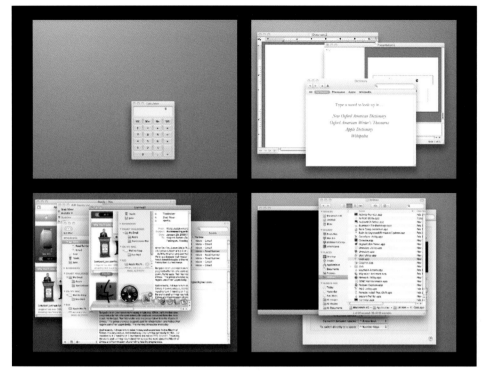

1.15 Here you see thumbnails for each of the four spaces I have configured.

Note that you can use the Spaces menu on the Finder menu bar to manage your spaces (see figure 1.16). The menu shows the number of the space in which you are currently working. Also, when you open an application that is not included in a space, you remain in the current space. Any applications not associated with a space can be used within any space, just like applications that are assigned to Every Space.

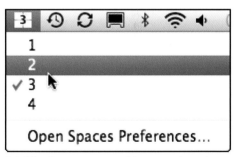

1.16 The Spaces menu enables you to jump into a space by selecting its number.

Using the Dashboard

The Dashboard is actually an application that is a collection of mini-applications, called widgets. By default, the Dashboard application is always running so that its widgets are always available to you. Unless you remove it from the Dock, the Dashboard's icon is located to the immediate right of the Finder icon on the Dock (or below the Finder icon if you use a vertical Dock).

Working with the Dashboard

When you open the Dashboard (press F12), the widgets that are configured to open when it is activated appear (see figure 1.17), and all other windows move into the background. You can then use those widgets or see the information they provide.

1.17 When you open the Dashboard, you get instant access to a set of widgets.

When you are done using widgets, deactivate the Dashboard again by pressing F12 or by clicking the desktop outside of any open widget. All the widgets disappear, the Dashboard closes, and you return to your desktop.

Getting weather information with the Weather widget

The Weather widget that displays current weather conditions and temperature forecasts for an area that you select is configured on the Dashboard by default. To use it, perform the following steps:

1. **Open the Dashboard by pressing F12.**

2. **Move the pointer over the Weather widget.** When you do, the Info button appears.

3. **Click the Info button (an "i" within a circle), located in the lower-right corner of the widget's window.** You see the widget's configuration tools.

4. **Enter the city and state or ZIP code for which you want to see weather information in the box.**

Note The widget's default city is Cupertino, CA. Can you think of any reason why?

5. **Choose the unit of temperature you want to be displayed on the Degrees pop-up menu.**

6. **If you want lows to be included in the six-day forecast, check the Include lows in 6-day forecast check box.**

7. **Click Done.** You return to the widget. You see the city you selected and an icon representing the current weather conditions in that area. Also displayed are the current temperature and the current day's temperature forecast, along with the six-day forecast if you enabled that option (see figure 1.18).

8. **When you're done, close the Dashboard by pressing F12.**

Calculating with the Calculator widget

Okay, it's a bit lame compared to the state of today's calculators and it certainly won't replace Excel, but you might be surprised how handy this simple widget is (it's installed on the Dashboard

1.18 Not bad for mid-March in Indiana.

by default). When it appears on the screen, you can use it to perform basic calculations.

Calculate your numbers by opening the Dashboard (press F12), clicking the Calculator widget to make it active, and clicking the keys on the widget with the trackpad.

Tracking your days with the iCal widget

You can learn about the iCal calendar application in Chapter 10, where you'll see that it's a powerful time management application. The iCal widget, however, isn't the most aptly named one. From its name, you might think you can access all of your iCal calendar information from it. However, that isn't the case. The iCal widget presents an on-screen calendar that you can use to view dates, such as today's date or any date in the past or future. You can see the iCal events you've scheduled for a day when you click that date on the calendar.

This isn't much and it's just about as easy to jump into iCal itself, where you get a lot more function-ality. But if you want to check it out, open the Dashboard by pressing F12 and follow these steps:

1. **Click the iCal widget to make it active.** In the left part of the widget, you see the current date highlighted in green. In the center part, you see a calendar view.

2. **To move ahead in the calendar, click the right- or left-facing arrows next to the month and date at the top of the widget.**

3. **To see your iCal events, click the current date.** A third pane appears, and you see the iCal events for the current date.

4. **Click an event's title to move into iCal to see its details.**

Managing widgets

The Widgets Manager is not shown by default, but you can open it using the following steps:

1. **Open the Dashboard by pressing F12.**

2. **Click the Manage Widgets button (+) located in the lower-left corner of the window.** The Widget bar appears.

3. **Drag the Widgets Manager from the Widget bar onto the Dashboard.** The widget waves to show you that it's installed, and you see its window (see figure 1.19).

Following are some ways you can use the Widgets Manager:

● The widget's list shows all of the widg-ets that are installed under the current user account.

● You can disable a widget by unchecking its check box. This causes the widget to be removed from the Dashboard (if it's been added there) and to be removed from the Widget bar. This doesn't actu-ally remove the widget from your com-puter, however. You can restore a widget by checking its check box again.

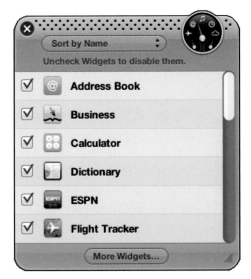

1.19 Use the Widgets Manager to work with your widgets.

○ Widgets marked with a red circle with a hyphen in its center are available only under the current user account.

Note Many widgets, such as the Weather and World Clock widgets, require an Internet connection to work. Others, such as the Calculator, don't.

Setting the Dashboard keyboard shortcut and hot corner

Like Exposé, you can set the hot corners used to open or close the Dashboard by performing the following steps:

1. **Choose Apple menu ⇨ System Preferences.** The System Preferences application appears.

2. **Click the Exposé & Spaces icon.** The Exposé & Spaces pane appears.

3. **Click the Exposé tab.**

4. **To open the Dashboard by pointing to a corner of the desktop, use the pop-up menu located next to each corner of the desktop thumbnail at the top of the pane to select Dashboard for the corner you want to make the hot corner.**

5. **To change the Dashboard keyboard shortcut, open the Hide and show pop-up menu and choose the function key you want to use.**

Configuring the widgets on the Dashboard

One of the nice things about the Dashboard is that you can configure the exact set of widgets that you want to use and how those widgets appear on the screen. Here's how to customize your own Dashboard:

1. **Press F12 to activate the Dashboard.** The widgets that are currently configured to open appear.

2. **Click the Manage Widgets button (+).** The Widget bar opens and you see all of the widgets that are currently installed. Each widget contains the Close button (x) that indicates you are in Dashboard management mode. At the bottom of each widget's icon on the Widget bar, you see the widget's name. Widgets are shown in alphabetical order from left to right (see figure 1.20).

3. **To add a widget to your Dashboard, drag its icon from the Widget bar onto the screen at the location where you want it to appear.** The widget appears on the screen with a cool rippling effect.

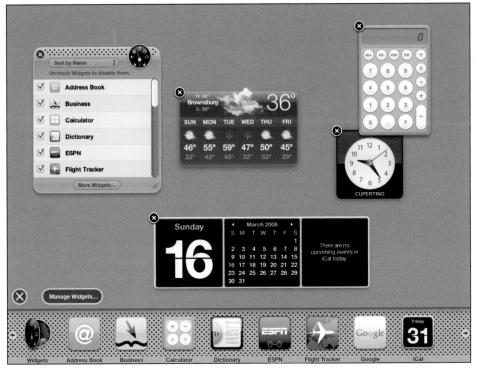

1.20 The Widget bar at the bottom of the Dashboard shows all the widgets that are installed on your MacBook Pro.

Genius

You can add multiple instances of the same widget to the Dashboard. Each time you add a widget, a new version of that widget is added to the Dashboard. This is useful for widgets that you configure with specific information, such as a location (the Weather widget is a prime example).

4. **Close any widgets that you don't want to open when you activate the Dashboard by clicking their Close button (the "x" located in the upper-left corner of each widget's window).** The widget disappears from the Dashboard, but remains on the Widget bar.

Configuring installed widgets

To see if a widget has configuration options, move the pointer over the widget in which you are interested. If it has options, the Info button appears; this button is usually a lowercase "i," sometimes inside a circle, sometimes not. The location of the button varies, and sometimes they are kind of hard to see, so just watch closely when you hover over a widget.

When you click the Info button, the widget's configuration tools appear (see figure 1.21). You can use those tools to make the widget work or look the way you want it to. When you're done, click the Done button and the widget is updated accordingly. You should always check out the Info options for any widgets that you use because they will probably make those widgets even more useful to you.

Installing more widgets

The Dashboard includes quite a few widgets, but there are thousands of widgets available on the Apple widget Web site that you can download and install. Here's how to do it:

1. **Open the Dashboard.**

2. **Open the Widget bar.**

3. **If the Widgets Manager isn't installed on your Dashboard, click the Manage Widgets button.** The Widgets Manager appears.

4. **In the Widgets Manager, click the More Widgets button.** Your default Web browser opens and takes you to the Apple widgets Web page (see figure 1.22).

5. **Browse or search until you find a widget you want to try.**

6. **Download the widget.** In most cases, the widget is downloaded directly and you're prompted to install the widget after it's been downloaded. If this is the case for a widget you download, skip to step 8.

7. **If the file is downloaded to your Downloads folder, move to and open it.** Widget files have the file extension .wdgt. If you don't see this extension, you might have to double-click the file you downloaded to expand it.

8. **Click Install at the prompt.** You move to the Dashboard and see the new widget that you installed.

9. **Click Keep to keep the widget, or Delete to get rid of it.** If you click Keep, it is installed on your Dashboard. If you click Delete, it is not installed on your Dashboard.

10. **Configure the new widget.**

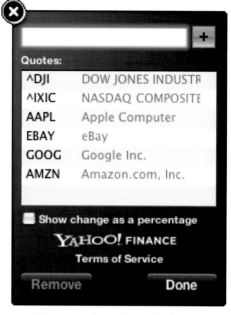

1.21 You can configure the stocks that the Stocks widget tracks for you.

29

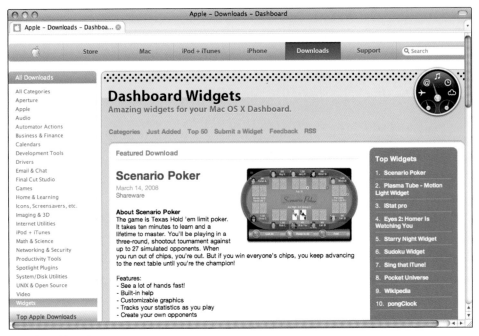

1.22 Got widgets?

Genius

When you install a widget from the Apple Web site, it is installed only in the current user's Widgets folder. To make it available to everyone who uses your MacBook Pro, move it from the Widgets folder in your Home folder to the Widgets folder in the System folder. Then, everyone who uses your MacBook Pro is also able to use the widget.

Note

You have to use Safari to create Web widgets.

Creating your own Web widgets

While you have to do some basic programming to create a widget like those you see on the Apple widget Web site, you can create your own widgets by capturing parts of Web sites that then appear as widgets on your Dashboard. Follow these steps:

1. **Open Safari.**

2. **Move to a Web page containing information or tools that you want to capture in a widget.**

3. **Do one of the following:**

   - Click the Add this page to the Dashboard button on the Safari toolbar (it looks like a pair of scissors cutting paper).

   - Choose File ⇨ Open in Dashboard.

   A selection box and capture toolbar appear (see figure 1.23).

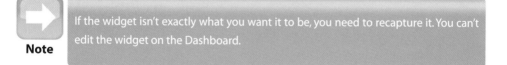

1.23 Use the selection box to choose the part of the Web page that you want to capture in a widget.

Note

If the widget isn't exactly what you want it to be, you need to recapture it. You can't edit the widget on the Dashboard.

4. **Make the selection box enclose the part of the page that you want to be a widget by dragging the box to the general area you want to capture, clicking the trackpad button to lock the selection box, and then dragging its resize handles to enclose the part of the page you want as a widget.**

5. **Click the Add button on the toolbar.**
   The Dashboard opens and the part of
   the page you selected becomes a
   widget (see figure 1.24).

6. **Click the new widget's Info button.**

7. **Use the resulting tools to select a
   theme.** The theme determines the border of the widget.

8. **If the clip has audio and you want it
   to play only while the Dashboard is
   open, check the Only play audio in
   Dashboard check box.**

9. **Click Done.**

10. **Place the widget on your Dashboard.**

For more tips about Web widgets, see the
following list:

Forecast Conditions		High/Low °F	Precip Chance	High Tempe
Today Mar 16	Partly Cloudy	44°/32°	10%	Check Your Loca Forecast
Mon Mar 17	PM Showers	51°/44°	30%	
Tue Mar 18	T-Storms	57°/41°	80%	
Wed Mar 19	Showers / Wind	43°/32°	50%	Check Flight Del
Thu Mar 20	Mostly Sunny	50°/34°	20%	
Fri Mar 21	Showers	41°/29°	40%	
Sat Mar 22	Mostly Cloudy	47°/31°	20%	Get the Gamed
Sun Mar 23	Showers	48°/33°	40%	

1.24 I captured a forecast from weather.com as a widget.

- The Web capture selection tool captures
  a static portion of the Web page, based on what you select. If the information changes on
  the source Web page, it might shift what's shown in the widget you create. You'll need to
  re-create the widget to fix any problems that result.

- To get rid of a Web capture widget, open the Dashboard and then open the Widget bar.
  Then click the Close button for the widget. Unlike other widgets, when you close a
  widget you've captured, it's gone forever.

How Do I Manage User Accounts?

Mac OS X is a multi-user operating system, meaning that MacBook Pro is designed to be used by more than one person at a time. Each person has his own user account that includes a Home folder for storing files; system preferences for things like Dock configuration, the desktop picture, and screen resolution; application preferences; and security settings. When you log in, Mac OS X configures itself based on your preferences and, in effect, becomes your personalized computer. Understanding how to create and manage user accounts is an important part of getting the most out of your MacBook Pro.

Creating and Managing User Accounts

You will use the System Preferences application to create and manage most of the user accounts on your MacBook Pro. Before jumping in there, understand that there are a number of different types of user accounts:

- **Administrator.** Administrator accounts are the second-most powerful type of account; when logged in under an Administrator account, you have complete access to the System Preferences application to make changes to the operating system, such as to create and manage user accounts and change network settings. Administrators can also install software at the system level, where it can be used by others. The user account that you create the first time you start your MacBook Pro is an Administrator account.

> **Note**
>
> By default, your MacBook Pro uses Automatic Login; this logs in the default user account (the one you created when you first started your MacBook Pro) automatically, which can disguise the fact that you are accessing a user account.

- **Standard.** Someone logged in under a Standard user account can only make changes related to that account. Standard users can't change other user accounts or perform other system-wide administration actions.

- **Managed with Parental Controls.** The Mac OS X Parental Controls feature enables you to limit the access that a user has to various kinds of content, such as e-mail and Web sites. When you create this kind of account, you determine specific types of content, applications, and other areas that the user can access. They are prevented from doing all actions not specifically allowed by their Parental Control settings.

- **Sharing Only.** This type of account can only access your MacBook Pro to share files across a network and has no access to your MacBook Pro operating system or other resources.

- **Group.** Access to folders and files on your MacBook Pro is determined by each item's Sharing and Permissions settings. One of the ways you can assign privileges to an item is by configuring a group's access to it; a group user account is a collection of user accounts and is used only to set access privileges.

- **Root.** Mac OS X is built on the UNIX operating system and so has extensive security architecture that specifically controls what each user account can do and the resources that user can access. The Root user account is a unique user account that bypasses all the limitations that are inherent to the other types of user accounts (even Administrator user accounts). When you log in under the Root user account, the system doesn't limit anything you try to do. Because of this, the Root user account is the most powerful kind of user account and is also the most dangerous because you can do things that might damage the system or files that it contains. You typically only use the Root user account during troubleshooting tasks. Unlike the other user accounts, you don't administer the Root user account using the System Preferences application; you can learn how to use the Root user account at the end of this chapter.

Creating new Administrator or Standard user accounts

The following steps show you how to create a new Administrator or Standard user account:

1. **Choose Apple menu ⇨ System Preferences.**

2. **Click the Accounts icon.** The Accounts pane opens (see figure 2.1). In the accounts list on the left side of the window, you see the accounts that currently exist. The user account under which you are logged in appears at the top of the list, and its details appear in the right part of the pane, along with the tools you use to configure those details. At the bottom of the user list are the Add and Remove buttons, which enable you to add or remove user accounts. In the lower-left corner of the window is the Authentication status Lock icon; if the Lock is closed (the text next to it says "Click the lock to make changes"), you need to authenticate yourself before you can create a new account. If the Lock is open (the text next to it says "Click the lock to prevent further changes"), you can skip to step 7.

2.1 Using the Accounts pane, you can create and manage user accounts on your MacBook Pro.

3. **Click the Lock icon.** The Authentication dialog appears and the current username is entered in the Name field.

4. **If the current username isn't the name for your Administrator account, change it to be your user account name.**

5. **Enter your password.**

6. **Click OK.** You are authenticated as an Administrator and you return to the Accounts pane, on which the Lock icon is now open.

7. **Click the Add button, which is the + located just above the Lock icon.** The New Account sheet appears.

8. **On the New Account pop-up menu, choose Standard to create a Standard user account, or Administrator to create an Administrator account.**

Genius

You can change a Standard user account into an Administrator account or vice versa after it's been created.

9. **Enter a full name for the account in the Name field.** This can be just about anything you want, but usually the person's name works best; this is one of the names that the user enters to log in or authenticate the account (if it is an Administrator account). Mac OS X creates a short name, based on the full name you entered.

10. **Edit the short username if you want to change it.** This appears in a number of places, such as in the path to the user's Home folder and in the URL to that user's Web site on the MacBook Pro (each user account can publish a Web site on the local network).

11. **If you want to create a password yourself, enter it in the Password box and skip to step 16.**

Genius

While it isn't good practice from a security standpoint, you don't have to have a password for a user account. If you leave the Password and Verify fields empty, the user leaves the field empty and clicks the Login or other button to complete the action he is performing.

12. **If you want to use the Password Assistant to help you create a password, click the Key icon.** The Password Assistant appears (see figure 2.2).

13. **Choose the password's type on the Type pop-up menu.** There are a number of options, such as Memorable and Letters & Numbers. After you choose a type, the Assistant generates

a password for you and this password is entered in the Password field on the New Account sheet.

14. **Drag the slider to the right to increase the length of the password, or to the left to decrease its length.** The longer a password is, the more secure it becomes. As you make changes, the Quality gauge shows you how secure the password is.

15. **When the password is what you want to use, leave the Password Assistant open and click back in the New Account sheet.**

16. **Re-enter the password in the Verify field.**

17. **Click Create Account.** The user account is created and appears on the list of accounts.

18. **To associate an image with the user account, click the Image well, located to the left of the Change Password button.**

19. **Choose an icon from the pop-up menu or choose Edit Picture.** If you selected an icon, it appears in the Image well, and you can skip to step 23. If you clicked Edit Picture, the Edit Picture sheet appears (see figure 2.3).

20. **Choose the user's picture from the desktop, or click Choose and browse for an image, or take a photo with the MacBook Pro's iSight camera.**

21. **Configure the user's picture by using the tools on the Edit Picture sheet.**

2.2 The Password Assistant is useful when you don't want to create passwords manually.

2.3 An image that you associate with the user account appears in several locations, such as the Mac OS X Login screen.

39

22. **When you're happy with the image, click Set.** The Edit Picture sheet closes and you see the image in the Image well on the Accounts pane.

23. **If you previously selected the Standard account type, but changed your mind, check the Allow user to administer this computer check box.** This changes the type to an Administrator account.

The user account you created appears on the list of accounts and is ready to use (see figure 2.4).

2.4 Following good practice, I've created a troubleshooting account on my MacBook Pro.

Limiting user accounts with Parental Controls

The Mac OS X Parental Controls feature enables you to limit the access a user has to functionality and content, including the following:

- **Simple Finder.** When you limit a user to the Simple Finder, they can only access their own documents and specific applications that you choose.

- **Selected applications.** You can use Parental Controls to create a list of applications to which the user has access.

- **System functions.** You can prevent a user from administering printers, burning CDs or DVDs, changing their password, or changing the Dock.

- **Dictionary.** You can hide profanity in the Mac OS X Dictionary application.

- **Web Sites.** You can prevent the user from visiting specific Web sites.

- **E-mail and iChats.** You can specify the people with whom the user can e-mail or chat.

- **Time Limits.** You can determine when the user is able to access their user account.

Using Parental Controls is a two-step process. First, create the user account that you want to limit; you can only use Parental Controls with accounts of the Standard or Managed with Parental Controls types. Second, configure the controls you want to use with the account; each of these controls is covered in its own section.

Creating Managed User Accounts is similar to creating Standard or Administrator user accounts. Just choose Managed with Parental Controls on the New Account pop-up menu. When you are done with the creation process, you see that the Enable Parental Controls check box is checked.

You are now ready to use the Parental Controls pane to configure the restrictions the user account has. Open the System Preferences application and click the Parental Controls icon. Select the user account (only accounts of the Managed type are shown) on the list of accounts in the left part of the window that you want to configure. Once you've opened the Parental Controls pane with the appropriate user selected, you're ready to configure that user's limitations by using the tabs at the top of the pane.

Restricting system resources for Managed user accounts

You can determine the Finder's behavior, the applications a Managed user can use, and access to certain system functions by using the System tab.

1. **Click the System tab.** You see the System controls in the pane (see figure 2.5).

2. **To enable the Simple Finder for the user, check the Use Simple Finder check box.** When the user logs in, they see a very simple desktop. The Dock contains only three folders; when the user clicks a folder, it opens on the Desktop and the user has access to the applications that you enable and to documents that they create. Within Finder windows, everything opens with a single click.

3. **To limit the access of the user to specific applications, check the Only allow selected applications check box.**

2.5 Use the System tab to configure a user's access to various system resources, such as applications.

4. **Uncheck the check boxes for the categories or individual applications that you don't want the user to be able to use, and check the check boxes for the categories or individual applications that you do want the user to be able to use.**

5. **Check the check boxes at the bottom of the pane to allow (or uncheck them to prevent) access to selected system actions, such as administering printers or burning CDs.**

Restricting content for Managed user accounts

You can limit the user's access to various kinds of content by performing the following steps:

1. **Click the Content tab.** You see the Content controls in the pane (see figure 2.6).

2. **To prevent profanity from appearing in the Mac OS X dictionary, check the Hide profanity in Dictionary check box.**

3. **Limit the user's access to Web sites by clicking the Try to limit access to adult websites automatically option, or clicking the Allow access to only these websites option.** The list of allowed Web sites (bookmarks) appears at the bottom of the pane. To add a site to the list (so the user is able to visit it), click the Add button (+) at the bottom of the list and choose Add bookmark.

2.6 If you don't want the user to access profanity in the Dictionary or selected Web sites, use the Content controls.

Limiting e-mail and chats for Managed user accounts

Another area of activity that you can limit for a Managed user account is e-mail and chatting. You can define specific e-mail addresses and chat accounts with which the user can communicate. To provide more flexibility, you can set up a notification that you receive when someone not on the approved list attempts to communicate with the user; on the notification, you can choose to allow the contact, in which case the person is added to the approved list, or to reject it, in which case the communication is blocked.

In the Mail & iChat tab (see figure 2.7), you can limit e-mail and chats, and add approved contacts as shown in figure 2.8. Enter contact information on the sheet manually or select a contact from your Address Book by clicking the downward-facing triangle. If you want to receive a permission e-mail when someone not on the list is involved in an e-mail exchange, check the Send permission requests to check box and enter your e-mail address.

Caution The e-mail and chat controls only work with Mail and iChat. If the user can access other applications for these functions, the controls won't limit any access. Use the System controls to ensure the user can only access Mail for e-mail and iChat for chatting.

Parental Controls

Show All

System | Content | Mail & iChat | Time Limits | Logs

Marcus Aurelius

☑ Limit Mail   ☑ Limit iChat

This user can exchange email and chat
with only the addresses added to the list.

Only allow emailing and instant messaging with:

Name	Email & Instant Messaging Address
Morgan Earp	another_earp@mac.com (home)
	another_earp@mac.com (home)
Ike Clanton	dont_like_lawdawgs@mac.com (home)
Wyatt Earp	lawman_kansas_city@mac.com (work)
Doc Holliday	i_am_a_dentist@mac.com (home)

+ −

☑ Send permission requests to: bradmacosx@mac.com

Sends an email notifying the recipient that this user is attempting to exchange
email with a contact that is not in the list.

Click the lock to prevent further changes.

2.7 Use the Mail & iChat tab to control the people with whom a user can e-mail or chat.

Setting time limits for Managed user accounts

You can use the Time Limits tab to limit the amount of time for which the user can use the MacBook Pro. When a time limit is reached or when the time is outside of an allowed window, the user can't log into their user account, or if they are currently logged in, they are logged out after a brief warning that allows them time to save open documents. Here's how to set time limits:

First Name: Morgan

Last Name: Earp

Allowed accounts:

another_earp@mac.com   Email   − +

another_earp@mac.com   AIM   − +

☑ Add person to my address book

Cancel   Add

2.8 Configure the Contact sheet to allow the user to communicate with someone in particular.

1. **Click the Time Limits tab (see figure 2.9).**

2. **To set the amount of time for which the user can be logged in on weekdays and/or weekends, check the top Limit Computer use to check box and set the time on the slider for each option.**

2.9 Using a MacBook Pro can be a lot of fun; use the Time Limits feature to make sure it doesn't replace other important activities.

3. To prevent the user from being logged into the user account for specific periods of time Sunday to Thursday, check the School nights check box and enter the time period during which user activity should be prevented using the two time boxes.

Note When a user has been logged out because of time limits, a red circle with a hyphen in it appears next to the user's name in the Login window. The time at which the user can log in again is also shown.

4. To prevent the user from being logged into the user account for specific periods of time on Friday and Saturday, check the Weekend check box and enter the time period during which user activity should be prevented using the two time boxes.

Setting Login Items for a user account

Any file added to the Login Items list for a user is opened when the user logs into their account. For example, if a user opens Safari and Mail every time they use the MacBook Pro, you can add these applications to the user's Login Items so that they open automatically. Here's how you can make life easier for users (including yourself):

1. **Log in under the user's account (you can set Login Items for your own account by logging into your account).**

2. **Open the System Preferences application and click the Accounts icon to open the Accounts pane.**

3. **Click the Login Items tab, as shown in figure 2.10.**

4. **Add items to the list by clicking the Add button at the bottom of the pane.** Use the resulting dialog to browse for the items you want to add, select them, and click Add.

5. **Check the check box for any items you want to be hidden by default.**

2.10 Any file you add to the Login Items tab is opened automatically when a user logs in.

Creating Sharing Only user accounts

Typically, you create Sharing Only user accounts for groups of people who need to get to files on your MacBook Pro. Creating a Sharing Only user account is similar to creating other types of accounts; just choose Sharing Only on the New Account pop-up menu. When you are done with the creation process, you see that the only tools for the Sharing Only account are for the user name, image, password reset, and .Mac user name.

You don't use a Sharing Only user account from your MacBook Pro; its purpose is to enable people to log into your MacBook Pro from other computers. Provide the username and password to each person whom you want to allow to access your MacBook Pro, and they can log in to access files that you share.

Creating Group user accounts

Creating a Group user account is much simpler than the other types. Here's how:

1. **Open the System Preferences application.**

2. **Click the Accounts icon.**

3. **Click the Add button.**

4. **On the New Account pop-up menu, choose Group.**

5. **Enter the group's name in the Name field.**

6. **Click Create Group.** You move to the group's screen, on which you see all the user accounts on your MacBook Pro (see figure 2.11).

7. **Check the check box for each user whom you want to be a member of the group.** The group is ready to be used to assign access permissions.

2.11 Pick a user to add to the group.

Checking Up on Managed Users

On the Logs tab, you can view a Managed user's activities, such as Web sites visited, Web sites blocked, and applications used. To see user activity, click the Logs tab. On the Log Collections list, select the kind of activity you want to see, such as Applications. In the right part of the pane, you see a list of all the applications the user has accessed. To see each instance of application use, click the expansion triangle next to the application's name. Under its icon, you see each date and time that the application was used, and the amount of time for which it was used. When you select an application or activity, use the Open or Restrict buttons to change the permissions for that application or activity.

Changing user accounts

You change existing user accounts using the same set of tools that you use to create accounts. To make changes, perform the following steps:

1. **Open the System Preferences application.**

2. **Click the Accounts icon.**

3. **Select the user whose account you want to change.**

4. **Use the tools in the right part of the pane to make changes to the user account, such as resetting a forgotten password.**

Note

The only way to change an account's short name is to delete the account and recreate it with a different short name.

Deleting user accounts

If you no longer need a user account, you can delete it.

1. **Open the System Preferences application and click the Accounts icon.**

2. **Select the account that you want to delete.**

3. **Click the Remove button (–) at the bottom of the user list.** A sheet appears with three options for handling the user's Home folder, as follows:

   - **Save the home folder in a disk image.** All the files in the user's Home folder are saved into a disk image located in the Deleted Users folder under the Users folder. You can access the files in the disk image by opening it.

   - **Do not change the home folder.** If you choose this option, the user's Home folder remains in its current location under the user's folder in the Users folder, but its permissions are changed so that you can access it from an Administrator user account.

   - **Delete the home folder.** If you choose this option, all traces of the user are removed from your MacBook Pro.

4. **Click OK.** The user account is deleted and the user's Home folder is handled according to the option you selected.

Using Automatic Login

The Mac OS X Automatic Login feature does just what it says. You can choose to log into a specific user account each time your MacBook Pro restarts. Enable Automatic Login by following these steps:

Caution

Enabling Automatic Login makes your MacBook Pro less secure because anyone who has access to it can use it because they don't have to provide information needed to log in. While this feature is convenient, you should only enable Automatic Login if your MacBook Pro is in an area that you can control and you're sure other people won't be able to use it without your knowledge.

1. **Open the System Preferences application and click the Accounts icon.**

2. **Click Login Options.** The Login Options pane appears, as shown in figure 2.12.

3. **On the Automatic Login pop-up menu, choose the name of the user that you want to be automatically logged in.**

4. **Enter the user's password.**

5. **Click OK.** Each time your MacBook Pro starts or restarts, the user you selected is logged in automatically.

```
○ ○ ○                          Accounts
◄  ►   Show All                                    Q

My Account
    Brad Miser
    Admin                Automatic login ✓ Disabled
▼ Other Accounts                          Brad Miser
    Emily Miser         Display login wi   Emily Miser      ►
    Admin                                  Marcus Aurelius
    Marcus Aurelius                        Troubleshooting Account
    Managed             ☑ Show the Res...                ...s
    Troubleshooting ...
    Admin               ☐ Show Input menu in login window
    Guest Account       ☑ Show password hints
    Sharing only        ☐ Use VoiceOver at login window
    Maximus
    Sharing Only        ☑ Enable fast user switching
▼ Groups                   View as:  Name         ⬍
    Project_X_Files

   Login Options

+  −

 🔓  Click the lock to prevent further changes.              ?
```

2.12 Use the Automatic Login pop-up menu to select a user account to automatically log in to your MacBook Pro.

Configuring the Login Window

The Login window appears to prompt a user to log in. If Automatic Login is disabled, it appears when your MacBook Pro starts up. If a user logs out of their user account, the Login window also appears. You can also make it appear by choosing Login Window on the Fast User Switching menu (this is covered in the next section). There are a number of options you can configure for the Login window through System Preferences ➪ Accounts, including what information displays in the Login window.

If you want to be able to restart your MacBook Pro, put it to sleep, or shut it down from the Login window. Then check the Show the Restart, Sleep, and Shut Down buttons check box.

Caution If you've enabled Automatic Login, don't check the Show the Restart, Sleep, and Shut Down buttons check box. If you do, someone can gain access to your MacBook Pro when the Login window is displayed without having a user account, by choosing the Shut Down button and then restarting the MacBook Pro.

Working with Fast User Switching

The Fast User Switching feature is great because it allows multiple users to be logged in at the same time. Instead of having to log out of your account for someone else to log in, the other user can log in by using the commands on the Fast User Switching menu. This is good because when you log out of an account, all processes are shut down, meaning that all open documents and applications are closed. If you have a lot of work on-going, this can be a nuisance. With Fast User Switching, other users can log in while your account remains active in the background. When you log back into your account, it is in the same state as when the other user logged in, and you can get back to what you were doing immediately.

Enabling Fast User Switching

Fast User Switching is disabled by default; to enable it, do the following:

1. **Open the System Preferences application and click the Accounts icon.**

2. **Click Login Options.**

3. **Check the "Enable fast user switching" check box and click OK in the warning prompt.**

Using Fast User Switching

Using Fast User Switching is simple. Open the Fast User Switching menu on the menu bar by clicking the current user's full or short name or the silhouette. The Fast User Switching menu appears (see figure 2.13).

On this menu, you see the following:

- **List of user accounts.** Each user account configured on your MacBook Pro appears on the list.

- **Login Window.** Choose this command to cause the Login window to appear.

- **Account Preferences.** Choose this command to move to the Accounts pane of the System Preferences application.

To switch to a different user account, select it on the menu. The password prompt appears. If the password is entered correctly, that user account becomes active. The current account remains logged in, but is moved into the background.

2.13 The Fast User Switching menu makes it easier to share your MacBook Pro with others.

51

You can have as many user accounts logged in simultaneously as you want. However, remember that each account that is logged in can have active processes, which use your MacBook Pro's resources. So, you don't want to get carried away with this idea.

Working with the Root User Account

Because Mac OS X is based on UNIX, it includes the Root user account. In a nutshell, the Root user account is not limited by any security permissions. If something is possible, the Root user account can do it. This is both good and bad. It's good because you can often solve problems using the Root user account that you can't solve any other way. It's bad because you can also cause problems that it might not be possible to recover from, at least, not easily. By contrast, when you use an Administrator account, you have limited access to certain system files, and so there is no way you can delete them; however, under the Root user account, anything goes, and so it's possible for you to do things that cause your MacBook Pro to be unusable.

You should only use the Root user account for troubleshooting. While you shouldn't use the Root user account often, when you need to use the Root user account, you'll really need it.

By default, the Root user account is disabled. You must enable it before you can log in to use it.

Enabling the Root user account

You can enable the Root user account with the Directory Utility application, as described in the following steps:

1. **Open the Directory Utility application, which is located in the Utilities folder within the Applications folder.**

2. **Click the Lock icon.**

3. **Enter an Administrator username (if necessary) and password, and click OK.**

4. **Choose Edit ⇨ Enable Root User.** You're prompted to create a password for the Root user account.

5. **Enter a password in the Password and Verify fields (see figure 2.14).** I recommend using a different password than what you use for your normal user account so that it's more secure.

Directory Utility

Please enter a new password for the root user.

Password: ••••••••

Verify: ••••••••

Cancel   OK

+ −

Click the lock to prevent further changes.   (?)   Show Advanced Settings

2.14 Create a secure password for the Root user account to prevent unintended access to it.

6. **Click OK.** The New Password sheet closes, but nothing else appears to happen. Don't worry, the Root user account is now enabled and you can use it.

7. **Quit the Directory Utility application.**

Using the Root user account

Because the Root user account has unlimited permissions, you can add or remove files to any directory on your Mac while you are logged in under the Root user account, including those for other user accounts. You can also make changes to any system file, which is where the Root user account's power and danger come from.

Note

The full name of the Root user account is System Administrator. You therefore see that term instead of Root wherever the full account name is shown.

To log into the Root user account, start from the Login window by choosing Login Window on the Fast User Switching menu, logging out of the current account, or restarting your MacBook Pro (if Automatic Login is disabled). If the window is configured to show usernames, scroll down and select the Other username; the Name and Password fields appear (these appear immediately if the window is configured to display them instead of user accounts). Enter root as the name and the password you created for the Root user account, and click Login. You log in as the Root user account (or under root, as UNIX aficionados would say). The Root user account's desktop appears, and you can get to work.

When you are logged into the Root user account, you can use your MacBook Pro as you can with other user accounts, except, and this is a big exception, you have no security limitations. You can place files into any folder, delete any files, or complete any other action you try, regardless of the potential outcome.

How Can I Connect a MacBook Pro to the Internet?

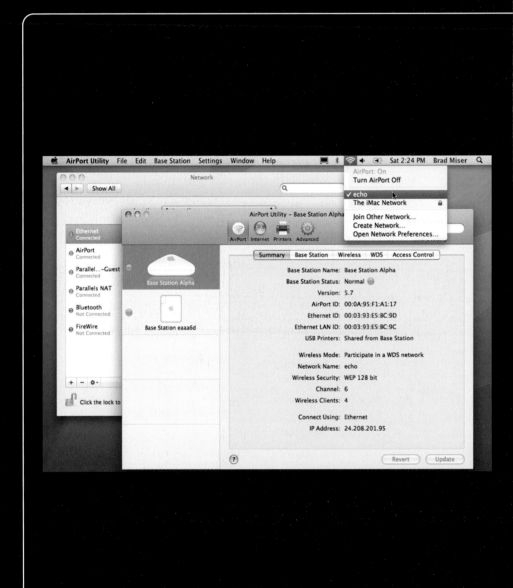

Being able to take advantage of the Internet is almost as important a skill as being able to read (of course, you have to be able to read to be able to use the Internet, and so reading still wins on the importance scale). Fortunately, your MacBook Pro is a perfect tool for getting the most out of the Internet. In order to use the Internet, you must be able to connect to it, which is where this chapter comes in.

Setting Up a Local Network with Internet Access

There are many ways to connect your MacBook Pro to the Internet. Fortunately, one of the great things about using a MacBook Pro and related Apple technology is that you don't have to worry about all the technical details involved. It's quite easy to create and manage a local network that provides Internet access and other services, including file sharing, to multiple computers.

This chapter focuses on networks built around an Apple AirPort Extreme Base Station (see figure 3.1) because it makes managing a network easy while providing all the features that most people need for a local network. MacBook Pro networking technology supports wireless and wired networking standards, so you can use just about any network components designed to the same standards to accomplish the same purposes, but with a bit more effort and complexity, and who needs that?

There are two general steps to creating a local network. First, install and configure the AirPort Extreme Base Station. Second, connect devices, such as computers and printers, to the wireless or wired network provided by the base station.

Installing and configuring an AirPort Extreme Base Station

The Apple AirPort Extreme Base Station is a relatively simple device. It contains a transmitter that broadcasts the signal over which the wireless network is provided, and it has four Ethernet ports. One, the WAN (Wide Area Network) port, connects to a broadband Internet connection, which is most commonly connected to a cable or DSL modem. The other three ports connect to an Ethernet network or to Ethernet-equipped devices, including computers, printers, and Ethernet hubs. Along with the power adapter port, the base station offers a USB port to which you can connect a USB printer or USB hard drive to share a printer or a hard drive with the network.

Installing an AirPort Extreme Base Station

After you have placed the base station in its location, attach its power adapter to the base station and plug it into a wall outlet. Use an Ethernet cable to connect the cable or DSL modem to the WAN Ethernet port.

You can connect an Ethernet device to each of the three LAN (Local Area Network) Ethernet ports on the base station (see figure 3.1). For example, you can connect a network printer and a computer, or to add more than three devices, you can connect one of the ports to an Ethernet hub.

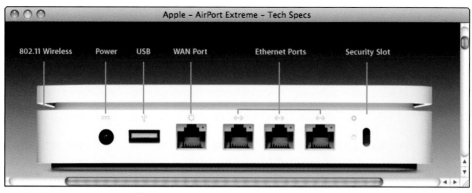

3.1 The three LAN ports enable you to create a wired network to go along with the wireless one.

Configuring an AirPort Extreme Base Station

After you have installed the base station, you need to configure it. You can configure it manually through the AirPort Utility application, or you can use the same application with a guided approach. With either method, configure the base station from a computer with which it can communicate, either through AirPort or through an Ethernet network. To configure the base station wirelessly, make sure AirPort is enabled on your MacBook Pro (see "Connecting to wireless networks" later in this chapter for the details). To configure the base station through Ethernet, connect your MacBook Pro to one of the Ethernet ports on the base station.

Genius

To use the guided approach, open the AirPort Utility application located in the Utilities folder in the Applications folder. Select the base station and click Continue. Follow the on-screen instructions to complete the configuration.

You must use the manual approach to configure certain aspects of the base station (and it's often easier and faster to use this approach anyway); the following steps show you how to configure a base station manually:

1. **Open the AirPort Utility located in the Utilities folder in the Applications folder.** The base stations with which your MacBook Pro can communicate are shown in the left pane of the window.

2. **Select the base station you want to configure.** If there is only one base station in range, it is selected automatically.

3. **Click Manual Setup.** You're prompted to enter the base station's password.

59

Note Two passwords are associated with a base station. One password is required to be able to administer the password. The other password is required to join the wireless network provided by the base station.

4. **Enter the password and click OK.** You next see a window that has the base station name as its title and that includes several tabs. The upper tabs provide access to general configuration areas, such as Internet, while the lower tabs provide the configuration tools for the selected area.

5. **Select the AirPort tab.**

6. **Click the Base Station sub-tab shown in figure 3.2.**

3.2 The Base Station sub-tab allows you to configure basic attributes, such as the base station's name.

7. **Enter the base station name in the Base Station Name field.** This is the name of the base station itself, not the name of the network it provides.

8. **Enter the administration password in the Base Station Password and Verify Password fields.** Again, this is the password you use to configure the base station, not the one you use to access the network it provides.

9. **Check the Remember this password in my keychain check box.** This causes your MacBook Pro to remember the password so that you don't have to enter it each time you connect to the network.

10. **To allow the base station to be configured over its Ethernet WAN connection, check the Allow configuration over Ethernet WAN port check box.**

Genius

To enter the contact information for the base station and its location, click the Base Station Options button.

11. **Click the Wireless sub-tab.** On this tab, you configure the wireless network being provided by the base station (see figure 3.3).

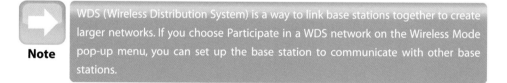

3.3 Use the Wireless sub-tab to create a wireless network.

12. **Use the Wireless Mode pop-up menu to choose Create a wireless network.**

Note

WDS (Wireless Distribution System) is a way to link base stations together to create larger networks. If you choose Participate in a WDS network on the Wireless Mode pop-up menu, you can set up the base station to communicate with other base stations.

13. **Enter the network name in the Network Name field.** This is the name that you choose to access the network being provided by the base station.

14. **Use the Radio Mode pop-up menu to determine the wireless standards supported on the network.** The more standards you allow, such as 802.11b/g/n compatible, the more types of devices are able to connect to the network.

15. **Use the Channel pop-up menu to select the channel over which the base station communicates.** Generally, the default channel works fine.

16. **Use the Wireless Security pop-up menu to choose a security option.**

17. **Enter the network password in the Wireless password and Verify Password fields.**

18. **Check the Remember this password in my keychain check box.** This causes your MacBook Pro to remember the network's password so that you don't have to enter it when you connect.

19. **Click the Wireless Options button.** The Wireless Options sheet appears, as shown in figure 3.4.

Wireless Options

Multicast Rate: 2 Mbps

Transmit Power: 100%

☐ Create a closed network

The name of a "closed" network is hidden. To join the network, a user must know the name of the network.

☐ Use interference robustness

Interference robustness can solve interference problems caused by other devices, such as cordless phones or wireless video monitors. Using interference robustness may affect overall network performance.

Done

3.4 The Wireless Options sheet enables you to configure more advanced options for a wireless network.

20. **Use the Multicast Rate pop-up menu to set the multicast rate.** Choosing a higher value improves performance but also reduces range.

21. **Use the Transmit Power pop-up menu to change the strength of the base station's signal.** If many base stations exist in the same physical area, reduce the signal strength to limit the interference of these stations with one another.

22. **If you want to create a closed network, check the Create a closed network check box.** A closed network does not appear on other users' AirPort menus. To join closed networks, users have to know the name and password for that network.

23. **Click Done.** Your changes are saved and you return to the Wireless sub-tab.

24. **Click the Internet tab.** You use this tab to configure the Internet connection on the base station.

25. **Click the Internet Connection sub-tab, as shown in figure 3.5.**

3.5 Use the Internet Connection sub-tab to configure your Internet account on the base station.

26. **Choose Ethernet on the Connect Using pop-up menu.**

27. **Choose Using DHCP on the Configure IPv4 pop-up menu.**

28. **On the Connection Sharing pop-up menu, choose Share a public IP address.**

29. **Click the NAT sub-tab.** Make sure the Enable NAT Port Mapping Protocol check box is checked. The base station uses NAT (Network Address Translation) to shield devices that are connected to it from Internet attacks. In order to hack a device, you need its address, and NAT hides the addresses of the devices connected to the base station. Make sure that NAT is enabled for your network.

30. **Click Update.** The base station is configured according to the settings you entered. When the process is complete, the base station restarts and the network becomes available.

Building a local network

The base station is the heart of the local network. In addition to providing an Internet connection to the other devices on the network, it makes many other services available, such as file sharing and printer sharing. To add devices to the network being provided by the base station, build the network by adding wireless devices, adding a USB printer or hard drive, adding a network printer, or adding an Ethernet router.

Connecting to the Internet through a Wireless Network

To be able to connect to an AirPort network, you first enable AirPort on your MacBook Pro. Once AirPort is enabled, you can find and connect to a wireless network.

Enabling AirPort

To configure your MacBook Pro to use AirPort, follow these steps:

1. **Open the System Preferences application and click the Network icon to open the Network pane.**

2. **Click the AirPort option in the list of available network options in the left part of the pane.** The AirPort tools appear in the right part of the pane.

3. **If AirPort is currently off, turn it on by clicking the Turn AirPort On button.** AirPort services start and AirPort moves to the top of the list of network options.

4. **Check the Show AirPort status in menu bar check box to put the AirPort menu on your menu bar.** You can use this menu to quickly select and control your AirPort connection.

Genius

Put the network you want to use most at the top of the list, and your MacBook Pro connects to that one first when it is available to you.

5. **Close System Preferences.** Your MacBook Pro is ready for wireless communication.

Connecting to wireless networks

To manage your wireless network connections, open the AirPort menu (see figure 3.6).

The AirPort menu contains the following:

- **Signal strength of the current network.** When you are connected to a wireless network, the number of black waves at the top of the menu indicate the strength of the signal.

- **AirPort status.** You see either AirPort: On or AirPort: Off.

- **Available networks.** The second section of the menu shows you all the networks within range of MacBook Pro.

- **Join Other Network.** You use this command to join a closed network for which you must know the network name and, almost always, the password.

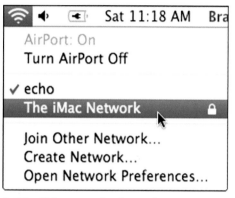

3.6 The AirPort menu is a fast and easy way to identify wireless networks in range of your MacBook Pro.

- **Create Network.** This command enables you to set up a wireless network between computers.

- **Open Network Preferences.** This command opens the Network pane of the System Preferences application.

Connecting to open wireless networks

If a network is open, meaning that its information is broadcast publicly, then it appears on the AirPort menu. To join an open network, perform the following steps:

1. **Open the AirPort menu.**

2. **Select the network you want to join.**

3. **Enter the network's password.**

4. **Click OK.** You join the network and its resources become available to you.

Connecting to closed wireless networks

In order to be able to access a closed network, you need to know it exists, what its name is, the kind of security it uses, and its password. If you have all that information, you can join it:

1. **Open the AirPort menu.**

2. **Select Join Other Network.** A network information dialog appears (see figure 3.7).

3. **Enter the network's name in the Network Name field.**

4. **Choose the kind of security the network uses on the Security pop-up menu.**

5. **Enter the network's password.**

6. **Click Join.** You join the network and its resources become available to you.

Enter the name of the network.

Enter the name of the network you want to join, and then enter the password if necessary. You can also click Show Networks to see a list of available networks.

Network Name: HiddenForAReason

Security: WEP Password

Password: APassword

☑ Show password
☑ Remember this network

(Show Networks)   (Cancel) (Join)

3.7 Use this dialog to join closed networks.

Connecting to the Internet with an Ethernet Connection

Ethernet connections are fast; in fact, your MacBook Pro can perform better with an Ethernet connection than it does with a wireless connection. This might not be too noticeable for Internet activity, but transferring files within a local network is much, much faster. Ethernet connections are also more secure because their signals travel over a cable, so you have to be physically connected to the network with a wire, making it much harder for someone to intercept or interfere with the signal. Of course, the problem with Ethernet connections is that your MacBook Pro has to be physically connected to the network to be able to use an Ethernet connection.

Genius It's a good idea to carry an Ethernet cable with you as part of your MacBook Pro toolkit. While some locations that offer an Ethernet connection also provide a cable, others don't.

To connect your MacBook Pro to an Ethernet network, perform the following steps:

1. **Connect one end of an Ethernet cable to an available Ethernet port on the network.**

2. **Connect the other end to the Ethernet port on your MacBook Pro, which is located on the right side of the computer.**

3. **Open the System Preferences application and click the Network icon.** The Network pane appears.

4. **Select Ethernet on the list of available connections.** Status information is shown at the top of the right part of the pane (see figure 3.8).

3.8 Select Ethernet on the list of available connections to see the status of that connection.

Connecting to the Internet with a Wireless Broadband Card

Using a wireless broadband card, you can get a high-speed Internet connection from anywhere within the service area covered by the card and service plan you are using.

If you travel regularly, a wireless broadband card can be a much more convenient way to connect to the Internet while you are on the move. Because the connection is the same for you no matter where you are located, you don't have to find and sign onto networks in various locations, making a wireless broadband card much easier to use. A wireless broadband card can also be less expensive to use than purchasing temporary accounts.

The primary downside of wireless broadband cards is that the networks they access aren't available in every location. Like cell phones, you need to be within a covered area to be able to access the service provided on the network. The other downside of a wireless broadband card is that its connection can be a bit slower than some wireless or wired connections that are available to you. Even with this usually minor limitation, you may find a wireless broadband card to be an indispensable part of your MacBook Pro toolkit.

Obtaining a wireless broadband card

Obtaining a wireless broadband card is a lot like buying a cell phone; you need to purchase the card and also sign up for a service plan.

Most of the major cell phone providers also offer wireless broadband cards, so visit their Web sites to research the available cards. When you look for a wireless broadband card, consider the following factors:

- **Mac compatibility.** Most cards are compatible with Mac OS X version 10.4 and higher.
- **Card type.** Your MacBook Pro is compatible with a USB or Express Card wireless broadband card.
- **Coverage areas.**
- **Connection speed.**
- **Contract terms.**

Installing and configuring a wireless broadband card

After you've obtained a wireless broadband card, you need to install and configure it. The general steps to do this are as follows:

1. **Install the wireless broadband card's software.** This software includes the drivers and other software associated with the operating system and the application you use to connect to the network.
2. **Plug the card into your MacBook Pro.**
3. **When prompted, restart your MacBook Pro.**

The details of these steps depend on the specific card and the service provider that you use. The following steps provide the details for a Verizon Wireless UM150 USB modem; installing and configuring other kinds of wireless broadband cards should be similar.

1. **Insert the CD provided with the card into your MacBook Pro.**
2. **Launch the installer application provided on the CD.**

3. **Work through the steps of the installer application until you've finished installing the card's software.**

4. **If required, restart your MacBook Pro.**

5. **Insert the wireless broadband card into an available USB port or into the ExpressCard slot (located on the left side of the computer).**

6. **Extend the antenna on the card if it has one.**

7. **Click Check for Updates.** If the software finds an updated version, it downloads and installs the update.

8. **Click Continue.** The Select Hardware screen appears.

9. **Choose Detect both AirPort and WWAN (Wireless Wide Area Network) devices and click Continue.**

10. **Click Continue.** The software identifies your hardware and presents options for the kind of access the card has.

11. **Select the account option with the broadest and fastest coverage areas and click Continue.**

12. **Authenticate yourself as an Administrator.** You are prompted to set up your wireless account.

13. **Follow the on-screen instructions to set up your account.**

14. **When setup is complete, click Continue.**

15. **Click Continue on the Wireless Account Setup Complete screen.** You now move into the AirPort part of the process.

16. **Click Continue to enable AirPort support in the software.**

17. **Click Close on the Complete screen.** The installer application quits, the application launches, and you're ready to start using the wireless broadband card to connect to the Internet.

Using a wireless broadband card to connect to the Internet

Once the broadband card is installed and configured, connecting to the Internet is usually pretty simple. The general steps are as follows:

3.9 You can use Verizon's VZAccess Manager software to manage your wireless broadband card and AirPort connections.

1. **Launch the wireless broadband card's connection application.** In the application's window, you see the types of wireless connections that are available to you, including those available through AirPort (see figure 3.9).

2. **Select the connection you want to use.**

3. **Click Connect.**

Managing Multiple Network Connections

With Mac OS X, you can have multiple connections active at the same time. In this section, you learn how to configure the connections that you use. You can also use Locations to create sets of connections so that you can easily reconfigure your MacBook Pro for connectivity by choosing a location.

Configuring network connections

You use the Network pane of the System Preferences application to manage your MacBook Pro connections. Follows these steps:

1. **Choose Apple menu ➯ System Preferences and click the Network icon.** The Network pane appears. Along the left side of the pane, you see all the connections configured on your MacBook Pro (see figure 3.10). Connections marked with a green dot are active and connected. Connections marked with a red dot are not active. Connections marked with a yellow dot are active, but not connected to anything. The connection at the top of the list is the currenzt one.

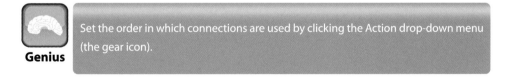

3.10 The Network pane provides you with detailed information about, and control over, your network connections.

2. **Select a connection.**

3. **Remove a connection that you don't use by selecting it and clicking the Remove button (–) located at the bottom of the connection list.**

> **Genius**
>
> Set the order in which connections are used by clicking the Action drop-down menu (the gear icon).

4. **Choose Set Service Order.** The Services sheet appears.

5. **Drag services up and down in the list until they are in the order that you want your MacBook Pro to use them, starting at the top of the list and moving toward the bottom.**

71

6. **Click OK.** Your changes in the Services sheet are saved and the sheet closes.

7. **Click Apply.** The changes that you've made on the Network pane are saved and they take effect.

Using locations to manage network connections

In addition to having multiple connections active, you can use locations to define different sets of connections so that you can easily switch between them. For example, you may use one Ethernet configuration to connect to the Internet at home, and a different one to connect when you are at work. Creating a location for each set of connections makes switching between them simple because you have to configure them only once and can switch between them by simply choosing a different location. (Without locations, you'd have to re-configure the Ethernet connection each time you change the location of your MacBook Pro.)

As you've seen, you can have multiple connections active at the same time.

Creating locations

Your MacBook Pro includes one default location, which is called Automatic. You can create new locations when you need them (you can also change or delete existing locations).

To configure a new network location, use the following steps:

1. **Open the Network pane of the System Preferences application.** The current location is shown on the Location pop-up menu at the top of the pane.

2. **On the Location pop-up menu, choose Edit Locations.** The Locations sheet appears. In the top pane of the sheet, you see the current locations that are configured on your MacBook Pro.

3. **Click the Add button (+) located at the bottom of the sheet.** A new location, called Untitled, appears.

Genius If one of the current locations is similar to the one you want to create, select it on the Locations sheet, open the Action drop-down menu, and choose Duplicate Location. Then give the copy a different name. This is faster than recreating the location from scratch.

4. **Enter a name for the new location.**

5. **Click Done.** The new location is saved and you return to the Network pane. The location you created is shown on the Location pop-up menu (see figure 3.11).

3.11 The location called Work is currently selected on the Location pop-up menu and is ready to be configured.

6. **Configure the location by doing any of the following.** You can select a connection and configure it, or add a connection by clicking the Add (+) button located at the bottom of the list of connections.

7. **When you're done, click Apply.** Your changes are saved and the location becomes active.

Changing locations

To change the location you are using, do one of the following:

- Open the Network pane of the System Preferences application and choose the location you want to use on the Location pop-up menu. If the Apply button becomes active, click it to apply the location; some configuration changes require this, while others don't.

- Choose Apple menu ⇨ Location ⇨ *locationname*, where *locationname* is the name of the location you want to use. After you've selected a location, it is marked with a check mark on the menu to show you that it is active.

Changing or deleting locations

You can edit or remove locations by following these steps:

1. **Open the Network pane of the System Preferences application.**

2. **Choose Edit Locations from the Location pop-up menu.** The Locations sheet appears.

3. **Rename, move, or delete a location.**

4. **Click Done.** You return to the Network pane.

Troubleshooting an Internet Connection

The time will come when you try to connect to a Web site or send e-mail and you'll see error messages instead (see figure 3.12). While this probably won't happen very often, you do need to know what to do when a good Internet connection goes bad. In general, the solutions to most connection problems are relatively straightforward.

3.12 Houston, we have a problem.

One of the difficulties in solving an Internet/network problem is that there are typically a number of links in the chain, the minimum of which are your MacBook Pro, an AirPort Base Station, and the cable or DSL modem that you use to connect to the Internet. There are likely to be more devices connected to the network, such as other computers, an Ethernet hub, printers, and anything else you've connected. After you've identified where the problem is, you can take some action to try to solve it.

Solving a network problem

Solving a network problem can be tricky because there are a number of potential sources of problems within the network and some that reside outside of the network and outside of your control.

Start with basic steps to see whether you can determine which part of the network is causing you problems so that you can begin to solve them. Working from the first element in the chain, do the following:

1. **Check the status of the modem.** Most modems have activity lights that indicate whether the modem is powered up and has a working connection. Check these lights to make sure the modem appears to be powered up and connected to the Internet. If the modem does appear to be working, move to step 2. If the modem doesn't appear to be working, move to step 7.

2. **Check the status of the AirPort Base Station.** It also has a light that uses color and flashing to indicate its status (see figure 3.13). If the light indicates the base station is working (in the current version, the status light is solid or flashing green when the base station is working correctly), move to step 3. If not (for example, if the status light is flashing amber), move to step 8.

Apple - AirPort Extreme - Performance

3.13 If the status light on the base station is green, all systems are go.

3. **Disconnect power from the base station and from the modem.**

4. **Wait at least 20 seconds.**

5. **Connect power to the base station and then to the modem.** These simple steps often reset a network and restore the connection.

Note When you can't access a Web page because of a network issue, Safari presents the Network Diagnostics button. Click this button to start the diagnostics application, and follow its instructions to try to solve the problem.

6. **Try what you were doing when you first encountered the problem.** If it's successful, you're done and you can go on about your business. If not, continue with the next steps.

7. **If the modem's power light is on (which it probably is) but the connection light is not, contact your Internet Service Provider to make sure service is available.**

8. **Remove power from the base station, wait 10 seconds, and connect it again.**

9. **Check the status light.** If the light goes green, the problem is solved. If not, you need to further isolate the problem.

10. **Ensure the firewall is set on your MacBook Pro.**

11. **Connect the MacBook Pro directly to the cable or DSL modem using an Ethernet cable.**

Caution To get a connection directly from the modem, your MacBook Pro must have the Ethernet connection enabled. Never connect MacBook Pro directly to a modem without first enabling its firewall.

12. **Try an Internet activity.** If it works, you know the problem is with the base station, and you can continue with these steps. If you can't get an Internet connection directly from the modem, you know the problem is with the modem or the Internet connection itself; contact the provider for assistance.

13. **Troubleshoot the base station until you solve its problem.** You might need to reset it and reconfigure it. See the documentation that came with the base station or use the Apple support Web site at www.apple.com/support/airport for help.

Solving a MacBook Pro problem

When you know the network is performing and other devices have connectivity, you can focus on the MacBook Pro to solve the issue.

1. **Try a different Internet application.** If one application works, but the other does not, you know the problem is related to a specific application and you can troubleshoot that application. If no Internet application works, continue with the following steps.

2. **Open the Network pane of the System Preferences application.**

3. **Check the status of the various connections.** If the status is Not Connected for a connection (see figure 3.14), you need to reconfigure that connection to get the connection working.

3.14 This MacBook Pro isn't connected.

4. **If the status is Connected, choose Apple menu ⇨ Restart.**

5. **Click Restart at the prompt.**

6. **After the MacBook Pro restarts, try the activity again.** Restarting when you have a problem is always a good thing to try because it's easy to do and solves a lot of different issues.

None of these steps helped. Now what?

While the steps in this section help with many problems, they certainly won't solve all problems. When they don't work, you have a couple of options. First, find a computer that can connect to the Internet and move to www.apple.com/support. Search for the specific problem you are having and use the results you find to solve it. Second, disconnect everything from your network and connect your MacBook Pro directly to the modem (ensuring the firewall is on first). If the connection works, you know the problem is related to the network; add other devices one-by-one, starting with the base station, until you find the source of the problem. If the connection doesn't work, you need help from your Internet provider to be able to solve the problem.

What Can I Do on a Local Network?

If you connect your MacBook Pro to the Internet with an AirPort Extreme Base Station as described in Chapter 3, you create a local network at the same time. Any devices connected to your local network, whether through a wired Ethernet connection or a wireless one, can communicate with the other devices on your network. This is a good thing because Mac OS X includes a lot of network features that you'll find to be very useful. Perhaps the most useful of these features is the ability to share files, but there are plenty of other powerful network features to explore and use.

Sharing Files

If you have more than one computer on your local network, the ability to share files among those computers is really useful because you can easily move files between the computers on the network. You can also store files on one computer and work on them while using any other computer on the network. The three general sharing skills you'll learn in this section are:

- Configuring your MacBook Pro to share files with other computers.
- Accessing files that are being shared with you.
- Sharing files with Windows computers.

Sharing your files with others

To enable other computers to access files stored on your MacBook Pro, you need to accomplish the first two tasks below, while the third task is optional:

- Configure user accounts to access your MacBook Pro from other computers.
- Configure file-sharing services on your MacBook Pro.
- Set specific security privileges on the files and folders you share.

Configuring Sharing user accounts for your MacBook Pro

To be able to access files on your MacBook Pro, a user must have a valid user account on your MacBook Pro that he uses to log into your computer to access the files that you are sharing. Group is the only type of account you can't use to share your files. The Sharing type of user account is especially intended to provide only sharing access to your MacBook Pro.

Note By default, a user account called Guest Account exists on your MacBook Pro (and every Mac, for that matter). This is a Sharing Only account that doesn't require a password to use.

If sharing files is all you want the user to be able to do while logged into your MacBook Pro, create a Sharing user account (see figure 4.1). If you want to provide broader access to your computer, use a Standard or Administrator account instead.

4.1 A Sharing account, like the Maximus account highlighted here, is ideal for enabling people to access the files on your MacBook Pro.

Configuring file sharing on your MacBook Pro

The second part of enabling file sharing is to configure your MacBook Pro to share its files, choose the folders you want to share, and determine the user accounts and permissions with which you want to share those folders. Here's how to perform these tasks:

1. **Open the System Preferences application.**

2. **Click the Sharing icon.** The Sharing pane opens.

3. **To set the name by which your computer is recognized on the network, enter a name for the computer in the Computer Name field.**

4. **Check the On check box next to the File Sharing service in the left pane of the window.** File sharing starts up, you see its status change to On, and you see your computer's address and name just below the Status text.

5. **To share a folder, click the Add button (+) at the bottom of the Shared Folders list.** The Select sheet appears.

6. **Move to and choose the folder you want to share.** You can only share folders for which you have Read & Write access.

7. **Click Add.** You return to the Sharing pane, and the folder you chose is added to the Shared Folders list.

8. **To allow a user account to access the folder, click the Add button (+) at the bottom of the Users list.**

Genius If you click the Address Book option in the User Account sheet, you can access any person in your Address Book.

9. **Select the user accounts (see figure 4.2) with which you want to share the folder.**

10. **Click Select.**

11. **Select a user on the Users list on the Sharing pane.**

12. **On the pop-up menu at the right edge of the Users list, choose the permissions for the folder that this user account has, such as Read & Write or Read Only (figure 4.3).**

4.2 Choose the users with whom you want to share the selected folder on this sheet.

4.3 Maximus and Brad Miser can see and change items in the Pictures folder, Marcus Aurelius can only view things there, and all other accounts can't do anything with it.

Say Hello to Bonjour

Bonjour is the name of the Apple technology that makes it possible for devices on a network to automatically find each other. This means you don't have to bother with addresses or browsing though various paths to find the Mac or printer you want to work with. Even Windows computers can use Bonjour, as long as they have the Apple Bonjour for Windows software installed.

Genius

You can provide different levels of access to items within a folder.

13. **To remove a user's access to the folder, choose the user, click the Remove button (-) at the bottom of the Users list, and click OK in the warning sheet.**

14. **To unshare a folder, choose it on the Shared Folders list, click the Remove button (-) at the bottom of the Shared Folders list, and click OK in the warning sheet.**

After you've completed these steps, all that remains is to provide the user account information to the people with whom you'll be sharing your files.

Accessing files shared with you

While it is better to give than receive, there's also the expression share and share alike. You can access files being shared with you in a couple of ways:

- Browsing using the Sidebar.
- Moving directly to a shared source by its address.

Both of these methods work, but the browsing option is the easiest and fastest. If you are accessing a device that supports Bonjour, browsing is definitely the way to go.

Using the Sidebar to access shared files

Thanks to Bonjour, as soon as your MacBook Pro is connected to a network, any computers that are sharing files are immediately recognized and mounted on your desktop, making it easy to access the files they are sharing. When you want to access shared files, perform the following steps:

1. **Open a Finder window.**

2. **In the Shared section of the Sidebar, select the computer with the files that you want to access.**

Genius

You don't need to log in to access Public files and folders because you are automatically logged in under the Guest account.

3. **Click the Connect As button.** The Login dialog appears. The Registered User option is selected automatically.

4. **In the Name field, enter the name of the user account you want to use to log in.**

5. **Enter that account's password in the Password field.**

6. **Check the Remember this password in my keychain check box.** This enables you to log in automatically.

7. **Click Connect.** Your MacBook Pro connects to the computer and mounts all the folders being shared with you in the Finder window; the resources you see are those for which the user account you are using has Read, Write Only (Drop Box), or Read & Write permissions (see figure 4.4).

4.4 I've logged into the computer called Brad Miser's iMac under the bradm account.

8. **Select the folder containing the files with which you want to work.** The files in that folder become available to you if you have Read Only, Read & Write, or Write Only permissions.

Accessing shared files using a URL

For those computers that are not using Bonjour, you can move directly to a computer that is sharing its files using its address on the network. Try this:

1. **If the computer you want to access is a Mac, open the Sharing pane of the System Preferences application and select File Sharing.** You see the computer's address (starting with afp://) under the File Sharing status information. Use the address to log into the computer.

Note

You'll learn how to access a Windows PC in the next section.

2. **From your MacBook Pro's desktop, choose Go ⇨ Connect to Server.** The Connect to Server dialog appears (see figure 4.5).

3. **Enter the address of the computer you want to access in the Server Address field.**

4. **Click Connect.** The Login dialog appears.

4.5 Using the Connect to Server command, you can log into a file-sharing computer through its network address.

5. **In the Name field, enter the name of the user account you want to use to log in.**

6. **Enter that account's password in the Password field.**

7. **Check the Remember this password in my keychain check box.** This enables you to log in automatically.

8. **Click Connect.** The Volume Selection dialog appears. In this dialog, you see the folders and volumes that are available to your user account on the computer you are logging into.

9. **Select the volumes you want to use.**

10. **Click OK.** Your MacBook Pro connects to the other computer, and each volume you selected is mounted on your desktop.

Genius

If you regularly use an address to connect to a computer, add it as a favorite by clicking the Add button (+) in the Connect to Server dialog; the address is added to the list of favorites shown under the Server Address field.

Sharing files with Windows PCs

If your network includes both Macs and Windows PCs, you can share files between them. The process is similar to sharing files between Macintosh computers, but there are some differences (which you could have probably guessed).

Sharing files on a MacBook Pro with Windows PCs

Configuring files to share with Windows PCs is accomplished very similarly to sharing files with Macs, but you need to enable Windows file sharing by also doing the following:

1. **On the Sharing pane, click the Options button.** The Options sheet appears (see figure 4.6).

2. **Check the Share files and folders using SMB check box.**

3. **Check the On check box for a user account that you want to be able to access files on your MacBook Pro from a Windows PC.** The Password dialog appears.

4. **Enter the user account's password in the Password field.** This is the same password you provided when you created the account.

4.6 Activate Windows file sharing on the Options sheet.

Note

You can't enable Windows sharing for a user account that is a Sharing Only account.

5. **Click OK.** The dialog closes and you return to the Options sheet.

6. **Click Done.** The selected files are available from Windows PCs on the network.

Genius

You can't share some folders with only Windows or only Macs. You can only enable file sharing for Windows by user account and control access to those files using the Shared Folders and Users tools.

Accessing files on your MacBook Pro from a Windows PC

After you've configured your MacBook Pro to share files with Windows computers, you can access them from a Windows PC by performing the following steps:

1. **On the PC, open the My Computer folder in a Windows Explorer window.**

2. **Click the My Network Places link in the Other Places section.**

3. **Click the Add a network place link in the Network Tasks section.** The Add Network Place Wizard opens.

4. **Click Next.**

5. **Select the Choose another network location option.**

6. **Click Next.**

7. **Enter the path to and name of the shared folder you want to access on the Windows PC in the Internet or network address field (see figure 4.7).** The path starts with \\ followed by the computer's name and the specific folder you want to access.

4.7 Enter the path to the folder you want to share with Windows PCs.

8. **Click Next.** You're prompted to log into the MacBook Pro.

9. **Enter the username for an account on the MacBook Pro in the User name field.**

10. **Enter the account's password in the Password field.**

87

11. **Click OK.** You see the Name screen.

12. **Enter a name for the shared folder.** This can be any name you want and is how you recognize the shared folders on the PC.

13. **Click Next.** You see the Complete screen. This confirms that you have successfully accessed the shared folder.

14. **Click Finish.** The shared folder opens on the Windows desktop, and you can access its contents based on your user security.

Caution If the Windows PC is connected to a Virtual Private Network (VPN), disconnect from that network before setting up sharing on the local network. Some VPN software can block Macs from being able to access a Windows computer.

Sharing files on a Windows PC with Macs

To share a folder and its files that are stored on a Windows PC, perform the following steps:

1. **Right-click the folder on the Windows PC that you want to share.**

2. **Choose Properties.** The Properties dialog box appears.

3. **Click the Sharing tab.**

4. **Click the Share this folder radio button.**

5. **Click the Permissions button.** The Permissions dialog box appears.

6. **Choose a user or group at the top of the dialog box.**

7. **Check the Allow check box to allow, or the Deny check box to deny various permissions.**

8. **Click OK.** You return to the Sharing tab (see figure 4.8).

9. **Click OK.** You're ready to access the shared folder from another computer on the network.

4.8 Use the Sharing tab to share folders on a Windows PC.

Accessing files on a Windows PC from your MacBook Pro

To be able to access shared files on a Windows PC, you need to know its address on the network and have a username and password. To log on, perform the following steps:

Genius To determine the address of a Windows PC, choose Start menu ⇨ All Programs ⇨ Accessories ⇨ Command Prompt. At the command prompt, type **ipconfig** and press Enter. The IP address appears in the resulting information.

1. **From the desktop, choose Go ⇨ Connect to Server.** The Connect to Server dialog appears.

2. **Enter the address of the computer you want to access in the Server Address field.** The address should start with smb:// which is followed by the computer's IP address and the name of the shared folder. So, if the computer's IP address is *1.2.3.4* and the folder you are accessing is called *books*, the address you enter would be *smb://1.2.3.4/books* (see figure 4.9).

3. **Click Connect.** The Login dialog appears.

4. **In the Name field, enter the name of the user account you want to use to log in.** If your user account is part of a domain on the Windows PC, you must add the domain and \ as a prefix to the user account, as in *xyz\useraccount*, where *xyz* is the domain with which *useraccount* is associated.

4.9 Logging into a Windows PC is very similar to logging into a Mac.

5. **Enter that account's password in the Password field.**

6. **Check the Remember this password in my keychain check box.** This enables you to log in automatically.

7. **Click Connect.** The shared folder is mounted on your desktop and you can access it according to your permissions.

Sharing Screens

With screen sharing, you can control a Mac over the local network just as if you were sitting in front of it. This is very useful for helping other users on your network. Instead of moving to their locations, you can simply log into their computer to provide help.

Like file sharing, you can configure screen-sharing permissions on your MacBook Pro. You can also share the screens of other Macs that have screen-sharing permissions configured.

Sharing MacBook Pro with other Macs

To share your MacBook Pro screen with other Macs on your network, configure screen-sharing permissions:

1. **Open the Sharing pane of the System Preferences application.**

2. **Choose the Screen Sharing service on the service list.** The controls for screen sharing appear.

3. **In the Allow access for section, choose one of the following options:**

   - Click All users to allow anyone who can access your MacBook Pro over the network to share its screen.

   - Click Only these users to create a list of user accounts that can share your screen. To create the list, click the Add button (+) at the bottom of the user list.

4. **Check the On check box for Screen Sharing.** Screen sharing services start (see figure 4.10), and your MacBook Pro is available to users on your local network according to the access permissions you set.

4.10 This MacBook Pro is sharing its screen with three user accounts.

Note If you allow anyone to request to share your screen, then when someone wants to share your MacBook Pro, you see a permission dialog on your screen. To allow your screen to be shared, click Share Screen.

Accessing another Mac from MacBook Pro

You can access other Macs being shared with you by browsing the network for available comput-ers or by moving to a specific address.

Accessing a shared Mac by browsing

To connect to another Mac to share its screen, perform the following steps:

1. **Open a Finder window.**

2. **In the Shared section of the Sidebar, select the Mac whose screen you want to share.**

3. **Click Share Screen.** The Share Screen Permission dialog appears (see figure 4.11).

4. **Use one of the following options to share the other Mac's screen:**

   ○ To request permission to share the screen, click the By asking for per-mission radio button and click Connect and wait for the other per-son to grant you permission.

   ○ To log in using a user account with screen-sharing permissions, click the As a registered user radio button, enter the username in the Name field.

4.11 Use the Share Screen Permission dialog to access another Mac on your network.

5. **Once the other person's desktop appears within the Screen Sharing window on your MacBook Pro desktop, you can work with the shared Mac as you would your own.**

Accessing a shared Mac by address

You can also connect to a Mac to share its screen by entering its address on the network. To deter-mine the address of a Mac whose screen you want to share, open its Sharing pane, select the Screen Sharing service, and note the address just under the Screen Sharing status information. The Mac's screen-sharing address starts with vnc://.

Once you have the other Mac's address, you can share its screen using the following steps:

1. **From the desktop, choose Go** ➪ **Connect to Server.** The Connect to Server dialog appears.

2. **Enter the address of the computer whose screen you want to share in the Server Address field.** This address is something like *vnc://1.2.3.4*.

3. **Click Connect.** The Share Screen Permission dialog appears.

4. **Use one of the following options to share the other Mac's screen:**

   ● To request permission to share the screen, click the By asking for permission radio button and click Connect and wait for the other person to grant you permission.

   ● To log in using a user account with screen-sharing permissions, click the As a registered user radio button.

Sharing a Mac's screen

When you share a Mac's screen, you use the Screen Sharing application. Its window, which has the name of the Mac whose screen you are sharing as its title, contains the desktop of the Mac whose screen you are sharing, including open Finder windows, applications, and documents (see figure 4.12). When your cursor is inside the Screen Sharing application window, any action you take is done on the Mac whose screen you are sharing. When you move outside the window, the cursor for your MacBook Pro separates from the shared Mac's cursor and the shared Mac's cursor freezes (unless, of course, the user at that Mac is doing something, in which case you see the results of their actions).

When you access a shared Mac, its screen is automatically scaled to fit into the Screen Sharing application window. The desktop you see in the Screen Sharing window depends on the resolution of the Mac's desktop you are sharing. If it is very large, such as a 24-inch iMac that also has an external display connected to it, the information in the shared window is quite small so that it all fits on your MacBook Pro screen. You can access the Display pane of the System Preferences application on the shared Mac to decrease its resolution so that the image appears larger on your desktop. You can choose View ➪ Turn Scaling Off to make the screen its actual size; if the shared Mac's screen is larger than yours, you have to scroll to see all of it.

Caution   If you use the shortcut ⌘+Q to quit applications, don't do so when you are using the Screen Sharing application because that closes the active application on the shared Mac, not the Screen Sharing application itself. Use the Quit command on the File menu instead.

4.12 This Screen Sharing window shows the desktop of an iMac on the MacBook Pro network.

To move information from the shared computer to yours, copy that information on the shared computer and choose Edit ➪ Get Clipboard. This copies what you pasted to the clipboard on your MacBook Pro, where you can paste it into your applications. To move information in the other direction, copy it on your MacBook Pro and choose Edit ➪ Send Clipboard. This moves the data from your Clipboard to the Clipboard on the shared Mac, where it can be pasted into documents that are open there.

Sharing Printers

Printers are a great resource to share on a network because you seldom need one printer for each computer. There are two basic ways to use printer sharing to make printers available on a network. You can connect a USB printer to an AirPort Extreme Base Station and share it from there, or you can connect a USB or Ethernet printer directly to your MacBook Pro and share it with the network.

Note

If a printer is networkable, you don't need to share it. Instead, connect the printer to the network through an Ethernet or wireless connection. This is better than printer sharing because no computer or base station resources are required for the networked printers.

Sharing USB printers connected to a base station

To share a USB printer from a base station, perform the following steps:

1. **Connect the printer to the USB port on the AirPort Extreme Base Station.**

2. **Open the AirPort Utility located in the Utilities folder in the Applications folder.** The base stations with which your MacBook Pro can communicate are shown in the left pane of the window.

3. **Select the base station to which the printer is attached.**

4. **Click Manual Setup.** You're prompted to enter the base station's password (if its password is saved on your keychain, it is entered automatically). The Manual Setup screen appears.

5. **Click the Printers tab.** The connected printer is shown under the USB Printers field.

6. **Enter the name of the printer in the Name field.** This is the name that users select to configure the printer on their Macs.

7. **Click Update.** The base station is updated and restarts. Any computers on its network can use the printer connected to it.

Sharing printers connected to a Mac

If a Mac has a printer connected to it directly, through Ethernet or USB, you can share that printer with the network. However, in order for other computers to use that printer, the Mac to which it is connected must be active (it can't be asleep) and currently connected to the computer. Because you'll probably move your MacBook Pro around a lot, this isn't convenient. However, if your network includes a desktop Mac to which a printer is connected, you can share it using the following steps:

1. **Connect and configure the printer to the Mac from which it is being shared.**

2. **Open the Sharing pane of the System Preferences application.**

3. **Check the On check box for the Printer Sharing service.** The service starts up.

4. **Check the check box for the printer you want to share.** Other computers can use the printer by adding it; the printer's name is the current printer name with @*yourmacbookpro*, where *yourmacbookpro* is the name of the computer to which the printer is attached (see Chapter 15 for detailed information about adding a printer).

Sharing an Internet Connection

Any Mac can share its Internet connection with other computers, similar to a base station. While I don't recommend this for a permanent network (one reason is because the Mac has to be active all the time for the network to be available), it can be very useful when you are traveling with your MacBook Pro. You can share an Internet connection that you are getting through Ethernet with other computers using AirPort, or you can share an Internet connection that you are getting through AirPort over your MacBook Pro Ethernet port. Here's how:

1. **Connect and configure your MacBook Pro to access the Internet.**

2. **Open the Sharing pane of the System Preferences application.**

3. **Select the Internet Sharing service.** Its controls appear in the right part of the pane.

4. **On the Share your connection from pop-up menu, choose Ethernet if you get your connection through Ethernet, or AirPort if you get your connection through AirPort.**

5. **Check the On check box for the connection that other computers use to get their Internet connection from you.** For example, if your MacBook Pro is using Ethernet for Internet access, check the On check box for AirPort.

6. **If you selected AirPort in step 5, click AirPort Options.** The AirPort Options sheet appears (see figure 4.13).

7. **Enter a name for the network you are creating in the Name field.** This is how others identify the network you provide.

8. **Choose the channel for the network on the Channel pop-up menu.** Automatic is usually the best choice, but you can choose a specific channel if your network has problems.

Network Name:	TemporaryInternet
Channel:	Automatic
	☑ Enable encryption (using WEP)
Password:	••••••••
Confirm Password:	••••••••
WEP Key Length:	128-bit

If you plan to share your Internet connection with non–Apple computers, use a 5 character password for a 40–bit WEP key, and a 13 character password for a 128–bit WEP key.

(Cancel) (OK)

4.13 Use the AirPort Options sheet to create an AirPort network over which you can share an Internet connection.

9. **Check the Enable encryption (using WEP) check box.** I recommend that you always create a secure network.

10. **Enter a password for the network in the Password and Confirm Password fields.** If you're sharing your connection with Windows computers, make the password exactly 13 characters long.

11. **On the WEP Key Length pop-up menu, choose 128-bit.**

12. **Click OK.** The sheet closes, and you return to the Sharing pane.

13. **Click the On check box for the Internet Sharing service (see figure 4.14).**

4.14 This MacBook Pro is sharing its Internet connection over AirPort.

14. **Click Start in the resulting confirmation sheet.** Your MacBook Pro creates a wireless network and starts sharing its Internet connection over it. Other computers can connect to the Internet by joining your wireless network.

Sharing with Applications

A number of applications also provide sharing on a local network. Using iTunes, you can share your library with the network so that other people can listen to and view its contents. You can also share your iPhoto libraries on the network so that people can access the photos in your database. Of course, you can access iTunes and iPhoto libraries that are being shared by others on the network, as well.

To set up sharing in those applications, open the Sharing tabs of their Preferences dialogs. Check the Look for shared libraries/photos check boxes to access resources that are being shared with you. Check the Share my library/photos check boxes to share your libraries on the network. Use the controls on the tab to define what you share, its share name, and whether a password is required.

How Do I Take Advantage of MobileMe?

To become a genius, take advantage of the Apple MobileMe services to expand your MacBook Pro to encompass (literally) the Internet. With MobileMe, you aren't just an Internet consumer; the Internet becomes an extension of your MacBook Pro desktop. A MobileMe account provides a number of great features that I think you'll find indispensable, examples include: iDisk, e-mail, and data synchronization. In order to access these features, you need to have a MobileMe account, which you can easily and inexpensively obtain and configure on your MacBook Pro in just a few minutes.

Obtaining a MobileMe Account

To use MobileMe, you must have a MobileMe account. A MobileMe account includes, by default, 20GB of storage space on Apple servers, an e-mail account, space for online galleries of your photos, and more. You can also purchase a family account that provides several different user accounts under a single MobileMe account (for distinct e-mail addresses and iDisks). At the time of this writing, the cost of an individual MobileMe account is $99 per year, while the cost of a family account is $149 per year. You can also add disk space by upgrading accounts.

Note The disk space included with a MobileMe account is used for two purposes: iDisk and e-mail storage space. The total space included with a MobileMe account is the total space for both kinds of data; you can choose how this space is allocated.

To get your MobileMe account, perform the following steps:

1. **Select Apple menu ⇨ System Preferences.**

2. **Click the MobileMe icon.** The MobileMe pane appears (see figure 5.1).

5.1 Use the MobileMe pane to obtain a MobileMe account and to configure it on your MacBook Pro.

3. **Click Learn More.** Your Web browser opens, moves to the MobileMe Web site, and you see the Login dialog.

4. **Click sign up for a free trial.** The first page of a two-step form appears.

5. **Fill out the information on this page.**

Caution Be thoughtful about what you choose as your member name; in addition to using this to log in to MobileMe, it becomes part of your e-mail address You can't change this name after you've created an account.

6. **Click Continue.**

7. **In a similar way, complete the second page of the form.** The Welcome to MobileMe screen appears, and provides information that you need to use your MobileMe account.

Configuring a MobileMe account

Now that you have a MobileMe account, configure its information in the System Preferences application so that you can automatically access your iDisk from the desktop and so the MobileMe e-mail account is configured in the Mail application for you too.

1. **Select Apple menu ➪ System Preferences.**

Genius If you didn't quit the System Preferences application when you completed the previous steps, hold the ⌘ key down and press Tab until the System Preferences application icon is highlighted on the Application Switcher so that you jump back to the MobileMe tab instead of doing steps 1 and 2.

2. **Click the MobileMe icon.**

3. **Enter your member name.**

4. **Enter your password.**

5. **Click Sign In.** Your account information is configured and you can access MobileMe services from your desktop (see figure 5.2).

Note You don't actually have to configure your MobileMe account in the System Preferences application to be able to use it because you can access most MobileMe services directly from the MobileMe Web site. About the only tool that does require you to have configured your account on your MacBook Pro is your iDisk. So, if you are using a computer other than your MacBook Pro, just move to the MobileMe Web site and log into your account (you'll learn how to do that in the section called "E-mailing from the Web" a bit later in this chapter).

5.2 After you have entered your MobileMe account information, the MobileMe pane changes indicating that you have successfully configured a MobileMe account.

Managing a MobileMe account

As you work with MobileMe, you might need to change your account. For example, you might want to convert a trial account to be a full account or you might upgrade your disk space. To make these sorts of changes, you can manage your account on a Web page dedicated to this purpose. Here's how:

1. **Move back to the MobileMe pane if you aren't there already.**

2. **Click the Account tab if it isn't selected.**

3. **Click Account Details.** You move to the MobileMe login Web page.

4. **Enter your member name (if required) and password.**

5. **Click Continue.** You move to the Account Settings Web page. This page shows various information about your account, such as its type, your e-mail address, and how much disk space you have. Along the left side of the window are tabs you use to configure different aspects of your account (see figure 5.3).

5.3 To change various aspects of your MobileMe account, click the related Account Settings tabs along the left side of the window.

6. **To make changes in any of these areas, click the appropriate tab, make the changes on the resulting Web form, and click Save.** The changes you make take effect immediately.

Working with an iDisk

An iDisk provides you with disk storage space on the MobileMe servers. Why is this a good thing? For starters, you need to store files on your iDisk to be able to create and publish Web sites using HomePage. Even better, an iDisk is a great way to store files because you can easily access the same files from multiple computers, such as from your MacBook Pro and from an iMac. You can also easily share files on your iDisk and even provide a place for people to store files they want to share with you.

Finally, because your iDisk is stored remotely, it's a great way to protect critical files because even if something really bad happens to your MacBook Pro, the files will be available to you on your iDisk. Your iDisk is remote so it works a bit differently than the disk in your MacBook Pro or an external hard drive to which the MacBook Pro is connected, but the tools you need to work with it are built into Mac OS X.

Configuring and managing an iDisk

There are two basic modes for an iDisk: unsynced or synced.

In the unsynced mode, you access the iDisk online, meaning that any files you move to or from the iDisk move across the Internet immediately. The benefit of this approach is that the iDisk doesn't take up any space on your MacBook Pro's hard drive. The downside is that you have to be connected to the Internet to be able to access the disk, so if you are someplace where net access isn't available, you can't get to the disk. If you want to store files there, you have to wait until you can connect, and then manually move the files to the iDisk.

In the synced mode, a local copy of the iDisk resides on your MacBook Pro's desktop. You move files to and from this local copy of the iDisk; the files aren't actually moved onto the online iDisk until it is synced with the local version (this can be done manually or automatically). This approach has a couple of benefits. One is that you can access the iDisk at any time because the local copy is always available. Another is that the speed of the iDisk is much faster because you are really just using your MacBook Pro's hard drive instead of working over the Internet (the sync process takes place in the background so it doesn't interfere with your other tasks). The downside of this approach is that you have to store all the files on the iDisk on your MacBook Pro's hard drive. If you have plenty of disk space, this isn't a problem, but if you have a lot of large files on your iDisk and the space on your MacBook Pro's hard drive is limited, you might have enough space to have a local copy.

In addition to choosing the mode for your iDisk, you need to configure how the Public folder on the iDisk can be accessed. You have a couple of choices here. You can determine if other people can only read (copy) files from your Public folder or if they can read files from and write files to the Public folder. You can also determine if a password is needed to be able to access the Public folder.

You configure and manage your iDisk from the MobileMe pane of the System Preferences application as the following steps demonstrate:

1. **Select Apple menu ⇨ System Preferences.**

2. **Click the MobileMe icon**.

3. **Click the iDisk tab.** At the top of the pane, you see a gauge showing how much of your iDisk space you are currently using; the green part of the bar represents the space being used (see figure 5.4). Immediately under the gauge, you see the total size of the iDisk, how much is being used, and how much is available.

MobileMe

Show All

MobileMe stores your email, contacts, calendar, photos and files in an online "cloud," and keeps your Mac, PC, iPhone, or iPod touch up to date.

Account   Sync   iDisk   Back to My Mac

iDisk Usage

0   9.51 GB   19.02 GB

19.02 GB total, 558 MB used, 18.48 GB available   (Upgrade Storage...)

Your iDisk Public Folder

You can connect to your iDisk public folder at http://idisk.mac.com/bradmacosx-Public

Allow others to: ● Read only   ○ Read and Write
☑ Password-protect your public folder   (Set Password...)

iDisk Sync: Off

(Start)   Click Start to keep a copy of your iDisk on this computer, so you can access it even when you're not connected to the Internet.

Update: ● Automatically   ○ Manually

5.4 Configure your iDisk on the iDisk tab of the MobileMe pane.

Genius

If the usage gauge shows that your iDisk is full or getting close to being full, move to the iDisk and delete files from it to free up more space. However, make sure you don't delete files that you use on your Web sites or removing files might have consequences you didn't intend. If you can't find files to remove and the disk is full, click the Upgrade Storage button to add more space to your iDisk.

4. **If you want people who access your iDisk to be able to store or change files in your Public folder, click Read and Write.**

Caution

You should protect your public iDisk with a password, especially if you allow others to read and write to the disk. If you don't require a password and allow read and write, anyone who stumbles across your iDisk can store files there. That's not a good idea for a number of reasons, the most obvious of which is that you are paying for the space and probably don't want strangers to be able to use it for free.

5. **To put a password on your Public folder, check the Password-protect your public folder check box.** The Password sheet appears.

6. **Enter the password for the folder in the Password field.** Passwords must be between 6 and 8 characters long can can't be the same as the password for your MobileMe account.

7. **Confirm the password by entering it again in the Confirm field.**

8. **Click OK.**

Genius

To see your iDisk's Public folder on the Web, click the link shown on the MobileMe pane or enter the address in a Web browser (it is public.me.com/*membername*, where *membername* is your MobileMe member name). You move to the folder's Web page. If required, a Name and Password sheet appears. Enter public in the Name field and the folder's password in the Password field. Click Log In. The contents of the Public folder are shown; you can download files by clicking their links. If enabled, you can upload files by clicking the Upload button.

9. **To use your iDisk in the synced mode, click the Start button.** A copy of your iDisk is made on your MacBook Pro's hard disk.

10. **If you want the sync process to happen automatically, click the Automatically radio button. If you want to manually sync the iDisk, click the Manually radio button.** Your iDisk is ready to use.

Using an iDisk

Working with an iDisk is similar to using the hard disk in your MacBook Pro. You can open it in any of the following ways:

- Open a Finder window and click iDisk in the Devices section of the Sidebar.
- On the Finder's menubar, choose Go ⇨ iDisk ⇨ My iDisk.
- Press Shift+⌘+I.

When you open the iDisk, you see its contents in the resulting Finder window as shown in figure 5.5. These include a set of default folders similar to those in your Home folder, such as Documents, Movies, and Music. Like your Home folder, you can create new folders, move files around, create new files, and so on. In this respect, using an iDisk is just like using your MacBook Pro's hard drive.

5.5 Using an iDisk is just like using your MacBook Pro's hard drive — almost.

If you use the iDisk in the Unsynced mode, files you move to or from the iDisk are moved across the Internet. This can take some time, so don't expect the kind of response you get from your hard drive. If files are larger than a MB or two, you'll see the Copy dialog on the screen for a while; copying works in the background so you can just ignore the window. When the copy process is complete, the window closes.

Note The first time you sync an iDisk can take a long time, especially when large amounts of data are on the disk. Subsequent syncs are much faster because only files that have changed are involved.

If you use the iDisk in the Synced mode, you see the Sync button next to its icon on the Sidebar; you also see the time and date of the last synchronization at the bottom of the window. To manually sync the disk, click the Sync button. Files on the local version are copied to the online version and vice versa until the two versions are duplicates of each other. If you selected the Automatic option, Mac OS X takes care of this for you, but you can manually sync the disks at any time.

Other Useful iDisk Commands

There are a couple of interesting commands on the iDisk sub-menu on the Finder's Go menu: Other User's iDisk and Other User's Public Folder.

If you choose Go ⇨ iDisk ⇨ Other User's iDisk, you're prompted to enter the other user's member name and password. When you do so, the other user's iDisk is mounted on the desktop. This is really useful if you want to access your own iDisk on someone else's computer. Just choose the command and enter your own member name and password; your iDisk mounts just like when you use it from your MacBook Pro. (Make sure you eject the iDisk when you're done using it.)

If you choose Go ⇨ iDisk ⇨ Other User's Public Folder, you're prompted to enter the other user's member name. When you do and click Connect, you're prompted to enter a password (if required) and then that user's Public folder appears on the Sidebar, where you can open it and add files (if you have write permission).

E-mailing from the Web

Your MobileMe account includes a full-featured e-mail account that you can use with Mac OS X's Mail or other e-mail application. Your MobileMe e-mail address is *membername*@me.com, where *membername* is your MobileMe member name. Using your MobileMe e-mail with an e-mail application is great, and you'll learn some tricks for the Mail application in Chapter 7. However, your MobileMe e-mail is also easily accessible from the Web, which is nice because that means you can work with your e-mail from any computer with Internet access (including Windows computers).

Using MobileMe Webmail

Using the Web to access your MobileMe e-mail is simple as you see in the following steps:

1. **Open Safari or other Web browser and move to me.com.** You see the MobileMe Login dialog.

2. **Enter your MobileMe member name.**

3. **Enter your password.**

4. **If you're using a computer you control, check the Keep me logged in for two weeks check box.**

5. **Click Login.** Your MobileMe applications appear.

6. **Click the Mail button (the envelope on the far left end of the toolbar).** The MobileMe Mail page appears as shown in figure 5.6.

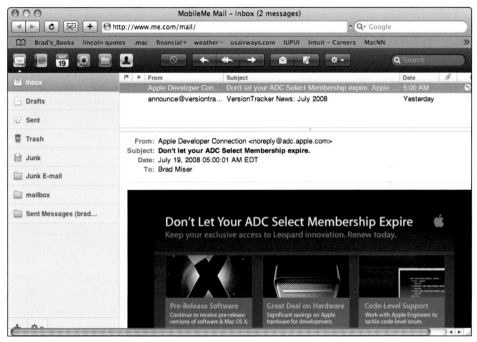

5.6 If you've used Mac OS X's Mail application, MobileMe Mail on the Web should look quite familiar.

7. **Select an email to read it.** The message body appears in the lower pane of the window.

8. **To reply, click the Reply button and complete the reply.**

9. **To create a new message, click the New Message button (paper and pencil icon) and complete the new message.**

10. **To check for new e-mail, click Get Mail (the envelope).**

As you can see from these steps, using MobileMe Web e-mail is very similar to working with e-mail in an e-mail application, especially if you are familiar with Mail.

Setting Webmail preferences

While the basics of using MobileMe Web e-mail are pretty straightforward, there are a lot of ways to customize how it works for you using the not-so-obvious preferences controls. Check them out:

1. **Open the MobileMe Mail application.**

2. **Open the Action pop-up menu (the gear icon) and choose Preferences.** The Preferences window opens (see figure 5.7).

5.7 If you use Web e-mail much, take some time to configure its preferences to suit yours.

3. **Configure the following settings on the General tab:**

   ● **Appearance.** These tools enable you to determine the appearance of the Mail page, including the number of panes used and whether all folders are shown when you log in.

   ● **Mailboxes.** Use these check boxes and pop-up menus to determine how sent and deleted messages are stored. If you want to conserve the space used to store e-mail, uncheck the Move deleted messages to check box; when you delete messages, they are removed from your account immediately so that they don't consume disk space.

● **Junk Mail.** You can use the junk mail filter to try to cut back on the amount of spam with which you have to deal.

4. **Configure the following settings on the Composing tab:**

● **Composing.** If you want the original message to be quoted when you replay, always a good idea, check the Quote original message when replying check box. The other important option is to enable spell checking by checking the Check spelling before message is sent check box and then choose the default dictionary you want to use.

● **Identity.** Here you can enter the name you want to be shown in the From field on e-mail you send; the default is the name you entered for your MobileMe account. To use a signature, check the Add signature to your mail check box and enter the signature you want to use in the text box.

5. **Configure the following settings on the Viewing tab:**

● **Inbox and Folders.** Choose how many messages you want to be shown per page and what kind of previews you want to see for each message in the Inbox (Short, Long, or No); if you choose No, you only see the message subjects.

● **Message Contents.** Determine how HTML e-mail is handled and whether long or short headers are shown at the top of messages.

6. **Skip over the Aliases tab for now; you'll learn about that in the next section.**

7. **Configure the following settings on the Other tab:**

● **External Account.** If you have another e-mail account that uses POP (Post Office Protocol, and no, I didn't make that up) and you want to be able to check e-mail from that account using MobileMe Mail, check the Check mail from an external POP account check box and enter the account's information in the resulting boxes. You can only add one additional account, but this can be useful if you want to be able to check two accounts using the Web interface.

● **Forwarding.** Use these tools to forward your MobileMe e-mail. Check the Forward my email to another email account check box and enter the address to which you want e-mail forwarded. Check the middle check box if you want to keep forwarded messages in your MobileMe e-mail Inbox. Use the bottom check box and text box to set up an automated reply to an e-mail you receive.

8. **Click Save.** The changes you made take effect immediately.

Using MobileMe e-mail aliases

E-mail aliases are a great tool in the fight against spam. You can create an alias address that points to your real MobileMe e-mail address. When you shop, participate in forums, or do other activity, provide an alias address. If that address gets spammed, you can simply delete it and create another one. Of course, you can use aliases for other reasons too. For example, if you are writing a book called *MacBook Pro Portable Genius*, you can create an alias I_Love_MacBook_Pro@me.com to show your preference in computers.

Creating e-mail aliases

Creating e-mail aliases is easy:

Note

You have to be using a full MobileMe account to be able to create aliases.

1. **Open your MobileMe Mail Preferences window.**

2. **Click the Aliases tab.**

3. **Click Add New Alias.** The alias creation tools appear.

4. **Enter the alias, which is everything before the "@" in the e-mail address.** The alias must be between 3 and 20 characters and can't have unusual symbols. If you try to use something you can't, you see an error message explaining the problem.

5. **Enter the name you want to be shown in the From field when you send e-mail using this alias.**

6. **Choose the color used to indicate e-mail sent to this alias.**

7. **Click Create.** The e-mail alias is checked. If it meets the requirements and is not being used already, it is created (see figure 5.8). If not, you have to change it until it does meet the rules and is not being used.

8. **To create more aliases, click Add New Alias.**

9. **Repeat steps 5 through 7.**

10. **Repeat steps 8 and 9 until you've created all your aliases.** You can have up to five aliases.

Mail Preferences

General · Composing · Viewing · **Aliases** · Other

Create or Delete an Alias
Disable or enable aliases and change their colors.

Active	Alias	Name (appears in "From")	Color
☑	i_am_a_dentist@me.com i_am_a_dentist@mac.com	Doc Holliday	○○○○○○○ ⊗
☑	dont_like_law_dawgs@me.com dont_like_law_dawgs@mac.com	Ike Clanton	○○◉○○○○ ⊗
☑	tombstone_lawman@me.com	Wyatt Earp	◉○○○○○○ ⊗
☑	i_love_macbook_pro@me.com	Mac Fan	◉○○○○○○ ⊗

(Add New Alias)

Cancel · Save

5.8 Your aliases can be just about anything you want them to be.

Genius

Use the Active check box to turn aliases off or on. When active, e-mail sent to the alias is delivered to it. When inactive, e-mail sent to the alias bounces. If you receive some spam at an alias that you don't want to delete, disable it to stop the spam. When you want to use it, make it active and then disable it again when you're done with it.

11. **Click Save.** The aliases are created and are ready to use (as long as they are active of course).

Using e-mail aliases

You can provide an e-mail alias just like you provided your real e-mail address, such as when you are making a purchase or registering on a forum.

You can also send e-mail using the alias:

1. **Create a new e-mail message as usual.**

2. **On the Account pop-up menu, choose the alias that you want the message to be from (see figure 5.9).**

113

5.9 Pick an alias, any alias.

3. **Complete and send the message.** The alias is associated with the message so if the recipient replies to it, the reply is sent to the alias.

If an alias does get spammed or you simply don't want to use it any more, you have two options. You can make it inactive or you can delete it. If you delete it, you won't be able to use it again so make sure you are really done with an alias before you delete. The steps to do either task are similar:

1. **Open your MobileMe Mail Preferences window.**

2. **Click the Aliases tab.**

3. **To disable an alias uncheck its Active check box.**

4. **To delete an alias, click its Remove button, which is the x located to the right of the last color radio button.**

5. **Click OK.** The alias is deleted.

6. **Click Save.** Any aliases you made inactive no longer are valid and any e-mail to those addresses bounces.

Synchronizing Data

One of the biggest benefits of MobileMe is that it provides you with a central, accessible location to store information. Using MobileMe, you can keep various kinds of information synchronized between MobileMe and your MacBook Pro, which is pretty useful. For example, when you add a contact on your MobileMe account, that contact can be automatically copied to your Address Book on your MacBook Pro.

You can also use this capability to synchronize data on multiple computers. Suppose you create a Safari bookmark on an iMac and want to use it on your MacBook Pro. You could recreate the bookmark on the MacBook Pro, but that would be a nuisance. With MobileMe synchronization, you can ensure that the same set of bookmarks is available on multiple computers automatically. Even better, if you have an iPhone, you can keep email, contact information, calendars, and other data in sync on that too.

The information you can keep in sync includes the following:

- Bookmarks
- Calendars
- Contacts
- Dashboard widgets
- Dock items
- Keychains
- Mail accounts
- Mail rules, signatures, and smart mailboxes
- Notes
- Preferences

In addition to selecting the kind of information you want to sync, you can also choose the direction in which information is synced, such as from MobileMe to a computer, from a computer to MobileMe, or in both directions. To configure synchronization, perform the following steps:

1. **Open the MobileMe pane of the System Preferences application and click the Sync tab (see figure 5.10).**

5.10 Use the Sync tab to choose the kind of information you want to synchronize.

2. **Check the Synchronize with MobileMe check box.**

3. **On the pop-up menu, choose how you want syncs to occur.** Choose Manually to sync manually or choose a time, such as Every Hour, to sync at those times, or Automatically to have syncs performed automatically when data in either location changes.

4. **Check the check box next to each item you want to include in the sync.** There are many options, including Bookmarks, Calendars, and Contacts.

5. **Click Sync Now.** The information you selected is copied onto MobileMe. If some of the information already exists, you see an alert.

6. **On the alert's pop-up menu, choose how you want data to be synced.** For example, if you want the data on MobileMe to be merged with the information on you MacBook Pro, choose Merge all data. Or, you can choose to replace data on MobileMe or on the computer.

7. **Click Sync in the alert box.** The sync process begins. As changes are made to data, you're prompted about what's going to be done.

8. **Click the Sync button to allow the sync to continue.**

9. **Repeat step 8 at each prompt.** When the process is complete, you see the time and date of the last sync at the bottom of the Sync tab

10. **Repeat steps 1 through 9 for each computer you want to include in the sync.**

Genius

Using the MobileMe synchronization works great for data, but doesn't do anything for documents. However, if you were paying attention earlier in the chapter, you learned how to use an iDisk. An iDisk enables you to keep documents on different computers in sync. On each computer, set up the iDisk so that it is synced automatically. Store the documents you want to keep in sync on your iDisk. As you make changes to the document, those changes are saved in the version stored on the iDisk. Since you can access the same iDisk and its documents from any Mac, you can easily make sure you are using the same version of the document no matter which computer you use.

How Can I Manage Contact Information?

The Mac OS X Address Book enables you to store contact information for people and organizations. While that's useful in itself, it's just the beginning. You can access and use your contact information in other applications, such as Mail, Safari, and iChat, to make what you want to do easier and faster. You can also act on information stored in Address Book directly, such as opening a Web page that shows a map of an address. Naturally, you'll also want to be able to access your contacts from your iPhone; synchronizing contacts between Address Book and an iPhone is a snap.

Adding Contact Information to Address Book

Address Book uses an address card model, which I suppose originated with the Rolodex way back in the analog era. Each contact, be it a person or an organization, is represented by a card containing contact information. Address Book cards are virtual (vCards), making them flexible because you can store a variety of information on each card; you can also store different information for various contacts.

In fact, each card in Address Book can hold an unlimited number of physical addresses, phone numbers, e-mail addresses, dates, notes, and URL addresses. Address Book only displays fields that have data in them so your cards aren't cluttered up with a lot of empty spaces.

Creating a contact manually

You can create address cards for contacts you want to add to Address Book manually. Use the following steps to guide you.

1. **Open the Address Book application (see figure 6.1).** The Group pane shows the groups that have been created in the application. The Name pane shows the cards in the selected group, and the Card pane shows the details for the card selected in the Name pane.

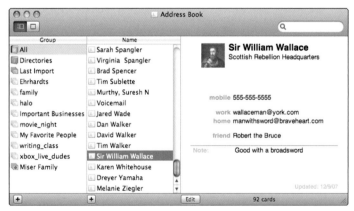

6.1 Address Book cards provide detailed information for each contact.

2. **Click the Add Card button at the bottom of the Name column.** A new, empty card based on the template appears in the Card pane.

3. **Enter the contact's information in the various fields.**

4. **Click the pop-up menu next to the first field (work by default) and select the type of contact information you want to enter.**

5. **To remove a field from the card, click the Delete button next to the field you want to remove.**

6. **To add another field of the same type to a card, click the Add button (+) next to a field of the type you want to add.** A new field appears, and you can select its type and enter the appropriate information.

7. **To add an image to the card, use one of the following options:**

Genius

If the information you want to enter isn't available on the pop-up menu, open it and choose Custom. Type the label for the field you want to add and click OK.

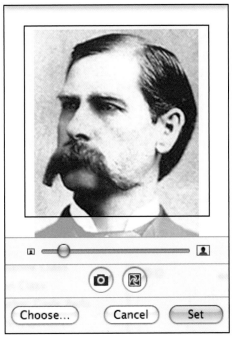

- Drag an image file from the desktop and drop it onto the Image well located immediately to the left of the name.

- Double-click the Image well, and the Image sheet appears allowing you to browse for an icon.

- Double-click the Image well, and the Image sheet appears. Take a picture with the MacBook Pro camera.

8. **Drag the slider to the left to make the image smaller, or to the right to make it larger.** Drag the image around the image box until the part of the image you want to be displayed is contained in the box (see figure 6.2).

9. **Click Set.** You return to the card and the image is stored on the card.

6.2 You can configure images for contacts; these images appear when you receive e-mail from the contact as well as calls from the contact on an iPhone.

10. **Click the Edit button.** The card is created (see figure 6.3).

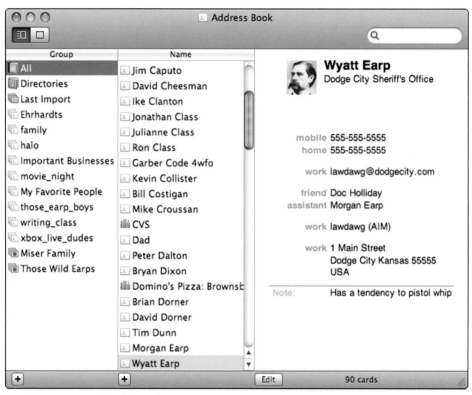

6.3 After you've completed the information on a card, it's available for you to refer to or use (such as to send an e-mail).

Note

When you select a data type, Address Book automatically creates a field in the appropriate format, such as for phone numbers when you select mobile.

Importing vCards

Creating vCards manually is a lot of fun and all, but it's a lot easier to import a vCard that you've received from someone else. One of the most common ways to receive vCards is through e-mail as attachments; vCard files have .vcf as their filename extension. Just drag the vCard from the e-mail onto your desktop.

To add a vCard to Address Book, drag the vCard file from the desktop and drop it onto the Address Book window. Click Add in the resulting sheet, and the contact information is added to your Address Book. You can edit cards created from vCards just like cards you have created manually.

Genius

If you have a MobileMe account, it's easy to keep your Address Book in sync on all your computers so that current contact information is available for you, regardless of the computer on which you created the card.

Adding contact information from e-mail

Many applications that involve contact information allow you to add that information to your Address Book. When you receive e-mail in Mail, you can add the sender's name and e-mail address to Address Book using the following steps:

1. **Move the pointer over the address shown next to From, Cc, or Bcc.**

2. **When the address becomes highlighted, click the trackpad button to open the action menu.**

3. **Choose Add to Address Book.** A new card is created with as much information as Address Book can extract, usually the first and last name along with the e-mail address.

4. **Use Address Book to edit the card, such as to add other information to it.**

Editing address cards

As time passes, contact information changes, and you might want to edit or add more information to existing cards. With Address Book, editing your cards is very similar to creating them in the first place.

1. **Select the card you want to edit in the Name pane.**

2. **Click Edit.** All the current fields become editable, and the empty fields that were on the template when the card was created appear.

3. **Use the edit tools to make changes to the card.**

4. **Click Edit.** Your changes are saved.

Your Address Card

One of the most important cards in Address Book is your own. When you first started your MacBook Pro and worked through the registration process, the information you entered was added to a card in Address Book. This card identifies your contact information in various places, including the Safari AutoFill feature that enables you to quickly complete Web forms. You should review and update your card as needed so that its information is current.

To jump to your card, choose Card ⇨ Go To My Card. Review the information on your card and make any changes necessary using the previous steps.

You can make any card your card by selecting it and then choosing Card ⇨ Make This My Card.

You can send your card to others as a vCard by dragging it from the Name list onto your desktop. A vCard is created, with your name as its filename.

Working with Cards

After your Address Book is full of cards, you start to get a lot of benefits from the work you've done.

Browsing for cards

Unless you have many, many cards in Address Book, browsing can often be the fastest way to find cards that you want to use.

Setting format and sort preferences

First, make sure Address Book displays names and sorts cards according to your preferences. Follow these steps:

1. **Choose Address Book ⇨ Preferences.** The Preferences dialog opens.

2. **Click the General tab (see figure 6.4).**

3. **In the Show first name section, click Before last name if you want names to be shown as first name then last name, or click Following last name if you prefer the last name-first name format.**

4. **On the Sort By pop-up menu, choose Last Name to have cards sorted by last name, or First Name to sort the Name pane by first name.**

5. **Close the Preferences dialog.**

Browsing for cards with three panes

When Address Book is displaying its three panes, you can browse for cards by doing the following:

1. **In the Group pane, select the group that you want to browse; to browse all your contacts, click All.**

2. **Use the scroll bar in the Name pane to browse up and down the list of cards.**

3. **Select the card that you want to use.** The card you selected displays in the Card pane.

6.4 Configure Address Book to display the first name first (or second).

Browsing for cards with one pane

Address Book has a one-pane mode that shows only the Card pane. You can browse your contacts using the one pane view, as you can see in the following steps.

1. **Choose View ⇨ Card Only.** The Group and Name panes are hidden, and you see only cards.

2. **Click the right-facing arrow at the bottom of the window to browse down one card, or the left-facing arrow to browse up one card, until you see the card you want to work with.**

Searching for cards

When you search for cards in Address Book, it searches all the fields on all your cards simultaneously. To search for cards, perform these steps:

1. **Select the group that you want to search; to search all your contacts, click All.** All the cards in the selected group appear in the Name pane.

2. **Type search text in the Search box.** As you type, Address Book starts searching all the fields in the cards; as it finds matches, it shows you the matching cards in the Name pane.

3. **Continue typing in the Search box until the card in which you are interested appears in the Name pane.**

4. **Select the card that you want to use (see figure 6.5).**

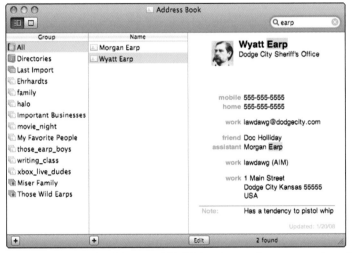

6.5 When you search, Address Book highlights the search term on each card that it finds.

To end a search, click the Clear button, which is the x within the gray circle in the Search bar. All the cards in the selected group appear again.

Using card information

While being able to see contact information is useful, Address Book enables you to really use the information on cards to perform specific actions. Following are some examples of useful things you can do with the information on cards:

● **Send e-mail.** Find the card for the person to whom you want to send e-mail. Hold the Ctrl key down and click the e-mail address you want to use. Choose Send Email.

- **Visit Web sites.** Find a card that contains a home page or other Web page URL. Click the URL you want to visit. Safari takes you to the URL that you clicked.

- **Find an address on a map.** Find the card containing the address you want to map out. Hold the Ctrl key down and click the address. Choose Map Of Safari takes you to a Google map showing the address that you clicked.

Genius You can share your Address Book with people who also have a MobileMac account. Open the Address Book menu and choose Preferences. Click the Sharing tab. Check the Share your Address Book check box. Click the Add button, which is a plus sign, and select the other MobileMac users with whom you want to share your Address Book.

Organizing Cards with Groups

Groups are useful because you can do one action and it will affect all the cards in that group. For example, you can create a group containing family members whom you regularly e-mail. Then, you can address a message to the one group, instead of addressing each person individually.

There are two kinds of groups in Address Book. Manual groups are those you create and then manually place cards in. Smart groups are a collection of criteria; Address Book places cards into smart groups automatically, based on their criteria.

Creating groups manually

To create a group, follow these steps:

1. **Click the Add button located at the bottom of the Group pane.** A new group appears in the Group pane with its name ready to be edited.

2. **Type the name of the group.** You can name a group anything you'd like.

3. **Browse or search for the first card you want to add to the group.**

4. **Drag the card from the Name pane and drop it onto the group to which you want to add it (see figure 6.6).**

6.6 Drag cards from the Name pane onto a group to add them to the group.

Genius

To add multiple cards to a group at the same time, hold the ⌘ key down while you click each card that you want to add to the group.

Creating smart groups

Smart groups are also collections of cards, but unlike regular groups, you don't have to manually add each card to the group. Instead, you define criteria for the cards you want to be included in the smart group, and Address Book automatically adds the appropriate cards. For example, suppose you want a group for everyone with the same last name; you can simply create a smart group with that criterion, and Address Book adds all the people with that last name to the group automatically.

Creating a smart group is quite different from creating a regular group, as you can see in the following steps.

1. **Choose File ⇨ New Smart Group.** The New Smart Group sheet appears (see figure 6.7).

2. **Type the name of the group.**

3. **Choose the first field you want to include in the criteria on the first pop-up menu, which is Card by default.** For example, to base a criterion on name, choose Name.

Smart Group Name:	Those Wild Earps		

Contains cards which match [all ⬍] of the following conditions:

[Name ⬍]	[contains ⬍]	earp	⊖ ⊕
[Name ⬍]	[is not ⬍]	clanton	⊖ ⊕
[Company ⬍]	[contains ⬍]	dodge city sheriff	⊖ ⊕

(?) ☑ Highlight group when updated   (Cancel) (OK)

6.7 This smart group includes all my contacts named "earp" whose company contains "dodge city sheriff" and whose name is not "clanton."

4. **Choose how you want the information you enter to be included on the center pop-up menu.** Going back to the Name example, the options on the center menu include the following: contains, does not contain, is, is not, and so on.

5. **Type the information that you want to be part of the criterion in the empty fields.** If you selected Name and contains on the pop-up menus, type the name you want the criterion to find.

6. **Click the Add button at the end of the criterion to add another criterion to the group.**

7. **If the group has at least two criteria, choose all on the top pop-up menu if all of the criteria must be met for a card to be included in the group, or choose any if only one of them does.**

8. **Click OK.** The smart group is created and all the cards that meet the criteria you defined are added to it automatically.

Changing groups

You'll probably want to change your groups over time. For example, with a manual group, you can add new cards or remove current ones. To change a smart group, just change the criteria it uses and the cards contained in the group are changed automatically.

Synchronizing Contact Information with an iPhone

If you have an iPhone, you can easily move your contact information from Address Book onto the iPhone by synchronizing it. You can also have changes you make on the iPhone be moved back into Address Book. Here's how:

1. **Connect the iPhone to your MacBook Pro.** iTunes opens if it isn't open already.

2. **Select the iPhone on the iTunes source list (see figure 6.8).**

6.8 Synchronizing your Address Book with an iPhone is a great way to ensure your contact information is always available to you.

3. **Click the Summary tab.**

4. **If you want the iPhone to synchronize each time you connect it to your MacBook Pro, check the Automatically sync when this iPhone is connected check box.**

5. **Click the Info tab.**

6. **Check the Sync Address Book contacts check box.**

7. **Choose either All contacts or Selected groups to determine which contacts are synced.**

8. **If you want contacts you create on the iPhone to be placed within a specific group in Address Book, check the Put new contacts created on this iPhone into the group check box and choose the group on the pop-up menu (see figure 6.9).**

9. **If you use Yahoo! Address Book and want to sync those contacts, check the Sync Yahoo! Address Book contacts check box and use the Configure button to set up the sync options.**

Contacts

☑ Sync Address Book contacts
  ◉ All contacts
  ○ Selected groups:
    ☐ Ehrhardts
    ☐ family
    ☐ halo
    ☐ Important Businesses

  ☑ Put new contacts created on this iPhone into the group: | Important Busi... ♦ |
  ☐ Sync Yahoo! Address Book contacts | Configure... |

Capacity						Cancel
7.27 GB	☐ Audio	☐ Photos	☐ Other	☐ Free Space		
	6.29 GB	11.7 MB	196.5 MB	803.4 MB		Apply

6.9 You can place contacts that you create on the iPhone into a specific group automatically.

10. **Scroll down the screen until you see the Advanced section.**

11. **If you want the contact information on the iPhone to be replaced by your contacts in Address Book the next time it is synced, check the Contacts check box.** If you don't check this check box, the contact information on the iPhone is merged with your Address Book information.

12. **Click Apply.** The changes you made are saved and the iPhone is synced.

Printing from Address Book

Address Book includes powerful printing functions that you can use to print mailing labels, envelopes, lists, and a pocket address book (if you don't have an iPhone). You can print each of these using similar steps. Because printing envelopes is the feature I find the most useful, I've used that as the example in the following steps:

1. **Select the cards for which you want to print envelopes.**

2. **Choose File ⇨ Print.** The Print dialog appears as shown in figure 6.10.

3. **Expand the dialog so that you can see all its options by clicking the downward-facing triangle next to the Printer pop-up menu.** The top half of the dialog contains printer controls, while everything underneath the Address Book pop-up menu is used to configure what and how you are going to print.

4. **On the Style pop-up menu, choose Envelopes.**

5. **Click the Label tab if it isn't selected already.**

6.10 Address Book provides powerful features for printing envelopes and other documents.

132

6. **If you want to include your return address, check the Print my address check box.**

7. **On the Addresses pop-up menu, choose All if you want to have an envelope for each of the addresses for each contact, or choose the specific address that you want to be used if you want to print only one envelope per contact.**

8. **Use the Print in pop-up menu to choose the order in which the envelopes are printed.** You can choose alphabetical order or order them by postal code. This is important if you've created a form letter so that the envelopes and letters are printed in the same order.

9. **To set the color of the text, click the Color button and use the Color Selector to choose the text color.**

10. **To include an image in your return address, click the upper Set button and use the resulting dialog to move to and select an image.**

11. **To set the font used, click the lower Set button.** The return and delivery addresses use the same font, but the size you set is only for the delivery address. The return address is scaled according to the size of the delivery address font.

12. **Configure the printer settings as needed and click Print.**

Genius

You can use the Layout tab to change the layout for different kinds of envelopes. Use the Orientation tab to change how the envelope feeds into the printer.

How Can I Go Beyond E-mail Basics with Mail?

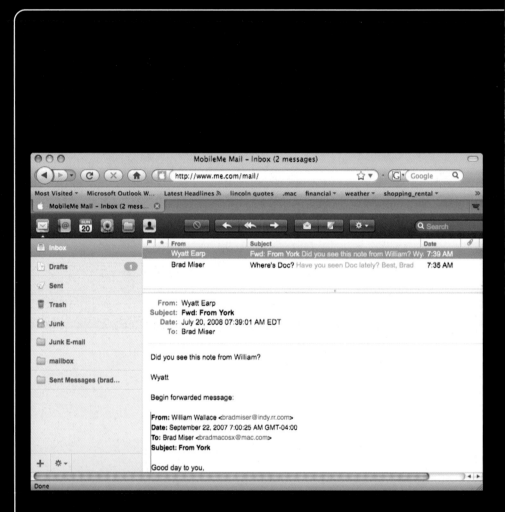

E-mail just might be one of the most powerful and convenient forms of communication ever. Okay, that might be a bit dramatic, but e-mail is definitely convenient for both sender and receiver because it can be sent and read according to their schedules. And, e-mail doesn't interrupt people; it waits patiently in their Inboxes until they have a chance to get to it. The Mac OS X Mail application is quite powerful, and you've probably already used it to send and receive e-mail. This chapter builds on those basic skills to show you how to go farther with your e-mail in Mail.

Configuring E-mail Accounts

One of Mail's benefits is that you can configure many different e-mail accounts in it and easily work with all, or just one, of those accounts at any point in time. There are many kinds of e-mail accounts with which Mail can work, including the following:

- **MobileMe.** If you have a MobileMe account, you also have a MobileMe e-mail account. This is convenient because you can use Mail to access your e-mail, or you can use the MobileMe Web site to work with it almost as easily (see figure 7.1).

7.1 A MobileMe e-mail account has a lot of benefits, including being able to access your e-mail within Mail or on the Web.

- **POP.** Post Office Protocol accounts are one of the most common types provided by many Internet Service Providers and other organizations that provide e-mail services.

- **IMAP.** Internet Message Access Protocol is a newer e-mail protocol.

- **Exchange.** Microsoft Exchange Server technology is dominant in the business world for managing e-mail.

There are a number of attributes that you need to know about in order to configure an e-mail account in Mail. These vary from account type to account type, but the following attributes are common:

- **E-mail address.**
- **Incoming mail server address.** Mail that you receive is delivered through an incoming mail server.
- **Username.**
- **Password.**
- **Outgoing mail server address.** E-mail comes in and e-mail goes out. To send e-mail, you need to configure the outgoing mail server through which it will be sent.
- **User authentication.** To configure an authenticated account, you need a username and password for the authentication.

When you obtain an e-mail account, you receive information for each of the attributes that you need to configure to be able to work with that account.

Configuring a MobileMe e-mail account

One of the benefits of MobileMe e-mail is that a MobileMe e-mail account is configured automatically when you register your account in the MobileMe pane of the System Preferences application. However, just in case you ever need to reconfigure it for some reason, perform the following steps to set up MobileMe e-mail:

1. **Launch Mail.**
2. **Choose Mail ⇨ Preferences.** The Mail Preferences dialog appears.
3. **Click the Accounts tab.** In the list on the left side of the Accounts pane are currently configured accounts. When you select an account on this list, the tools you use to work with the account are shown in the right part of the pane.
4. **Click the Add button located at the bottom of the list.** The Add Account sheet appears.
5. **Enter your name in the Full Name field.** This is the name that is shown as the From name on e-mail that you send.
6. **Enter the e-mail address for the account in the Email Address field.**
7. **Enter the password for the account in the Password field.**
8. **Uncheck the Automatically set up account check box.**
9. **Click Continue.** You see the Incoming Mail Server window.

10. **On the Account Type pop-up menu, choose MobileMe.**

11. **Enter a description of the account in the Description field.** This can be anything you'd like. This description enables you to easily identify the account on the list of accounts.

12. **Enter *mail.mac.com* in the Incoming Mail Server field.**

13. **Enter your MobileMe member name in the User Name field.**

14. **Enter your MobileMe password in the Password field.**

15. **Click Continue.** You see the Outgoing Mail Server window.

16. **Enter a description of the outgoing server in the Description field.**

17. **Enter *smtp.me.com* in the Outgoing Mail Server field.**

18. **Check the Use Authentication check box.**

19. **Enter your MobileMe member name in the User Name field.**

20. **Enter your MobileMe password in the Password field.**

21. **Click Continue.** You see the Account Summary window.

22. **Make sure the Take account online check box is checked.**

23. **Click Create.** The account is created and its mailboxes are added. You return to the Accounts window and see the account you created on the list.

Configuring a POP e-mail account

Many e-mail accounts use POP. You can add and configure a POP account in Mail with the following steps:

1. **Launch Mail.**

2. **Choose Mail ⇨ Preferences.** The Mail Preferences dialog appears.

3. **Click the Accounts tab.** In the list on the left side of the Accounts pane are currently configured accounts. When you select an account on this list, the tools you use to work with the account are shown in the right part of the pane.

4. **Click the Add button located at the bottom of the list.** The Add Account sheet appears.

5. **Enter your name in the Full Name field.** This is the name that is shown as the From name on e-mail that you send.

6. **Enter the e-mail address for the account in the Email Address field.**

7. **Enter the password for the account in the Password field.**

8. **Uncheck the Automatically set up account check box.**

9. **Click Continue.** You see the Incoming Mail Server window.

10. **On the Account Type pop-up menu, choose POP.**

11. **Enter a description of the account in the Description field.**

12. **Enter *popserveraddress*, where *popserveraddress* is the name of your incoming mail server, in the Incoming Mail Server field.** This is usually something like pop-server.*provider*.com, where provider is the domain name of your e-mail account provider, but this address can take other forms, as well. The important point is to use the address included in the account information provided to you.

13. **Enter your account's name in the User Name field.**

14. **Enter your account's password in the Password field.**

15. **Click Continue.** You see the Outgoing Mail Server window as seen in figure 7.2.

7.2 Use the Outgoing Mail Server window to configure your outbound e-mail.

16. **Enter a description of the outgoing server in the Description field.**

17. **Enter *smtp-server.provider.com*, where *provider* is the name of the account's provider, in the Outgoing Mail Server field.**

Note   SMTP stands for Simple Mail Transfer Protocol.

18. **If the provider uses authentication, check the Use Authentication check box and enter your account's authentication username and password.**

19. **Click Continue.** You see the Account Summary window.

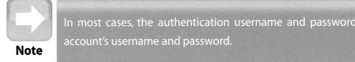

Note   In most cases, the authentication username and password are the same as your account's username and password.

20. **Make sure the Take account online check box is checked.**

21. **Click Create.** The account is created, and its mailboxes are added to the Accounts window.

Configuring an IMAP account

IMAP accounts can be configured in Mail by performing the following steps:

1. **Launch Mail.**

2. **Choose Mail ⇨ Preferences.** The Mail Preferences dialog appears.

3. **Click the Accounts tab.** In the list on the left side of the Accounts pane are currently configured accounts. When you select an account on this list, the tools that you use to work with the account are shown in the right part of the pane.

4. **Click the Add button located at the bottom of the list.** The Add Account sheet appears.

5. **Enter your name in the Full Name field.** This is the name that is shown as the From name on the e-mail you send.

6. **Enter the e-mail address for the account in the Email Address field.**

7. **Enter the password for the account in the Password field.**

8. **Uncheck the Automatically set up account check box.**

9. **Click Continue.** You see the Incoming Mail Server window (see figure 7.3).

Incoming Mail Server

Account Type: IMAP

Description: Gmail

Incoming Mail Server: imap.gmail.com

User Name: sorebruiser

Password: ••••••••

Cancel   Go Back   Continue

7.3 Here is the Incoming Mail Server configuration for a Gmail account.

10. **On the Account Type pop-up menu, choose IMAP.**

11. **Enter a description of the account in the Description field.**

12. **Enter *imap.provider.com*, where *provider* is the name of your account's provider in the Incoming Mail Server field.** The specific address you enter should be the one provided to you when you received your account information.

13. **Enter your account's username in the User Name field.**

14. **Enter your account's password in the Password field.**

15. **Click Continue.** You see the Outgoing Mail Server window.

16. **Enter a description of the outgoing server in the Description field.**

17. **Enter** *smtp.provider.com*, **where** *provider* **is the name of your account's provider, in the Outgoing Mail Server field.** As always, the specific address you enter should be the one provided to you when you received your account information.

18. **If the provider uses authentication, check the Use Authentication check box and enter your account's authentication username and password.**

Note

In most cases, the authentication username and password are the same as your account's username and password.

19. **Click Continue.** You see the Account Summary window.

20. **Make sure the Take account online check box is checked.**

21. **Click Create.** The account is created and its mailboxes are added. You return to the Accounts window and see the account you created on the list.

Configuring an Exchange account

You can easily configure Mail to work with an Exchange account if IMAP access to your Exchange e-mail is provided. If so, you can use the steps in the previous section to configure your Exchange account in Mail, with some small differences. You should choose Exchange on the Account type pop-up menu. If your organization uses an OWA (Outlook Web Access) server, you can configure this server with the e-mail account so that non-e-mail, such as calendar events or notes, can be filtered out by Mail. Otherwise, configuring the Exchange account is like configuring any other IMAP account.

If your organization doesn't provide IMAP access to your Exchange account, it is probably a Windows-only organization. In many cases, you can access your Exchange e-mail through the Web using an OWA Web site. Unfortunately, the current version of Safari is incompatible with OWA, so you need to use a different Web browser to access your Exchange e-mail; try Firefox, which you can download from www.mozilla.com. Using Firefox, you can work with your Exchange e-mail through a Web interface that is similar to the Microsoft Outlook application.

If the organization doesn't provide IMAP or OWA access to your Exchange e-mail, you have to run Windows on your MacBook Pro so that you can use Outlook to access it (see Chapter 18 for more information on how to run Windows on your MacBook Pro). You can do this using Boot Camp or one of the virtualization applications that are available, such as Parallel Desktop for Mac.

Note Ideally, you would be able to access Exchange e-mail in Mail, whether through IMAP or OWA. At the very least, Safari needs to be fixed so that it can access OWA e-mail. If you have a MobileMe account, you can sync your iPhone to an Exchange account to receive e-mail on your iPhone.

Testing e-mail accounts

After you've configured your e-mail accounts, expand the Inbox by clicking the right-facing triangle next to it. Under the Inbox, you see an Inbox for each e-mail account that you configured (see figure 7.4). If you don't see an icon containing an exclamation point, the accounts are properly configured and are ready to use. If you do see this icon, you need to correct the account configuration.

7.4 No caution icon means that I've successfully configured these three e-mail accounts in Mail.

Working with File Attachments

E-mail is one of the easiest and fastest ways to exchange files with other people. Using Mail, you can attach files of any type to e-mails that you send.

Sending compressed files through e-mail

I'm going to recommend something here that many people don't do as standard practice, which is that you compress files before attaching them to e-mail messages, even if you are sending only one file with a message. There are three reasons why I recommend this. One is that sending a compressed file requires less bandwidth to manage. Second, compressing files before you send them also reduces the chances that your message is screened out by spam or virus filters on the recipient's e-mail. Third, when you send a compressed file, it gives the user a single file to deal with, instead of an attachment for each file.

So, before moving into Mail, compress the files you want to send using the following steps:

1. **Move to a Finder window showing the files you want to send.**

2. **Select the files you want to send (remember that you can hold the ⌘ key down while clicking files to select multiple files at the same time).**

3. **Choose File ➪ Compress # items, where # is the number of files you selected.** The files you selected are compressed into a .zip file. Mac OS X uses .zip as its default compression scheme; this is a very good thing because it is also the dominant compression standard on Windows computers.

4. **Rename the .zip file.** The default name for .zip files is always Archive.zip.

After you've prepared the compressed file, you can attach it to an e-mail message by dragging the file onto the New Message window or by clicking the Attach button on the New Message window's toolbar (the Choose File sheet appears; use it to select the file you want to attach to a message).

Genius

If you need to transfer files larger than the recipient's gateway, there are a number of ways to do so. If you have a MobileMe account, you can provide access to your iDisk's Public folder, from which the recipient can download files.

Of course, I realize that many times, people attach non-compressed files to e-mail (and I do that more than occasionally myself). When you place a file that hasn't been compressed in a new message window, you see a thumbnail preview of the file with its icon, the filename, and its size in parentheses. If the file type is one that can be displayed in the message, such as a TIFF image or a PDF file, you actually see the contents of the file in the body of the message (see figure 7.5).

Preparing attachments for Windows users

7.5 Sending a non-compressed file.

Because Mac and Windows operating systems use different file format structures, Windows users sometimes end up with two files when you e-mail them attachments. One is the usable file and the other is unusable to them (the names of the files are filename and _filename). Recipients can use the first one and safely ignore the second one. However, it is still confusing.

You can choose to attach individual attachments as Windows-friendly by checking the Send Windows-Friendly Attachments check box in the Attach File dialog. If you always want to send files in the Windows-friendly format, choose Edit ➪ Attachments ➪ Always Send Windows-Friendly Attachments.

Genius You can use the Photo Browser in the New Message toolbar to easily find photos in your iPhoto Library and drag them into a new message window to attach them to an e-mail that you create.

Working with files you receive

When you receive a message that has files attached to it, you see the files in the body of the message. As when you send files in a message, you see the file's icon, name, and size. You can use the file attachments in the following ways:

145

● **Click the Quick Look button.** The Quick Look window opens and you can preview the contents of the files using the Quick Look window controls (see figure 7.6).

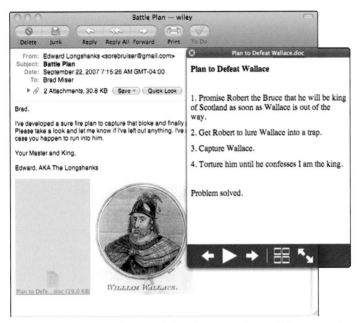

7.6 Here I am using the Quick Look function to preview the files attached to this message.

● **Choose File ⇨ Save Attachments.**

● **Click the Save button next to the attachment information at the top of the message.** The file is saved to your Downloads folder.

● **If multiple files are attached, click the expansion triangle next to the attachment line in the message's header and work with each file individually.**

● **Double-click a file's icon to open it.**

● **Drag a file's icon from the message onto a folder on your Mac's desktop to save it there.**

Genius

If the contents of the file are being displayed and you would rather see just an icon, open the file's contextual menu and select View as icon. The file is displayed as an icon instead. To view the file's content again, open the menu and select View in Place.

Organizing E-mail

As you send and receive e-mail, you'll end up with a lot of messages that you need to manage. Fortunately, Mail provides you with a number of ways to organize your e-mail, including mailboxes, smart mailboxes, and smart mailbox folders.

Using mailboxes to organize e-mail

You can create your own mailboxes to organize your messages; these are much like folders on your desktop. The mailboxes you create are shown in the Mailbox pane, below the Inbox and other special mailboxes. You can also create nested mailboxes to create a hierarchy of mailboxes in which you store your messages. Here's how:

1. **Click the Add button at the bottom of the Mailbox pane.**

2. **On the resulting pop-up menu, select New Mailbox.** The New Mailbox sheet appears (see figure 7.7).

New Mailbox

Enter name for new local mailbox to be created at the top level of the "On My Mac" section.

Location: 🖥 On My Mac

Name: Mail to Keep/Fan Mail

Cancel   OK

7.7 Here, I am creating a nested mailbox.

3. **On the Location pop-up menu, select the location where the mailbox you are creating will be stored.** If you select On My Mac, the folder is created on your computer. If you use an IMAP or MobileMe account, you can select that account to create a folder on that account's server.

4. **Enter the name of the mailbox you want to create in the Name field.**

5. **Click OK.** The mailbox is created and appears in the Mailbox pane in the location you selected.

Genius

After you create folders, you can place them within one another to create nested folders, by dragging a folder onto the folder in which you want to place it.

147

Using smart mailboxes to organize your e-mail

You can use smart mailboxes to organize your e-mail automatically, based on criteria you define. For example, you might want to collect all the e-mail you receive from a group of people with whom you are working on a project in a specific folder. Rather than having to place these messages in the folder by dragging them out of your Inbox individually, you can create a smart mailbox so that mail you receive from these people is automatically placed in the appropriate folder.

To create a smart mailbox, complete the following steps:

1. **Click the Add button at the bottom of the Mailbox pane.**

2. **On the resulting pop-up menu, select New Smart Mailbox.** The Smart Mailbox sheet appears (see figure 7.8).

7.8 Smart mailboxes organize your e-mail for you automatically; this smart mailbox collects all my e-mail from my pals in Tombstone.

3. **Name the smart mailbox by typing its name in the Smart Mailbox Name box.**

4. **Select the first condition for the mailbox on the first pop-up menu in the conditions box.** By default, this menu shows From, which bases the condition on the name or e-mail address in the From field.

5. **Select the operand for the condition on the second pop-up menu.** What you see on this menu depends on the condition you selected. For example, to create a smart mailbox for mail from a specific person, you would select Contains.

6. **Enter the condition text or date in the box.** For example, enter a person's name if you are creating a smart mailbox to collect mail from that specific person.

7. **If you have configured more than one condition, select all on the matching pop-up menu above the condition list if all the conditions must be true for mail to be stored in the smart mailbox, or select any if only one of the conditions must be true.**

8. **To remove a condition you no longer want to use, click the Remove button located on the condition's row.**

9. **Click OK.** The smart mailbox is created in the SMART MAILBOXES section of the mailbox pane. Any e-mail that meets its conditions is organized under that mailbox.

Using smart mailbox folders to organize your smart mailboxes

If you want to organize your smart mailboxes, you can create a smart mailbox folder and then place your smart mailboxes within it.

1. **Choose a folder in the ON MY MAC section.**

2. **Choose Mailbox ⇨ New Smart Mailbox Folder.** The Smart Mailbox Folder sheet appears.

3. **Name the new smart mailbox folder.**

4. **Click OK.** The smart mailbox folder appears in the SMART MAILBOXES section.

5. **Drag smart mailboxes into the smart mailbox folder that you created to place them there.** When you do this, an expansion triangle appears so that you can expand the smart mailbox folder to see its contents (see figure 7.9).

7.9 The My Email smart mailbox folder contains two smart mailboxes.

Using the Junk Mail Tool in Mail

E-mail is great, but it isn't perfect; its major imperfection is spam. Spam refers to any e-mail message you receive that you don't want to receive. You've no doubt seen messages for various products that are of little to no interest to you, such as fabulous money-making opportunities and other messages that require your time to manage.

The Junk Mail tool in Mail is designed to help you manage spam that you receive. You begin by configuring the tool. Once that's done, you can use the tool to manage your spam.

Configuring the Junk Mail tool

To configure the Junk Mail tool, perform the following steps:

1. **Open the Mail Preferences dialog.**

2. **Click the Junk Mail tab.** The Junk Mail tools appear (see figure 7.10).

7.10 To use the Junk Mail tool, configure it on the Junk Mail pane.

3. **Turn the tool on by checking the Enable junk mail filtering check box.**

4. **Choose one of the following options to determine what Mail does with junk mail:**

   - **Mark as junk mail, but leave it in my Inbox.** This option causes Mail to change the color of junk mail to an ugly brown, but leaves it in your Inbox.

- **Move it to the Junk mailbox.** When you choose this option, a Junk mailbox is created and any messages that are identified as junk are moved into it automatically.

- **Perform custom actions.** When you select this option, you can click the Advanced button to create a rule to deal with junk mail. You'll learn how to work with rules later in this chapter. When a message is identified as junk, the junk rule is implemented.

5. **Check the following check boxes to exempt mail from being identified as junk if it meets the related condition:**

   - **Sender of message is in my Address Book.**

   - **Sender of message is in my Previous Recipients.**

   - **Message is addressed using my full name.**

6. **Check the Trust junk mail headers set by my Internet Service Provider check box if you want to allow this option.** Many ISPs have filters in their e-mail systems that flag e-mail as junk. If you want Mail to treat messages with these flags as junk, check the check box. If this option is unchecked, Mail ignores these flags.

7. **If you want the junk mail filter to act before any rules you've created do, check the Filter junk mail before applying my rules check box.**

8. **Close the Mail Preferences dialog.** The Junk Mail tool starts working; any junk in your Inbox is marked or moved accordingly.

Managing spam with the Junk Mail tool

As the Junk Mail tool works, here's what happens and how you can use it:

- If a message should have been marked as junk, but wasn't, select the message and choose Message ⇨ Mark ⇨ As Junk Mail or press Shift+⌘+J. The message is marked as junk and moved to the Junk folder if that preference is set. Mail also tries to learn from this and will mark similar messages (such as those from the sender) as junk in the future.

- If a message shouldn't have been marked as junk but was, select the message and choose Message ⇨ Mark ⇨ As Not Junk Mail or press Shift+⌘+J. The junk tag is removed from the message, and Mail learns from this so that it won't identify similar messages in the future as junk. If the junk message is in the Junk folder, you have to manually move it back into the Inbox or other mailbox.

- You can also use the Junk or Not Junk buttons that appear at the top of messages in the Reading pane to change the junk status of individual messages.

Adding Signatures to E-mail

Like snail-mail messages, you probably want to sign your e-mail messages. With the Signature tools in Mail, you can configure signatures to be attached to your e-mail messages. You can have as many signatures as you would like, and you can select a default signature or select one each time you compose a new message. You can apply signatures to messages automatically or choose a signature for specific messages.

Here's how to set up your signatures:

1. **Open the Mail Preferences dialog.**

2. **Click the Signatures tab.** The Signatures tools appear as shown in figure 7.11. In the left pane, you see each e-mail account you've configured, as well as the All Signatures option.

3. **Select the account for which you want to configure a signature, or select All Signatures to make the signature available to all accounts.** In most cases, you should select All Signatures so that you can use the signature in any e-mail account.

4. **Click the Add button at the bottom of the signature list pane.** A new signature appears in the center pane.

5. **Name the signature by typing a name in the highlighted area and pressing Return.**

6. **With the new signature selected, edit the signature in the far-right pane for the new signature.** You can use just about anything you'd like for your signature, including text, your e-mail address, URLs, and graphics.

7. **If you want your signature to always appear in your default font, check the Always match my default message font check box.**

Genius

To provide your contact information in the signature, you can drag your address card from Address Book to the signature.

8. **Drag signatures onto the e-mail accounts from which you want to be able to use them.** If you create all your signatures under the All Signatures category, you can use the same signature in multiple accounts.

9. **Select one of the e-mail accounts in the far-left pane.** The signatures available under that account are shown.

7.11 You can configure many different signatures in Mail and use them manually or automatically.

10. **If you want a signature to be added to messages from that account automatically, select an option on the Choose Signature pop-up menu.**

11. **Check the Place signature above quoted text check box if you want your signature to be placed above any text that is quoted when you reply to a message.**

12. **Close the Mail Preferences dialog.**

Automatically Managing E-mail with Rules

You can automate your e-mail by configuring and using rules. For example, you might want to create a mailbox for the mail from a certain person and have that mail automatically transferred to and stored in that mailbox. Or, you might have the messages from a mailing list to which you are subscribed placed in a specific mailbox for later reading. There are a large number of actions you can perform with Mail Rules, so there is almost no limit to what you can do.

Like other Mail tools, you can start by configuring rules using the Mail Preferences dialog:

1. **Open the Mail Preferences dialog.**

2. **Click the Rules tab.** The Rules tools appear. In the pane, you see a list of all the current rules that are configured; those marked with a check mark are active.

3. **Click the Add Rule button.** The New Rule sheet appears (see figure 7.12).

Description: | Dump Brad's Email

If [any ⬍] of the following conditions are met:

From ⬍	Contains ⬍	sorebruiser@gmai	⊖ ⊕
From ⬍	Contains ⬍	bradmacosx@mac	⊖ ⊕
Message Content ⬍	Contains ⬍	ro Portable Genius|	⊖ ⊕

Perform the following actions:

| Move Message ⬍ | to mailbox: 🗑 Trash ⬍ | ⊖ ⊕ |
| Play Sound ⬍ | Submarine ⬍ | ⊖ ⊕ |

Cancel   OK

7.12 This rule moves mail from my e-mail addresses or containing this book's title to the Trash, and it plays the Submarine sound.

4. **Name the rule by entering a description.**

5. **Use the If pop-up menu to determine whether at least one criterion (select any) or all the criteria (select all) in the rule must be met for the actions in the rule to be taken.**

6. **Use the first condition pop-up menu to select the first criterion on which the rule acts.**

7. **Use the Contains pop-up menu to select how the criterion relates to the value you enter (for example, Contains and Is equal to).**

8. **Enter the value for which the rule will be implemented, if applicable, or use a pop-up menu to select a value.**

9. **To add another condition for the rule, click the Add button at the right side of the sheet.**

10. **Use the menus in the Perform the following actions area to select the actions that will be performed by the rule.** For example, if you choose the Move Message action, you would then choose the location to which the message is moved on the to mailbox pop-up menu.

11. **To add another action, click the Add button on the right side of the sheet.**

12. **Click OK.** The rule is created and you are prompted to apply the rule to the messages that are currently in selected mailboxes.

13. **Click Apply if you want the actions in the rule to be applied to the messages that are currently in your Inbox, or click Don't Apply if you want the rule to be ignored for your current messages.** You return to the Rules pane and see the rule you created.

14. **Close the Mail Preferences dialog.** The rules you created take effect for all the messages you receive in the future.

Working with RSS Feeds

RSS feeds are streams of information that change as time passes. Many Web sites, especially news sites, offer RSS feeds to which you can subscribe. You can use Mail to read RSS feeds, which is convenient because they are delivered to your Inbox automatically.

Note

By default, you're subscribed to the Apple Hot News RSS feed. To see the messages in this feed, expand the RSS section and select the Apple Hot News feed.

Adding RSS feeds to Mail

Before you can read RSS feeds in Mail, you need to subscribe to the feed. You can do this by choosing a Safari bookmark to the feed or by entering a feed's URL directly. Because it's the more flexible option, the following steps show you how to subscribe to a feed using its URL:

1. **Choose File ⇨ Add RSS Feeds.** The RSS Feeds sheet appears.

2. **Click the Specify a custom feed URL radio button.**

3. **Enter the feed's URL in the field.**

Genius

To find the URL of RSS feeds, visit an organization's Web site. Look for RSS feed links. These take you to the URL for various feeds that the organization provides. Some feeds come in various formats, such as short titles, so that you get the feed in a way that best meets your preferences. The URL for RSS feeds starts with feed://.

4. **If you want the feed's messages to appear in your Inbox, check the Show in Inbox check box.** In most cases, it's better not to check this option so that your Inbox doesn't get cluttered up with feed messages.

5. **Click Add (see figure 7.13).** You are subscribed to the feed and it is added to the RSS section of your Inbox.

○ Browse feeds in Safari Bookmarks
◉ Specify a custom feed URL

feed://www.macnn.com/rss/macnn.rss

☐ Show in Inbox   (Cancel   )   (Add   )

7.13 This feed provides a steady stream of Mac news.

Configuring RSS preferences

To complete your RSS experience, configure RSS preferences as follows:

1. **Open the Mail Preferences dialog.**

2. **Click the RSS tab.**

3. **Choose a selection on the Default RSS Reader menu to choose the application that you want to use by default to read feeds.**

4. **On the Check for Updates pop-up menu, choose how frequently Mail checks for updates to your feeds.**

5. **Use the Remove articles pop-up menu to determine when Mail removes articles in your feeds.**

6. **Close the Mail Preferences dialog.**

Reading RSS feeds

To read a feed, expand the RSS section. You see each feed to which you are subscribed. Select the feed you want to read; its messages appear on the Messages list (see figure 7.14). To read a message, select it; its contents appear in the Reading pane. Click the Read more link to open the full story in your Web browser.

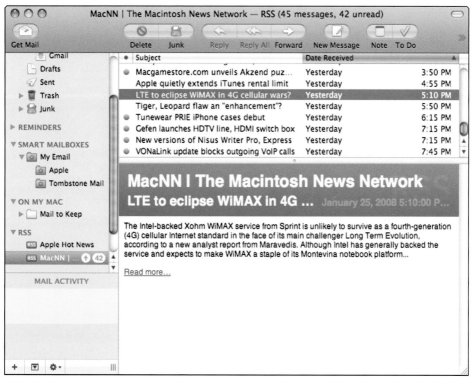

7.14 Here you see the current messages in the MacNN RSS feed.

There's something extremely compelling about having a high-quality video chat with someone who is far away; did I mention that it's free if you have a MobileMe account? Of course, you can also use iChat for text (you can use an AIM, Jabber, or Google Talk account for text chatting with iChat) and audio chats. Among its many useful features is that iChat allows users to share their desktops, which is great for helping someone, being helped yourself, or collaborating.

Configuring iChat

Before you start chatting, you need to do some basic configuration to prepare iChat. There are two basic paths. One is when you first start iChat and the Assistant walks you through the configuration steps. The other is manual configuration; even if you used the Assistant, you should work through a manual configuration so that you can tweak iChat to make it work as well as possible for you.

Configuring iChat with the Assistant

To get started, launch iChat and use the following steps to configure it through the Assistant, which starts with the Welcome screen:

1. **Review the information in the Welcome screen.**

2. **Click Continue.** The Set up a new iChat Account window appears. If you have a MobileMe account configured for the current user account, the account information is configured automatically to use that account.

3. **Enter the MobileMac or AIM account username and password information in the window.** You can also configure a Jabber or Google Talk account. The details of these account types are a bit different.

4. **Click Continue.** The Jabber Instant Messaging window appears.

Genius

If you want to apply for an iChat account, click the Get an iChat Account button and follow the on-screen instructions to register for a free iChat account.

5. **If you use Jabber Instant Messaging, check the check box, enter your Jabber account name and password, and click Continue; if not, just click Continue.** The Set up Bonjour Messaging window opens.

6. **If other Macs are on a local network with which you can communicate, click the Use Bonjour messaging check box.** This enables you to chat with others on your local network because all Bonjour devices are found automatically. If you use a wireless network in a public place, you might want to leave this option off.

7. **Click Continue.** The Set up iChat AV window appears. iChat shows you the image being captured by the built-in iSight camera. Just under the image is a volume level indicator that displays the relative volume of the audio input from the MacBook Pro microphone.

8. **Click Continue.** The Conclusion screen appears.

9. **Click Done.** The basic configuration of iChat is complete and you move into the chatting windows. You can start setting up buddies for chatting or move into the next section to learn how to configure iChat manually.

Configuring iChat with Preferences

iChat offers a number of preferences that you can use to configure the way it works. You don't have to set all of these preferences at once; you should plan on adjusting them over time to tweak the way iChat works. To access iChat preferences, choose iChat ⇨ Preferences. The Preferences window has a number of tabs that are summarized in the following sections (see figure 8.1).

8.1 Use the iChat preferences to make iChat work the way you want it to.

Note There are a number of preferences that you won't find described here. As you explore the preferences, watch for those that might meet your style. I've included only the ones that are most widely used.

Setting General preferences

The aptly named General tab of the iChat Preferences dialog enables you to configure some general behaviors. Here are some of the more useful settings:

⦾ **Show status in menu bar.** This places an iChat menu on your menu. From there, you can easily change your chat status, see which of your buddies is available, and move to your buddy lists.

⦾ **Confirm before sending files.** You can exchange files with others through chats. It's a good idea to enable this setting so that you don't send any files that you don't intend to.

⦾ **When fast user switching, set my status to.** Use this pop-up menu to automatically set your status when someone else logs into your MacBook Pro.

⦾ **When I return to my computer, if I set my status to Away.** Use these radio buttons to set an iChat status when you return to your user account.

⦾ **Save received files to.** Use this pop-up menu to select the folder into which files are stored when you receive them through iChat.

Setting Account preferences

You can use the Accounts tab to configure the user accounts that you use for chatting (see figure 8.2). You can create and use multiple kinds of accounts within iChat, including any on the following list:

8.2 Use the Accounts tab to configure your iChat accounts.

⦾ MobileMe

⦾ .Mac (free iChat accounts are .Mac as of this writing)

- AIM (AOL Instant Messenger)

- Jabber

- Google Talk

While each of these accounts is set up in a similar way, their details are slightly different. To configure iChat user accounts, open the Accounts tab of the Preferences window. Some of the more useful tools and settings are described in the following list:

- **Accounts.** In the left pane, you see a list of accounts that are currently configured. To add a new account, click the Add button (+) at the bottom of the Accounts list. Once configured, you can use the account to chat.

- **Use this account.** Select the account you want to primarily use for chatting and check this check box.

- **When iChat opens, automatically log in.** Check this check box if you want to log into your primary account as soon as you open iChat.

- **Add new buddies I chat with to Recent Buddies.** When you check this check box, anyone with whom you chat is added to your recent list, making it easier to chat with them again.

- **Security subtab.** You can set the privacy level here, which determines who can see when you are online. For example, if you click the Allow people in my Buddy List radio button, only people who are on your buddy list can see that you are available.

- **Bonjour.** Select the Bonjour account on the list and use the settings under the Account Information tab to enable it. This enables you to easily use iChat on your local network.

Setting Messages preferences

The Messages pane enables you to set various formatting options for your messages (see figure 8.3). Following are some useful controls:

- **Pop-up menus.** Use these menus to set the colors for your text balloons and the text that appears within them. If you leave the Reformat incoming messages option unchecked, then messages are formatted according to the sender's preferences.

- **Set Font buttons.** Use these buttons to select the font for your chats (sending and receiving).

- **Use keyboard shortcut to bring iChat to the front.** Check this check box and choose the keyboard shortcut on the pop-up menu to be able to bring iChat quickly to the front.

- **Remember my open chats across launch.** When you check this check box, iChat remembers the state of your on-going chats, even after you quit the application. When you start it up again, you can return to where you left off.

8.3 Use the Messages preferences to format how your text chats appear and to set options, such as automatic transcripts.

Setting Alerts preferences

Use the Alerts pane to set the alerts and notifications that iChat uses to get your attention. Select the event for which you want to configure an alert on the Event pop-up menu, and then select the specific alert on the check boxes and pop-up menus to configure it. You can choose a sound, bouncing the iChat icon on the Dock, running an AppleScript, or an announcement. There are many different events about which you can be alerted, including when you log in and log out.

Setting Audio/Video preferences

You can use these preferences to prepare for audio and video chats. Following are the important settings:

- **Image preview.** In this pane, you see the current image that is being received from your MacBook Pro iSight camera. If you can see yourself well, then people with whom you chat will also be able to.

Audio meter. Just under the image preview is an audio meter that provides a graphic representation of the volume level being received. You can use the built-in microphone or another audio input device, such as a Bluetooth headset.

○ **Play repeated ring sound when invited to a conference.** When this check box is checked and you are invited to an audio or video conference, you hear a ringing sound until you respond to the request.

Setting Up and Working with Chat Buddies

The people with whom you chat are called buddies, and in order to chat with someone, you must configure them as a buddy. There are two different kinds of buddies. One type is the people whom your MacBook Pro can see on a local network through Bonjour. The other type, and the one you are likely to deal with more often, is people who are configured in your Address Book and have a MobileMe e-mail address, a Jabber account, or an AIM screen name.

By default, when you open iChat, you see two windows: One is titled Bonjour List, and the other is labeled AIM Buddy List (see figure 8.4). The people shown on the Bonjour list are found automatically when your Mac searches your local network for Bonjour users. You add people with whom you want to chat on the AIM Buddy List. You can chat with people on either list in the same way.

Because using the AIM Buddy List is the more common way, I will focus on it for the rest of this chapter, but you can do anything with the Bonjour list that you can with the AIM Buddy List.

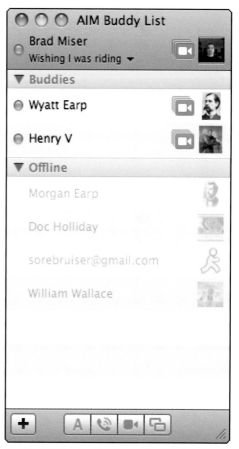

8.4 The AIM Buddy List shows the people with whom you can chat, along with their current status.

Working with the AIM Buddy List

At the top of the AIM Buddy List window, you see your information, including your name, status, video icon, and the photo associated with your name. The dot next to your name indicates your status. A green dot means you are available, and those who have permission to see your status know that you are available for an iChat. Text is also associated with each status, and you can have multiple text labels for the same status; the default is Available when you are online, but you can make it anything you want. A red dot means you are online, but unavailable; like the Available status, you can associate different text messages with the Unavailable status; the default is Away. When no dot is shown, you are Offline, meaning you aren't signed into chatting services. When a gray dot appears, it means that the buddy's messages are being forwarded to his phone. When the dot is yellow, the buddy is idle.

Genius

To change your status, open the pop-up menu immediately below your name at the top of the AIM Buddy List window, and choose the status you want to set.

In the AIM Buddy List window, buddies are organized, based on whether their status is Online or Offline. In the Buddies section, you see your buddies who are currently online. Someone who is online may or may not be available. If you see a green dot, the buddy is online and available for chatting; you also see their status message below their name. If you see a red dot, the buddy is online, but not available for chatting (you also see their current Away status message under their name).

The Offline category contains all your buddies who are currently offline. These buddies are disabled and you can't even try to chat with any of them.

Note

As buddies change status, you hear alerts as you have configured them on the Alerts tab of the iChat Preferences dialog.

Adding chat buddies

There are several ways to add people to your buddy list so that you can chat with one. You can create a buddy in iChat, or you can add someone who is in your Address Book as a buddy.

Creating a buddy in iChat

To create a new buddy in iChat, do the following:

1. **Click the Add button (+) located in the lower-left corner of the AIM Buddy List window.**

2. **Select Add Buddy.** The Add Buddy sheet appears.

3. **Choose the type of account the buddy uses on the pop-up menu on the right side of the sheet.** For example, if the buddy uses a .Mac account, select .Mac. If the buddy uses an AIM account, choose AIM.

4. **Enter the buddy's account name.** This will be whatever the person has provided to you. (If you selected .Mac in step 3, don't overwrite @*mac.com*.)

5. **Enter the buddy's first name in the First Name field and the last name in the Last Name field (see figure 8.5).**

6. **Click Add.** The buddy is added to your buddy list. If the buddy is online, they appear in the Buddies section. If not, they appear in the Offline section.

Enter the buddy's AIM or .Mac account:

Account Name: [ ]   AIM

Add to Group: Buddies

First Name:

Last Name:

Cancel   Add

8.5 To add a buddy to your list, complete the information on this sheet.

Caution

iChat doesn't check the account information that you enter to make sure it's correct. If the account information for a buddy is wrong, their status is always Offline.

Adding someone from your Address Book as a buddy

To add someone who is already in your Address Book as a buddy, use the following steps:

1. **Click the Add button (+) located in the lower-left corner of the AIM Buddy List window.**

2. **Select Add Buddy.** The Add Buddy sheet appears.

3. **Click the Expand button (downward-pointing triangle next to the Last Name field).** The lower pane of the sheet expands, and you see a mini-Address Book viewer.

4. **Search or browse for the person you want to add as a buddy.**

5. **Select the name and e-mail address or AIM account of the person you want to add.**

6. **Click Add.** The buddy is added to your buddy list. If the buddy is online, they appear in the Buddies section. If not, they appear in the Offline section.

Chatting with Text

Instant or text messaging is a preferred way of communicating for many people. Text chats are easy to do, fast, and convenient. Using iChat, start your own text chats or answer someone's request to text chat with you. You can also chat with more than one person at the same time.

Requesting a text chat

You can text chat with others by using the following steps:

1. **Select the buddy with whom you want to chat (see figure 8.6).** If the person is on the Offline list, they aren't available for chatting. Even if the person is online, make sure their status indicator shows that they are available for chatting before you initiate a chat session (look for the green dot).

2. **Click the Text Chat button, which is the A located at the bottom of the window.** An empty Instant Message window appears.

3. **Type your message in the text bar at the bottom of the window.**

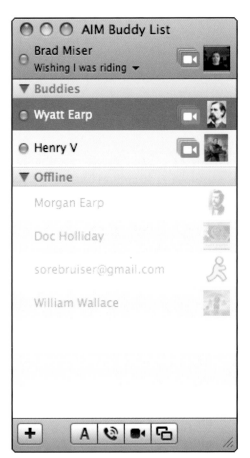

8.6 Think I'll check in with Wyatt.

Genius

You can use the pop-up menu (identified with a smiley) at the end of the text bar to add emoticons to what you type.

4. **When you are ready to send what you typed, press Return.** Your message appears in a text bubble in that user's iChat or other text messaging application. When you receive a reply to your message, you see the person's picture along with the text he sent (see figure 8.7).

5. **Continue chatting.**

6. **When you are done chatting, close the chat window.**

Responding to a text chat invitation

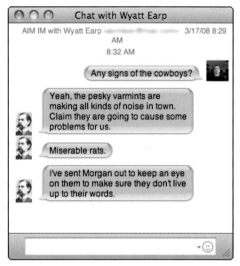

8.7 Things aren't looking so good in Tombstone.

You can respond to invitations that you receive to start a text conversation. When a person wants to chat with you, a box appears on your screen with the name of the person who sent it as its title and the text they sent. Respond to the request by following these steps:

1. **Click the initial text chat window.** It expands to a chat window that includes the text bar and the following buttons:

   - **Decline.** Click this button to decline the chat. Nothing is sent back to the person who is trying to chat with you.

   - **Block.** Click this button to decline the chat and block future requests from the sender.

   - **Accept.** Click this button to accept the chat.

2. **Type your response in the text bar.**

3. **Press Return.** Your text is sent.

4. **Continue the chat.**

When someone leaves the chat, you'll see a status message saying so at the bottom of the window.

169

Chatting with more than one person

You can include more than two people in a chat by performing the following steps:

1. **Select each buddy with whom you want to chat by holding the ⌘ key down while you click the buddy on your list.**

2. **Click the Text Chat button.** You see the text chat window, with each buddy that is included in the chat shown at the top of the window.

3. **Type your message.**

4. **Press Return.** The message is sent to each buddy.

   As a buddy responds, their message appears in your window. Everyone who joins the chat sees the messages from each participant as they come in (see figure 8.8).

8.8 You can text chat with multiple people at the same time.

Chatting with Audio

An iChat audio chat is pretty much like talking on the telephone. Starting an audio chat isn't any harder than starting a text chat, either, as you can see in the following steps:

1. **Select the buddy with whom you want to chat.**

2. **Click the Audio Chat button (the telephone receiver) at the bottom of the AIM Buddy List window.** If the button is disabled, the buddy isn't available for audio chats, and you have to change to a text chat instead. The Audio Chat window appears.

3. **When the buddy accepts the request, start chatting.**

4. **As you chat, use the following controls to manage your chat session (see figure 8.9):**

   - **Audio meter.** Use the Audio meter to gauge your own volume. As you speak, the green part of the bar should move to at least the halfway point. If not, you can use the Input level control on the Sound pane of the System Preferences application.

- **Add buddies.** Click the Add button (+) located in the lower-left corner of the window to add more people to the audio chat. Just like text chats, you can add multiple people to an audio chat. You can have up to ten people in the same audio chat.

- **Mute.** Click the Mute button (the microphone with a slash through it) to mute your end of the conversation. Click it again to unmute your sound so that people can hear you again.

- **Volume slider.** Drag to the right to increase the volume or to the left to decrease it.

When someone wants to audio chat with you, you see a window with the person's name as

8.9 Chatting with audio is as easy as it should be.

its title and the Audio icon. Click the window and then click one of the following buttons:

- **Text Reply.** Declines the audio invitation and starts a text chat.

- **Decline.** Declines the audio invitation. The person who sent it to you sees a status message stating that you declined.

- **Accept.** Accepts the invitation and starts the chat.

Note If you are listening to iTunes when you start an audio or video chat, it automatically pauses. It starts playing again when the chat ends.

Chatting with Video

Using iChat to videoconference is amazingly cool, and it is as simple to use as the other types of chatting. However, a video chat requires a lot of bandwidth, so it is more sensitive to the Internet connection of each person who is involved in the chat. Note that you can only video chat with someone who is using iChat or the most current version of Instant Messenger for Windows (assuming they have a working camera for their computer, of course).

To video chat, do the following:

1. **Select the buddy with whom you want to chat.**

2. **Click the Video Chat button (the video camera) at the bottom of the AIM Buddy List window.** If the Video Chat button doesn't become active when you select a buddy, the buddy is not capable of video chatting with you. The video chat window opens, and you see

the green "on" light next to the iSight camera. You see a preview of the view that others see of yourself, and a message that iChat is waiting for a response.

When the buddy accepts your chat invitation, you see their image in the larger part of the chat window. The smaller, inset preview window shows you what the other person is seeing in their chat window (see figure 8.10).

8.10 Why, I never knew Wyatt and Doc looked like this.

3. **Talk to and see the other person.**

4. **As you chat, you can manage your chat session in the following ways:**

- **Add buddies.** Click the Add button (+) to add more people to the video chat.

- **Mute.** To mute your end of the conversation, click the Mute button; click it again to unmute it.

- **Fill Screen.** To make the chat window fill the desktop, click the Fill Screen button (the arrows pointing away from each other). To see the toolbar while in full screen mode, move the pointer.

- **Effects.** When you click the Effects button, you see the Video Effects palette. You can browse the available effects and click one to apply it to your image. The preview updates, and other participants will see you as the effect changes you.

Applying Backgrounds During a Video Chat

You can apply backgrounds to video chats that make it appear as if you are someplace you aren't. A background can be a static image or a video. iChat includes some backgrounds by default, and you can also use your own images as backgrounds.

To add a default background, do the following:

1. **Start a video chat.** While you are waiting for the chat to start, you can use the following steps to set the background.

2. **Click the Effects button.**

3. **Scroll to the right in the Video Effects palette until you see the images and video that are provided by default.**

4. **Click the image or video that you want to apply as a background.**

5. **Move out of the camera view at the prompt.**

6. **When the prompt disappears, move back into the picture.** It will look as if you are actually in front of the background. The effect isn't perfect, but it is pretty amazing.

To add your own images or video as backgrounds, do the following:

1. **Choose Video ⇨ Show Video Effects.** The Video Effects palette appears.

2. **Scroll in the palette until you see the User Backdrop categories.**

3. **Drag an image file or video clip into one of the User Backdrop wells.**

4. **Click the image or video that you want to apply as a background.**

5. **Start a video chat and apply the background you added.**

Sharing Desktops During a Chat

You can share your desktop with people you chat with. When you do this, the person with whom you share it can control your computer. They see your desktop on their screen and can manipulate your computer using their keyboard and mouse (or trackpad). Using a similar process, you can share someone else's desktop to control their computer from afar.

Accessing a desktop being shared with you

You can share someone else's desktop to take control of their computer. Here's how:

1. **Start the sharing session in one of the following two ways:**

   - Select the buddy whose desktop you want to share. Click the Share Desktop button (the two boxes to the right of the camera button). Select Ask to Share *buddy*'s screen, where *buddy* is the name of the buddy you selected. When your request is accepted, you see a message that the sharing feature is starting , and two windows appear on your screen (see figure 8.11).

   - When you receive a request to share your screen, click Accept. You see a starting sharing message, and two windows appear on your screen (see figure 8.11). One window is the buddy's desktop, which is the larger window by default. The other, smaller window is a preview of your desktop, which is labeled with *My Computer.*

8.11 When you share someone else's desktop, you can control their computer.

2. **You can work with the buddy's computer just as if you were sitting in front of it.** For example, you can make changes to documents or use commands on menus. An audio chat is started automatically so you can communicate with the other person.

3. **To move back to your desktop, click the My Computer window.** The two windows flip-flop so that your desktop is now the larger window so you can control your MacBook Pro.

4. **Control your MacBook Pro again.**

5. **Click back in the other computer's window to control it again.**

6. **When you're done sharing, click the Close button on the My Computer window.**

Sharing your desktop with someone else

To share your desktop with someone else, perform the following steps:

1. **Select the buddy with whom you want to share your desktop.**

2. **Click the Share Desktop button (the two boxes to the right of the camera button).** If the Share Desktop button doesn't become active when you select a buddy, the buddy is not capable of sharing your desktop.

Caution

When you share your screen, you are sharing control of your MacBook Pro. Someone who shares your screen can do anything remotely that you can do directly.

3. **Select Share My Screen with *buddy*, where *buddy* is the name of the buddy you selected.** iChat sends a screen-sharing request to the buddy you selected, and you see the Screen Sharing window.

When the buddy accepts your invitation, the buddy with whom you are sharing your screen can now use your MacBook Pro. They can also talk to you because, when you share the desktop, you also have an audio chat session going. Expect to see your MacBook Pro do things without any help from you.

Sharing a Document During a Chat

In some cases, you might want to just share a document with someone else. You can do this with iChat Theater. This is ideal for making remote presentations. You can show the presentation and provide narration. Here's how to do your own remote presentations:

1. **Choose File ⇨ Share a File With iChat Theater.** You see the Share with iChat Theater dialog.

2. **Move to and select the document (such as a presentation) that you want to share.**

3. **Click Share.** You see a message stating that iChat Theater is ready to begin.

4. **Select the buddy with whom you want to share the document.**

5. Start a video chat.

When the buddy accepts your invitation, you see the Video Chat window. You also see a window showing the document you are sharing. In the lower-left corner of the window, you see a preview window showing the buddy with whom you're chatting (see figure 8.12).

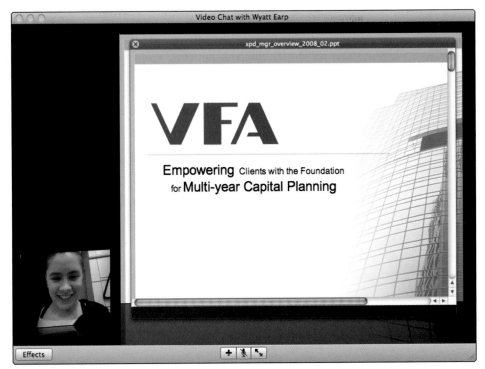

8.12 Here, I'm sharing a PowerPoint presentation.

Genius

If you want to see a preview window showing yourself, select Video ⇨ Show Local Video. A second preview window appears, and you see the image that your audience is seeing in their preview window.

6. Move through the document and speak to your chat buddy.
If you share a Keynote presentation, you can use the Keynote controls to present the document.

Chatting On

iChat is a powerful application that includes a lot of features and capabilities that I don't have space to cover here. Here is a brief description of some of them:

⦿ By default, when your MacBook Pro goes to sleep or when the screen saver activates, your status is changed to Away automatically.

⦿ You can have multiple chats of various types going on with different people at the same time. Each chat appears in its own independent chat window, unless you check the Collect chats into a single window check box on the Messages pane of the iChat Preferences dialog.

⦿ Use your status settings to prevent unwanted interruptions. For example, if you are online but busy with something, open your status menu and choose Away or one of the other unavailable statuses. You can also select the Offline status to prevent any invitations.

⦿ If you have trouble with a video chat, choose Video ⇨ Connection Doctor. The Connection Doctor opens and shows you statistics about the conference (see figure 8.13).

8.13 The Connection Doctor can help you understand problems you are having with chats.

⦿ Use the Video menu to configure and control various video and audio settings. For example, choose Video ⇨ Record Chat to record a chat session.

How Can I Get the Most from the Web?

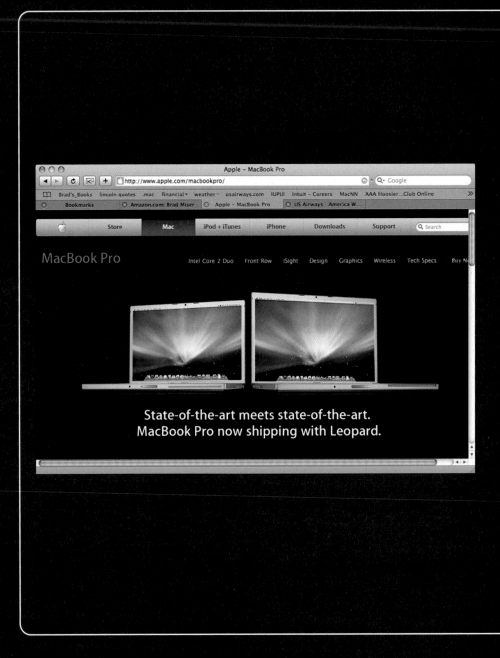

While I think of the pre-Web age, I don't understand how we got anything done without it; the Web has since become fundamental for information, finances, shopping, travel, and communication. With your MacBook Pro in hand, you're poised to get the most from the Web using Safari, the Mac OS X default Web browser. For speed, you should also check out Firefox. In this chapter, I assume that you know how to do the basics, such as move to Web sites. What you'll find here are techniques you can use to get more from the Web, faster and easier.

Setting, Organizing, and Using Bookmarks

Unless you are a glutton for punishment, you probably don't enjoy typing URLs into a Web browser to move to a Web page. Fortunately, using bookmarks, you can avoid having to type a URL more than once. In this section, you learn how to set, organize, and use Safari bookmarks to make your Web browsing more efficient and effective, not to mention more enjoyable.

Setting bookmarks

Like dropping breadcrumbs as you walk through the forest, you can set bookmarks for Web sites that you frequent regularly or only occasionally to lead you back to where you were before (of course, there aren't any birds on the Web that swoop in and eat your bookmarks, so bookmarks are much more reliable than breadcrumbs). To bookmark a site, follow these steps:

1. **Open Safari.**

2. **Browse the Web until you find a page that you want to bookmark.**

3. **Do one of the following:**

   - Choose Bookmarks ⇨ Add Bookmark.

   - Press ⌘+D.

   - Click the Add Bookmark button (+), which is located just to the left of the Address field in the Safari toolbar.

   The bookmark sheet appears (see figure 9.1).

4. **Type a name for the bookmark.**

5. **On the pop-up menu, choose to save the bookmark on the Bookmarks bar, the Bookmarks menu, or a folder that you've created or one of Safari's default folders.**

6. **Click Add.** The sheet closes and the bookmark is created in the location that you selected.

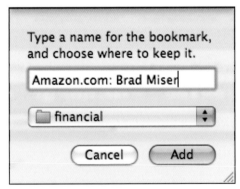

9.1 Use the bookmark sheet to name a bookmark and to choose where to save it.

Setting bookmarks preferences

There are several Safari preferences related to bookmarks. To configure them, choose Safari ➪ Preferences and click the Bookmarks tab. On the Bookmarks pane, you have the following options:

- **Bookmarks Bar.** The two Include check boxes in the Bookmarks Bar section determine whether Address Book and Bonjour sites are accessible from the Bookmarks bar. This enables you to quickly move to Web, FTP, or other resources on your local network.

- **Bookmarks Menu.** If you check the Include Bookmarks Bar check box, you can access any bookmarks on the Bookmarks bar by choosing that option on the Bookmarks menu.

- **Collections.** Safari collections are special folders of bookmarks, such as those on the Bookmarks bar. Checking the check boxes in this section adds URLs in your Address Book or available through Bonjour, to the collections in the Bookmarks window.

- **Synchronize.** If you have a MobileMe account, you can synchronize your bookmarks across many Macs so they all have the same bookmarks. To do this, check the Synchronize bookmarks with other computers using MobileMe check box.

Organizing bookmarks

You should use the tools in Safari to keep your bookmarks organized so you can use them more easily and quickly. You can determine the location of bookmarks, place them in folders (collections) to create hierarchical bookmark menus, and rename them. To do these tasks, open the Bookmarks window by clicking the Bookmarks button at the left end of the Bookmarks bar. The Bookmarks window replaces the contents of the page you were browsing (see figure 9.2).

At the top of the left pane is the Collections section, containing the Bookmarks Bar and Bookmarks Menu collections, the Address Book and Bonjour collections (if their Include preferences are enabled), the History collection, and the All RSS Feeds collection, which contains all your RSS feeds.

In the lower part of the left pane is the Bookmarks section, which shows folders of bookmarks. Safari includes several folders containing bookmarks by default. You can change these folders or add your own folders and bookmarks.

To create a new folder and add bookmarks to it, perform the following steps:

1. **Click the Add Folder button (+) located at the bottom of the left pane of the window.** A new untitled folder appears.

2. **Type a name for the folder.**

3. **Press Return.** The folder is ready for you to place bookmarks within it.

4. **Select a location containing bookmarks you want to move into the folder.** For example, if the bookmark is on the Bookmarks menu, select that option in the Collections section.

5. **Drag the bookmark from its current location and drop it onto the new folder.**

6. **Select the folder you created.** The bookmarks you placed in it appear on the list in the right pane.

7. **To create a folder within the selected folder, click the Add Folder button (+) at the bottom of the right pane.** A new, nested folder appears.

8. **Name the new folder and press Return.**

9. **Drag and drop bookmarks onto the nested folder to place them in it (see figure 9.2).**

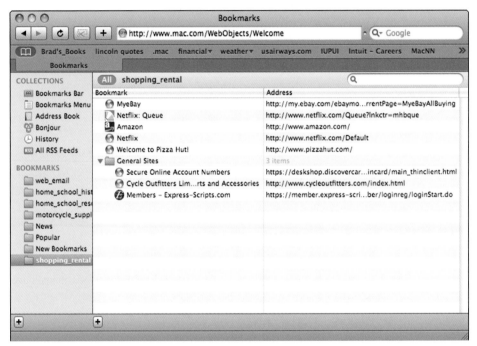

9.2 You can create folders within folders to achieve bookmark organization nirvana.

Adding a folder is just one of the bookmark organization tasks you can do. You can also perform the following techniques:

● Rename a collection, folder, or bookmark by selecting it, opening its contextual menu (Ctrl+click), and selecting Edit Name.

◉ Change the URL for a bookmark by selecting it, opening the contextual menu, and selecting Edit Address.

◉ If you check the Auto-Click check box for a folder in the Bookmarks Bar collection, then when you click the folder's button on the Bookmarks bar, all the bookmarks in that folder open, with each bookmark appearing in a separate tab.

◉ Delete a collection, folder, or bookmark by selecting it and pressing Delete.

◉ Search your bookmarks using the Search tool at the top of the Bookmarks pane.

Using bookmarks

You can use bookmarks to move to Web sites in many different ways, including the following:

◉ Click a bookmark or a folder of bookmarks on the Bookmarks bar.

◉ Select a bookmark on the Bookmarks menu.

◉ Press ⌘+1 to ⌘+9 to move to any of the bookmarks in the first nine positions on the Bookmarks bar. This only works for bookmarks on the bar, not for folders.

◉ Open the Bookmarks window and double-click a bookmark.

◉ Open the Address Book or Bonjour menu on the Bookmarks bar and select a site to visit.

◉ Open a bookmark's contextual menu and select Open, Open in New Window, or Open in New Tab.

Using Tabs to Browse

To make working with multiple pages at the same time more efficient, Safari windows can have tabs, with each open Web page being on its own tab.

Configuring tabbed browsing in Safari

To set Safari to use tabs, perform the following steps:

1. **Press ⌘+,.** The Safari Preferences open.

2. **Click the Tabs tab (see figure 9.3).**

3. **Check the top check box if you want to be able to press the ⌘ key down when you click a link to open a Web page in a new tab.**

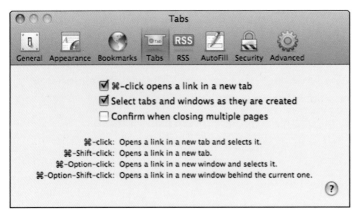

9.3 Configuring tabs requires just a few check boxes.

4. **Check the bottom check box if you want to confirm closing a window when it has multiple tabs open.** I find this prompt annoying, but it can prevent you from accidentally closing a page, such as one on which you are completing a form that you haven't saved.

Using tabs

Use the following pointers to work with Safari tabs (see figure 9.4):

9.4 Tabs make it neat and tidy to work with multiple Web pages at the same time.

- To open a new tab, press ⌘+T. You can move to a site in the tab by entering a URL or using a bookmark.

- Press ⌘+{ to move to the next tab, or press ⌘+} to move to the previous tab.

- Change the order of open tabs by dragging them to new locations.

- To close all tabs but the visible one, hold the Option key down and click the visible tab's Close button.

- To open a link in a new tab, Ctrl+click it and choose Open Link in New Tab.

- To create bookmarks for a set of open tabs, choose Bookmarks ➪ Add Bookmarks For These *X* Tabs, where *X* is the number of open tabs. Name the bookmark, choose a location in which to save it, and click Add. A folder containing a bookmark for each tab is created with the name and location you configured.

- To open multiple bookmarks in tabs, move to the Bookmarks window, select a set of bookmarks, and press the Space bar.

- To transform multiple Safari windows into a single set of tabs, choose Window ➪ Merge All Windows.

Opening many Web pages with one click

Using bookmarks, folders, and tabs, you can configure any collection of Web pages to open with a single click.

Create a one-click folder of bookmarks by doing the following:

1. **Set bookmarks for the pages you want to open with one click.**

2. **Open the Bookmarks window.**

3. **Create a folder for the bookmarks you want to open.**

4. **Place the bookmarks into the folder you created.**

5. **Drag the bookmarks up or down in the folder so they are in the order in which you want them to open on tabs.**

6. **Drag the folder you created in step 3 onto the Bookmarks Bar collection.**

7. **Check the Auto-Click check box.**

When you want to open all the bookmarks in this folder, click it on the Bookmarks bar. Each bookmark in the folder opens in its own tab.

Searching the Web

Searching for information on the Web is one of the most useful skills to have, and Safari is designed to make Web searches easy. You can access one of the best search engines, Google, directly from the Safari Address bar. This makes searching easier because you don't need to move to a page before you start searching, and it enables some great features, most notably the SnapBack button.

To search the Web using the built-in Google search tool, do the following:

1. **Type the text for which you want to search in the Search tool and press Return.** You jump to Google and the results of your search are displayed.

2. **Use a link on the results page to move to a page that looks promising.**

3. **If you view search results in the same window, click the SnapBack button, which is the curved arrow located at the end of the Search bar (see figure 9.5).** You return to the search results page.

```
  ○ ○ ○                    The Official Website of the Indianapolis Colts
 ◄  ►   C   ⬚   +    ⟳ http://www.colts.com/                       RSS  ·  Q indianapolis colts   ⊙
  ▯  Brad's_Books   lincoln quotes   .mac   financial▼   weather▫   usairways.com   IUPUI   Intuit – Careers   MacNN        »
```

9.5 Use the SnapBack button to return to your Google search results page.

As you can see, performing a Google search from within Safari is fast and easy. Here are a few more points for your searching pleasure:

- To repeat a previous search, click the magnifying glass icon in the Search tool; then, on the pop-up menu, select the search you want to repeat.

- To clear the searches you have performed, click the magnifying glass icon in the Search tool; then, on the pop-up menu, select Clear Recent Searches.

- To clear the current search, click the Clear button (the x) inside the Search field.

Snapping Back

Using the SnapBack button when you search with the Google search tool is great, but you can also use this feature when you are browsing. Safari marks the first page you visit on any site as the SnapBack page. As you move to other pages on the site, you can return to the SnapBack page by clicking the SnapBack button shown at the end of the URL of the page you are currently viewing.

You can mark a page to be the SnapBack page for a site by either selecting History ⇨ Mark Page for SnapBack or pressing Option+⌘+K. When you click the SnapBack button, you return to this page. (If you don't set a SnapBack page, you return to the first page on the site.)

You can also return to the SnapBack page by choosing History ⇨ Page SnapBack or pressing Option+⌘+P.

Downloading Files

Downloading files is an important part of using the Web. The files you download can be of any type, such as applications, graphics, PDF documents, audio files, text files, updaters, or any other file you can think of.

After you click a link to begin a download, the Downloads window opens, showing the progress of the file you are downloading (see figure 9.6). As a file is downloaded, you see its name, the download progress, and the file size. During the download process, you see the stop button for the files you are downloading; you can stop the process by clicking this button.

You can continue to browse the Web while your files are downloading. Your browsing speed decreases a bit, but at least you can do something while the file is downloading. If you use a fast connection, you probably won't notice the slowdown at all.

	Downloads
istumbler-98.tar 644 KB	
HandBrake 5.9 MB	
apple_iphone_guidedtour_20080115_848x480.mov 121 MB	
earp.html 1.2 KB	
Firefox.app 17.1 MB	
SnapzProX2.dmg 5.8 of 14.8 MB (632 KB/sec) — 14 seconds remaining	
Clear	6 Downloads

9.6 Use the Downloads window to monitor and control file downloads.

Genius

You can download as many files at the same time as you want. Each file downloads a bit more slowly because all the files share the same bandwidth.

As you download files, Safari continues to add them to the list in the Downloads window. You can clear them manually by clicking the Clear button. You can have Safari remove them automatically by selecting either When Safari Quits or Upon Successful Download on the Remove download list items pop-up menu, located on the General pane of the Safari Preferences dialog.

By default, Safari stores files you download in the Desktop folder in your Home directory, which also appears as a stack on the Dock. The file you most recently downloaded becomes the first one on the stack. If you click the Downloads stack, by default, the files in the folder open in a fan, with the most recent file you downloaded appearing on the bottom of the fan. Select its icon to open it.

Genius

If you want files that you download to be stored in some other location, open the General pane of the Safari Preferences dialog and use the Save downloaded files to pop-up menu to choose Other; then select the folder that you want to use instead.

Using AutoFill to Quickly Complete Web Forms

Like the real world, using the Web involves completing forms for various purposes, such as creating accounts on Web sites, shopping, and requesting help or information. Many of these forms require the same basic set of information, such as your name, address, and telephone number. Using the Safari AutoFill feature, you can complete this basic information with a single click. AutoFill can also remember usernames and passwords that you use to log into Web sites so that you don't have to retype this information each time you want to access your account.

Preparing AutoFill

Configure AutoFill with the following steps:

1. **Open the Safari Preferences window.**

2. **Click the AutoFill tab.**

3. **To complete forms using the information on your card in Address Book, check the Using info from my Address Book card option.**

4. **Click Edit.** You move to your card in Address Book.

5. **Use Address Book to update your information as needed.** You want to have the common items, such as address, e-mail address, and phone numbers, filled in so that AutoFill can complete these items for you.

6. **Move back to Safari.**

7. **To have Safari remember usernames and passwords for Web sites that you access, check the User names and passwords check box.**

8. **To have Safari remember information for forms on specific Web sites, check the Other forms check box.**

Using AutoFill

Using AutoFill is pretty straightforward (and if it wasn't, what would be the point?), as shown in the following steps:

1. **Move to a Web site that requires information on a form (see figure 9.7).**

```
○ ○ ○                    Personal Account Sign Up – PayPal

◀ ▶  C  ⟲  ✎  +   P https://www.paypal.com/us/cgi-bin/webscr?dispatch=5   Q▾ sign up

▢  Brad's_Books   lincoln quotes   .mac   financial▾   weather▪   usairways.com   IUPUI   Intuit – Careers   »

⊗   Bookmarks         ⊗  Personal Account Sign ...   ⊗   Google Accounts      ⊗  US Airways  America W...

                                              Log In  |  Help  |  Security Center

PayPal™

Create a PayPal Account                                           Secure 🔒

First Name:          [ Brad                                    ]
Last Name:           [ Miser                                   ]
Address Line 1:      [ 555 Main St                             ]
Address Line 2:      [                                         ]
(optional)
City:                [ Somewhere                               ]
State:               [ IN  ⬍ ]
ZIP Code:            [ 46555          ]
Home Telephone:      [                                         ]
                     This will not be shared    e.g. 555-555-5555
Mobile Telephone:    [                                         ]
(optional)
```

9.7 AutoFill takes a lot of repetitious data entry off your hands by entering common information for you.

2. **Activate AutoFill by doing one of the following:**

   - Choose Edit ⇨ AutoFill Form.

   - Press Shift+⌘+A.

   - Click the AutoFill button, which has a pencil within a box as its icon.

Genius

To add the AutoFill button to the toolbar, select View ⇨ Customize Toolbar. The Customize Toolbar sheet appears. Drag the AutoFill button onto the Safari toolbar. Click Done.

Safari completes as much information as it can, based on the form and the contents of your Address Book card. It highlights information that it enters in yellow.

3. Manually complete or edit any of the fields that AutoFill didn't complete correctly.

Saving and E-mailing Web Pages

Because the Web is always changing, there's no guarantee that a page you are viewing now will exist a day from now, or even five minutes from now. If you want to make sure you can view a page again in the future, you can save it on your MacBook Pro so that you can always view its content. In other situations, you might want to share Web pages with other people. Safari has tools for both of these tasks.

Saving Web pages

You can save a Web page to your MacBook Pro by performing the following steps:

1. Move to the Web page you want to save.

2. Choose File ⇨ Save As. The Save sheet appears (see figure 9.8).

9.8 Saving a Web page is a good way to convert dynamic information into static information.

3. **Enter a name for the Web page.**

4. **Choose the location in which you want to save it.**

5. **Choose Web Archive on the Format menu.**

6. **Click Save.** The page is saved in the location you specified.

You can view a saved Web page again later by double-clicking its icon. It opens in Safari, and the page appears as it was when you saved it. To see the current version of the page, you need to move back to it on the Web. You can tell which version of the page you are seeing by looking at its URL. If it starts with file://, you are viewing a saved Web page. If it starts with http://, you are viewing a live page on the Web.

E-mailing links to Web pages

E-mailing a link to a Web page is a great way to share it with someone else. To send a link, follow these steps:

1. **Move to a Web page you want to share.**

2. **Choose File ⇨ Mail Link to This Page.** A new e-mail message is created and a link to the page is added to the body of the message.

Genius

You can also e-mail a link by pressing Shift+⌘+I.

3. **Complete the message by adding recipients, editing the subject, and adding comments.**

4. **Send the message.** When the recipient receives it, they can click the link to view the page.

E-mailing Web pages

You can e-mail the content of a Web page you are viewing to someone else. This is better than sending a link if there is a chance that the page will change before the person with whom you want to share the page can look at it. The only downsides of sending content instead of a link are that the e-mail message is larger (not usually a problem for people with broadband access) and the recipient's e-mail application must be able to read HTML messages (most can).

To send a page's content, follow these steps:

1. **Move to a Web page you want to send to someone.**

2. **Choose ⇨ Mail Contents of This Page.** A new message is created and the content of the page is pasted into the body (see figure 9.9).

9.9 You can easily send the content of a Web page to someone using the Safari Mail Contents of This Page command.

Genius

The shortcut for e-mailing Web pages is ⌘+I.

3. **Complete the message by adding recipients, editing the subject, and adding comments.**

4. **Send the message.** When the recipient receives it, they can view the Web page in the message. Buttons and links on the page take the recipient to the Web.

Using Firefox to Surf the Web

While Safari is the Mac OS X default Web browser and also happens to be one of the best browsers available for any type of computer, it certainly isn't the only one available.

After using Safari ever since it was released, I've recently switched to Firefox as my primary browser. I find Firefox to be significantly faster than Safari for the Web sites I use regularly, and it is also more compatible with the sites I use. For example, Safari is unable to access an Outlook Web Access site I use for company e-mail, but Firefox gets to it perfectly. Other Web sites that give me trouble in Safari also work better in Firefox.

The good news is that if you have used Safari as the previous sections of this chapter describe, you won't have any trouble using Firefox because its interface is quite similar. Also, when you start Firefox for the first time, you can add Safari information, such as your bookmarks, to it so that you don't even have to start from scratch with the new browser.

Because Firefox is free, there's really no reason not to give it a try to see which you prefer. Of course, you don't really have to have a preference because you can use both browsers if you want to.

Downloading and installing Firefox

To give Firefox a try, download and install it:

1. **Use Safari to move to firefox.com.** You see the Firefox Home page.

2. **Click the Download link.** Firefox downloads. When the application's file has downloaded, you see the license screen.

3. **Click Accept (assuming that you accept the license terms, of course).** The Firefox disk image is mounted on your desktop, and a Finder window showing the Firefox application file appears.

4. **Drag the Firefox.app file to the Applications folder.** The application is installed.

5. **Click the Eject button for the Firefox disk image.** The image is unmounted.

6. **Delete the disk image file.** This step is optional, but you might as well save some space. You can always download the installer again should you ever need it.

Browsing with Firefox

As I mentioned, Firefox uses an interface that is quite similar to Safari. To browse with Firefox, use the following steps:

1. **Open the Applications folder.**

2. **Open Firefox.**

3. **Click Open in the security warning prompt.** The Import Wizard appears (see figure 9.10).

4. **Leave Safari selected.**

5. **Click Continue.**

6. **On the Home Page Selection window, choose either Firefox Start or import your Home page from Safari.**

7. **Click Continue.** After a few seconds you move into Firefox. You're prompted to set Firefox as your default browser.

9.10 The first time you open Firefox, you can import Safari information, such as your bookmarks.

8. **Uncheck the Always perform this check when starting Firefox check box.** If you leave this check box checked and Firefox isn't set as your default browser, you see this prompt each time you open Firefox. I find this annoying.

9. **If you want to make Firefox your default browser, click Yes; if not, click No.** You move to the Firefox window and see two tabs: one is a first run page that you only see the first time you run Firefox, while the second is the Home page you set.

10. **Review the first run tab and close it when you're done.** You see your Home page in Firefox (see figure 9.11). Notice that your bookmarks from Safari appear on the Bookmarks bar and menu, just as they are in Safari.

9.11 The Firefox Start page isn't much to look at, but it loads instantly and provides access to Google, which is a good starting point for many Web journeys.

11. **Begin to browse the Web as you would with Safari.**

Genius

To make Firefox your default browser, open the General tab of the Safari Preferences window and choose Firefox on the Default Web Browser pop-up menu. Any Web links you click open in Firefox automatically.

Setting and organizing bookmarks in Firefox

As you've seen, any bookmarks you created in Safari are imported into Firefox and you can use them as you do in Safari. Of course, you can also add more bookmarks in Firefox and organize them as you see fit.

To set a bookmark in Firefox, follow these steps:

1. **Move to a Web page for which you want to create a bookmark.**

2. **Do one of the following:**

- Choose Bookmarks ⇨ Bookmark This Page.

- Press ⌘+D.

The Bookmarks sheet appears.

3. **Enter a name for the bookmark in the Name field.**

4. **On the Create in pop-up menu, choose a location for the bookmark.** The options include the following:

- The Bookmarks Toolbar folder, which places the bookmark on the Bookmarks toolbar.

- A specific bookmarks folder; the available folders are those that have been configured using the Firefox Bookmarks tools.

5. **Click Add.** The bookmark is created in the location you selected.

Like Safari, Firefox includes tools you can use to organize your bookmarks. To access these tools, choose Bookmarks ⇨ Organize Bookmarks. The Bookmarks Manager appears (see figure 9.12) and you can use the Bookmarks Manager to get your Firefox bookmarks in order.

9.12 Use the Firefox Bookmarks Manager to organize all your bookmarks.

Genius

If you end up using both Safari and Firefox, you might want to use the same set of bookmarks in each application. Unfortunately, there's no easy way to keep the bookmarks synchronized between the two applications.

Browsing with Firefox tabs

Like Safari, Firefox is a tabbed Web browser. Also like Safari, there are Tabs preferences that you can set to influence how tabs work. Once configured, you can use tabs to view multiple pages.

Configuring Firefox tabs

To configure its tabs, perform the following steps:

1. **Choose Firefox ⇨ Preferences.** The Preferences window appears.

2. **Click the Tabs icon.** The Tabs preferences appear.

3. **Click the new window radio button if you want new pages to open in a new window, or the new tab radio button if you prefer new pages to open in tabs.**

4. **If you want to be warned when you close multiple tabs by closing a Firefox window, check the Warn me when closing multiple tabs check box.**

5. **Check the When I open a link in a new tab, switch to it immediately check box if you want new tabs to become active when they open because you clicked a link.** If you don't check this option, you need to click a tab to make it active.

Using Firefox tabs

To browse with tabs, do any of the following:

- Choose File ⇨ New Tab. A new tab appears. Move to a Web page in the new tab.

- Press ⌘+T. A new tab appears. Move to a Web page in the new tab.

- To move between tabs, press Ctrl+Tab to move forward in the tabs, or Shift+Ctrl+Tab to move backward in the tabs.

- To change the order in which tabs are shown in the window, drag them to the left or the right.

- Press ⌘+1 to ⌘+8 to select one of the first eight tabs. To jump to the last tab, press ⌘+9.

- To open a link in a new tab, hold the Ctrl key down, click the link, and select Open in New Tab.

How Can I Manage My Time Effectively with iCal?

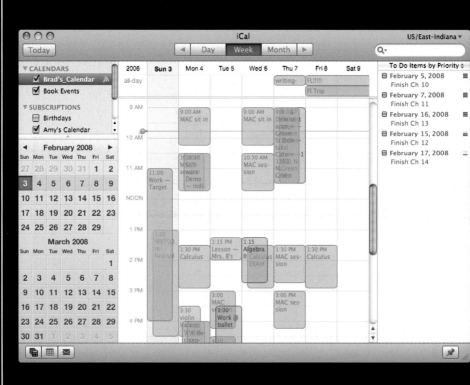

With iCal, you can manage your own time by creating calendars that help you to be where you're supposed to be when you're supposed to be there. You can also use To Do items to ensure that you accomplish important, or even not-so-important, tasks. As a personal calendar tool, iCal is very useful, and if it could only do that, it would be worth using. However, iCal is also designed for calendar collaboration. You can publish calendars so that others can view your calendars in iCal running on their Macs. Likewise, you can subscribe to other people's calendars so that you see their events.

Setting Up iCal

Before you jump into managing your calendars with iCal, take a few moments to configure some of its preferences so that it works the way you want:

1. **Launch iCal.**

2. **Choose iCal ⇨ Preferences.**

3. **Click the General tab.** Here you set general preferences relating to how the calendar appears and works (see figure 10.1) such as what day your week starts on, how many days are in your week, and whether or not you see birthdays listed for your Address Book contacts.

10.1 The General preferences enable you to configure how weeks and days are displayed.

4. **To keep your iCal calendar synchronized across multiple Macs using a MobileMe account, check the Synchronize my calendars with other computers using MobileMe check box.** See Chapter 5 for more information about MobileMe.

5. **Click the Advanced tab to configure choices about time zone support, hiding To Do items, and managing alarms.**

Creating Calendars in iCal

There are two levels of calendars that you deal with when you use iCal. First, there is the overall calendar, which is what you see inside the iCal window. This calendar includes all the information being managed or shown by the application. On the second level are the individual calendars on which you create events and To Do items. There are many good reasons that you might want to create multiple calendars for your events and To Do items. The classic example is one calendar for work events and one calendar for personal events. If there are some events that you don't want to show in a published version, then you can create a calendar for those events that you don't publish and another for those that you want to share.

To create a calendar, follow these steps:

1. **Click the New Calendar button (+) located in the bottom-left corner of the iCal window.**

2. **Enter a name for the new calendar and press Return.**

3. **Ctrl+click the new calendar and choose Get Info on the contextual menu.**

4. **Enter a description of the calendar in the Description field.**

5. **Click OK.** The changes you made are saved and you see the calendar's name in the color you selected.

To include a calendar's events and To Do items in the calendar being displayed in the iCal window, check its check box. If you uncheck a calendar's check box, its events and To Do items are hidden.

Most of the time, you're better off hiding a calendar because it won't appear in iCal anymore, but you can access its information at any time. When you delete a calendar, all its information goes with it.

Adding Events to Calendars

You can use iCal events to plan periods of time. If one of those periods of time is a meeting, you can invite others to join by sending them an invitation. In addition to the time and date, you can include all sorts of useful information in iCal events, such as file attachments, URLs, and notes. To add an event to a calendar, perform the following steps:

1. **Select the calendar on which you want the event to appear by clicking it.**

2. **While hovering over the date and time on which you want the event to occur, Ctrl+click and select New Event.** A new event appears on the calendar with its title selected. By default, the time of the event is the next hour on the calendar.

3. **Type the name of the event.**

4. **Press Return.** The event name is saved and it appears in the color of the calendar with which it is associated (see figure 10.2).

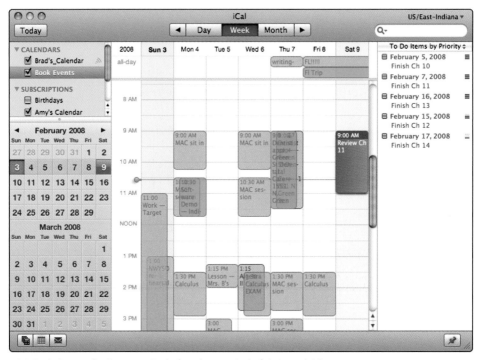

10.2 At their most basic, events include a date, period of time, and title.

5. **Double-click the event.** Its summary window appears. Here, you see the name, from and to dates and times, time zone, and alarm information.

6. **Click the Edit button.** The Edit sheet appears (see figure 10.3), allowing you to set start and stop times, and alarms.

7. **To add other people to the event, click Add Attendees.** A box for address information appears.

8. **Start typing the name (if the person is in your Address Book) or e-mail address of the person you want to add.**

9. **To associate a file with the event, click Add File and use the resulting Open dialog to browse for the file you want to attach.**

10. **If a URL is associated with the event, enter it in the url field or copy and paste it there.**

11. **If you added people to the attendees list, click Send; if not, click Done.** After you click Send, an e-mail is created in your default e-mail application and the event is attached to it. After you click Done, changes that you made to the event are saved.

Review Ch 11

location	Conference Room A
all-day	☐
from	02/09/2008 10:00 AM
to	02/09/2008 04:00 PM
time zone	US/East-Indiana ⬍
repeat	Every week ⬍
end	On date ⬍ 02/09/2008
calendar	■ Book Events ⬍
alarm	Message with sound ⬍ ◁) Basso ⬍ 15 minutes before ⬍
alarm	Email ⬍ bmiser@vfa.com (work) ⬍ 15 hours before ⬍
alarm	None ⬍
attendees	⊙ Marta Justak ⊙ sorebruiser@gmail.com
attachments	🗋 291702 Ch11.doc Add File...
url	http://www.bradmiser.com

Send

10.3 Use the Edit sheet to fully configure an event.

Genius

To choose people in your Address Book, select Window ⬉ Address Panel. You can drag people from the Addresses window onto the attendees list.

Check out these tips for managing events that you create:

● You can change the calendar on which an event occurs by opening its contextual menu (Ctrl+click the event) and selecting the event's new calendar.

● You can change the date on which an event occurs by dragging it from one date in the calendar to another date.

● You can e-mail an event to others by opening its contextual menu and selecting Mail Event.

● If you use the Send command, as people add the event to their calendars, you'll see a green check mark next to their names when you open the event's Information window. This indicates that the attendee has accepted the event by adding it to their calendar. If an attendee hasn't added the event to their calendar, their name is marked with a question mark icon. This tracking doesn't occur when you use the Mail Event command.

Creating and Completing To Do Items

You can use iCal To Do items to track just about any kind of action for which you are responsible. In this section, you learn how to create To Dos and how to complete them (by that, I mean how to mark them as complete — you're on your own to actually do the work).

Adding To Do items to a calendar

Creating a To Do item is similar to adding an event, as you see in the following steps:

1. **Select the calendar that you want the To Do item to be associated with.**

2. **Ctrl+click in the To Do pane and select New To Do, or press ⌘+K. A new, untitled To Do item appears.**

3. **Type the name of the To Do item and press Return.**

4. **Ctrl+click the To Do item and select Get Info.** The Information window appears (see figure 10.4).

5. **Use the priority pop-up menu to set the To Do item's priority.**

6. **If the To Do item has a due date, check the due date check box.** Use the date fields that appear to set the due date.

Finish Ch 15

completed ☐

priority High ⇕

due date ☑ 02/15/2008
alarm Message ⇕
the day before ⇕
at 11:45 PM

alarm None ⇕

calendar ■ Book Events ⇕

url bradmiser.com
note I need to get this chapter done by 2/15.

[Done]

10.4 Configuring a To Do item is similar to configuring an event, although there are fewer options.

7. **If a URL is associated with the To Do item, enter it in the url field.**

8. **Click Done.** The changes you made to the To Do item are saved.

Managing To Do items

You manage your To Do items in the To Do pane, which appears on the right side of the iCal window. (If you don't see this pane, click the pushpin button at the bottom of the window). As you work with To Do items, keep the following points in mind:

- The priority of a To Do item is indicated by the number of bars that appear to the right of its name on the To Do items list. A high-priority item has three bars, a medium-priority item has two bars, and a low-priority item has one bar.

- You can Ctrl+click a To Do item to open its contextual menu. With the commands on that menu, you can duplicate it, change the calendar with which it is associated, mark its priority, e-mail it, open its Information window, or change the sort order for the To Do items pane.

- When you e-mail an event or a To Do item to someone, the recipient can add the item to their calendar by clicking its link or by dragging it onto their iCal window.

   When the due date for an item is the current date or the due date has passed, its complete check box becomes a warning icon to indicate that the item is due or overdue (see figure 10.5).

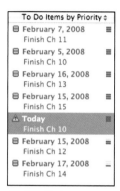

10.5 To Do items marked with a caution icon are due today or are overdue.

Working with Calendars on Your MacBook Pro

As you build your calendars in iCal, there are many ways you can view and manage events and To Do items. You can also print calendar information in a number of ways for those times when you'd like to have a hard copy.

Viewing calendars, events, and To Do items

Check out the following ways that you can control how information is displayed in the iCal window:

- If you want to focus on specific events and To Do items, uncheck the check boxes for the calendars that don't interest you, and their information is hidden.

- The Mini Months tool shows you one or more months at a glance. You can show or hide this section by choosing View ➪ Show Mini Months, or View ➪ Hide Mini Months, respectively.

- In the center pane is the actual calendar. There are three views for this: Day, Week, and Month. You can change the view by clicking the approach button.

- If Time Zone Support is enabled, you can change the current time zone by choosing a time zone on the pop-up menu above the Search tool. Open the menu and choose Other. The Change time zone sheet appears. Click the map near a city in the time zone you want, and then choose the specific time zone on the Closest city pop-up menu. Click OK. The times and dates are adjusted according to the new time zone.

- When you enter search text, iCal's Search Results pane opens at the bottom of the window automatically. This pane lists all events and To Do items that meet your search criterion. To see an event on the calendar, select it in the Search Results pane.

Genius

To change the calendar view to by Day, by Week, or by Month, press ⌘+1, ⌘+2, or ⌘+3, respectively. To move to the next day, week, or month, press ⌘+right arrow; move back by pressing ⌘+left arrow. Press ⌘+T to jump to today, or Shift+⌘+T to move to a specific date. You can show or hide the To Do List by pressing Option+⌘+T.

Printing calendars

While having your calendar in an electronic format is very useful and practical (because you can take your MacBook Pro with you), there may be times when you'd like to have a hard copy of calendar information. You can use the iCal Print command to create paper versions of your calendar information by following these steps:

1. **Choose File ⇨ Print.** The Print dialog appears (see figure 10.6).

10.6 iCal offers a number of printing options.

2. **Choose the view you want to print on the View menu.**

3. **Use the tools in the Time range section to define the time period to include in the printed version.**

4. **In the Calendars section, check the check box for each calendar whose information you want to be included in the printed version.**

5. **If you are printing to a black-and-white printer, check the Black and White check box.**

6. **On the Text size pop-up menu, choose the relative size of the text on the calendar.**

7. **Click Continue.** The Print dialog for the current printer appears.

8. **Use the controls in the Print dialog to configure the printer.**

9. **Click Print.**

207

Publishing and Subscribing to Calendars

iCal is designed to be a collaborative calendar tool, and you can publish your calendars; other iCal users can subscribe to them to see your calendar information in iCal on their computers. You can also share your calendars with Windows users or even with Mac users who don't use iCal. Of course, you can subscribe to other people's calendars to add their information to your iCal window.

Publishing calendars

There are two basic ways to publish calendar information. If you have a MobileMe account and everyone with whom you want to share your calendar uses iCal, you can use the iCal Publish tool to make your calendar easy to add to their calendars. If you want to share your calendar with people who use Windows (or Mac users who don't use iCal) or you don't use MobileMe, it gets a little more complicated.

Publishing calendars through MobileMe for iCal users

With your MobileMe account and iCal, it's simple to publish calendars for other people to view within their iCal application, as the following steps demonstrate:

1. **Select the calendar you want to publish.**

2. **Choose Calendar ⇨ Publish.** The Publish sheet appears (see figure 10.7).

10.7 Use the Publish sheet to share a calendar with other iCal users.

3. **Type the name of the calendar as you want it to appear to someone with whom you share it.**

4. **Select MobileMe on the Publish on pop-up menu.**

Genius

It's a good idea to remove any spaces in the calendar's name because in the URL for a calendar, spaces are replaced by %20, which makes the URL harder to deal with than it needs to be.

5. **If you want changes that you make to your calendar to be published automatically, check the Publish changes automatically check box.** In most cases, you should check this option so that your calendar is always up-to-date.

6. **Click Publish.** When the calendar has been published, you see the confirmation dialog (see figure 10.8).

Calendar Published

Your Calendar "Home" has been published successfully, and can be subscribed at URL:

webcal://ical.me.com/bradmacosx/Home.ics

or be viewed with a browser at URL:

http://ical.me.com/bradmacosx/Home

Visit Page   Send Mail   OK

10.8 This calendar can be viewed on the Web or subscribed to in iCal.

When a calendar is published, the published icon (which looks like radiating waves) appears next to the calendar's name on the list of calendars.

Publishing calendars for non-iCal users

Using MobileMe to publish calendars has two drawbacks. One is that you must have a MobileMe account, which seems kind of obvious. The other limitation is that your shared calendar can only be subscribed to by iCal users, which leaves Windows users out of the picture.

For either of these scenarios, you can publish your iCal calendars to a different server so that people can access them over the Web, including Windows users. While this isn't as convenient as subscribing to shared calendars in iCal, it does work.

You need to find and use a calendar server service to be able to publish calendars. There are many of these available, and a number of them are free to use. After you find the service you're going to use, create an account and then configure iCal to publish your calendars using that account.

The following steps explain how to publish an iCal calendar using the iCal Exchange service located at www.icalx.com (other services work similarly):

1. **Go to www.icalx.com.**

2. **Create an account.** Use any username and password that you want, as you only use this information to access your icalx account.

3. **Move back to iCal.**

4. **Select the calendar you want to publish.**

5. **Choose Calendar ⇨ Publish.** The Publish sheet appears.

6. **Type the name of the calendar as you want it to appear to someone with whom you share it.** It's a good idea to remove spaces in the name by deleting them or replacing them with underscores.

7. **On the Publish on pop-up menu, choose A Private Server.** The Base URL, Login, and Password fields appear.

8. **In the Base URL field, enter http://icalx.com/private/*your_icalx_username/*, where *your_icalx_username* is the username that you created in step 2.**

Genius Step 8 assumes that you want to create a private calendar, meaning one that requires a password to be able to view. If you don't want to require a password, replace *private* with *public* in the URL.

9. **Enter your icalx username in the Login field and your icalx password in the Password field.**

10. **If you want changes that you make to your calendar to be published automatically, check the Publish changes automatically check box.** In most cases, you should check this option so that your calendar is always up-to-date.

11. **Click Publish.** When the calendar has been published, you see the confirmation dialog (see figure 10.9).

10.9 This calendar has been published using the iCal Exchange service.

12. **Click OK.**

13. **Log into your icalx account.** You see the calendars that you've published on the Private Calendars or Public Calendars lists.

14. **Click the passwords link under the your account section on the left side of the screen.**

15. **Click add a password.**

16. **Enter the username that you want to provide to people to enable them to access your calendar.**

17. **Enter the password that you want to provide to people to enable them to access your calendar.**

18. **Select the calendars that you've published and want to share by checking their check boxes.**

19. **Click Save Changes.** The calendar is protected with the password you created.

Subscribing to published calendars

When people share their calendars with you through the iCal Publishing tools, you can subscribe to those calendars to add them to your iCal window:

1. **Choose Calendar ⇨ Subscribe.** The Subscribe sheet appears.

2. **Enter the URL for the calendar to which you want to subscribe.** URLs for calendars published with MobileMe start with webcal://ical.mac.com.

3. **Click Subscribe.** The Subscribing configuration sheet appears, where you can name the calendar, assign it a color, and choose whether you want the calendar's associated alarms, attachments, and To Do items.

4. **If you want the calendar's information to be refreshed automatically, select the frequency at which you want the refresh to occur on the Auto-refresh pop-up menu.**

5. **Click OK.** The calendar is added to the Subscriptions section of your iCal window, and you can view it just like your own calendars.

Subscribing to public calendars

Many public calendars are available to which you can subscribe. For example, most professional sports teams have calendars that show games and other events. You can also find DVD release calendars, TV schedules, and many other types of calendars to subscribe to. Just like personal calendars, when you subscribe to public calendars, the events on those calendars are shown in your iCal window. To find and subscribe to public calendars, do the following steps:

1. **Choose Calendar ⇨ Find Shared Calendars.** Your default Web browser opens and moves to the Apple Calendar library.

2. **Browse the available calendars by category, such as Most recent, Most popular, Alphabetical, or Staff picks.**

3. **Click the Download button for the calendar to which you want to subscribe.** You move into iCal and the Subscribe to calendar sheet appears. The calendar's URL is filled in automatically.

4. **Click Subscribe.** The Subscribe to configuration sheet appears, where you can name the calendar, assign it a color, and choose whether you want the calendar's associated alarms, attachments, and To Do items.

5. **If you want the calendar's information to be refreshed automatically, select the frequency at which you want the refresh to occur on the Auto-refresh pop-up menu.**

6. **Click OK.** The calendar is added to the Subscriptions section of your iCal window, and you can view it just like your own calendars. If you configured the calendar to be refreshed automatically, iCal keeps it current.

Moving iCal Calendars to an iPhone

If you have an iPhone, you can synchronize your iCal calendars with the Calendar on the iPhone. Here's how:

1. **Connect the iPhone to your MacBook Pro.**

2. **Move into iTunes.**

3. **Select the iPhone on the Source list.**

4. **Click the Info tab (see figure 10.10).**

| Summary | Info | Ringtones | Music | Photos | Podcasts | Video |

☑ Put new contacts created on this iPhone into the group: Important Busi... ◆

☐ Sync Yahoo! Address Book contacts   Configure...

Calendars

☑ Sync iCal calendars

◉ All calendars

◯ Selected calendars:

☐ Brad's_Calendar

☐ Book Events

☐ Amy's Calendar

☐ Jill's_Calendar

☑ Do not sync events older than 30 days

Put new events created on this iPhone into the calendar: Brad's_Calendar ◆

Mail Accounts

☐ Sync selected Mail accounts:

| Cancel |
| Apply |

pacity
7 GB

☐ Audio   ☐ Photos   ☐ Other   ■ Free Space
6.37 GB   11.7 MB   196.8 MB   720.9 MB

10.10 Keeping your iCal calendars in sync with an iPhone can make them even more convenient.

5. **Check the Sync iCal calendars check box.**

6. **Configure iCal to move all calendars or selected calendars on to your iPhone.**

7. **Click Apply.** Each time you sync your iPhone, its calendar is updated with changes that you make in iCal, and changes that you make on the iPhone calendar are moved into iCal.

213

How Can I Make Sure I Don't Run Out of Battery Power?

Energy Saver

Show All

Settings for: Battery

Optimization: Custom

Your energy settings are optimized for long battery life.
Current battery charge: 93% Estimated time remaining: 4:21

Sleep   Options

Put the computer to sleep when it is inactive for:

1 min   15 min   1 hr   3 hrs   Never

Put the display(s) to sleep when the computer is inactive for:

1 min   15 min   1 hr   3 hrs   Never

The display will sleep before your screen saver activates.
Click the button to change screen saver settings.

Screen Saver...

☑ Put the hard disk(s) to sleep when possible

Hide Details

Schedule...

Click the lock to prevent further changes.

Like all devices with batteries, a MacBook Pro can operate only as long as its battery continues to provide power. Once it runs out, your trusty MacBook Pro becomes so much dead weight to carry around. To get the most working time while you're mobile, you should practice good energy-management habits. These include a combination of using the Mac OS X battery management tools, conserving battery power, and being prepared to connect to an external power source whenever you have the opportunity.

Monitoring Battery Status

You can use the Battery menu to keep an eye on where your MacBook Pro power level is so that you know how much working time you have left and can take some action if it's clear you are going to run out of power soon.

Configuring the Battery menu

You can configure the Battery menu on your MacBook Pro by performing the following steps:

1. **Open the System Preferences application.**

2. **Click the Energy Saver icon.** The Energy Saver pane appears.

3. **Click the Show Details button.**

4. **Click the Options tab.**

5. **Check the Show battery status in the menu bar check box if it isn't checked already.**

6. **Quit the System Preferences application.**

7. **Open the Battery menu.**

8. **Select Show.**

9. **Choose one of the following display options:**

   - **Icon only.** This displays the battery icon at the top of the menu when you are on battery power or charging the battery. The amount of the icon that is dark represents the battery's current power level.

   - **Time.** This displays the battery icon and time at the top of the menu. When you are operating on a battery, the time indicates the approximate amount of working time remaining to you at the current power use level.

   - **Percentage.** This displays the battery icon and the percentage of power remaining.

Genius

You can check the current state of a battery by turning the MacBook Pro over and pressing the silver button on the battery. The number of lights indicates the state of the battery's charge.

Keeping track of power levels

As you work with your MacBook Pro, keep an eye on the Battery menu (see figure 11.1). If you open the Battery menu, the first item is the percentage of power remaining if you selected the Time view, or the time remaining if you selected the Icon or Percentage view.

When the battery gets close to being discharged, you see warnings providing an estimate of the remaining time and recommending that you save your work. If you keep going, the MacBook Pro eventually goes into Sleep mode and you won't be able to wake it until you connect it to a power source or insert a charged battery.

While it can remain in Sleep mode for a long time, a MacBook Pro eventually runs out of even the low level of power required to keep that going and shuts off. If you have any open documents with unsaved changes, they are lost when this happens. Beyond the possibility of losing unsaved changes, there really isn't any risk to you to let the MacBook Pro run completely out of power.

When you connect the MacBook Pro to a power source, the Battery menu displays information about the charging process instead of time remaining. The battery icon contains the lightning bolt symbol to indicate that it is currently being charged. The time displayed on the menu is the time until the battery is fully charged; when it is fully charged, the battery icon contains the electrical plug symbol.

| (4:56) | **Wed 6:56 AM** |

95%

Power Source: Battery
Better Battery Life
Normal
Better Performance
✓ **Custom**

Show ▶

Open Energy Saver...

11.1 Monitor the Battery menu as you work so that your MacBook Pro doesn't suddenly come to a grinding halt.

Genius

When you connect the adapter to the MacBook Pro, its status light is amber when the battery is charging. When fully charged, the status light is green.

Making the Battery Last Longer

You can use the Energy Saver to minimize power use while operating on battery power. You can also adopt simple practices to minimize the amount of power your MacBook Pro uses so that you get the most time possible from its battery.

Using the Energy Saver

You can use the Energy Saver pane of the System Preferences application to tailor how the computer uses power so that you can extend the working life of the battery as long as possible. There are two basic ways to configure power usage on a MacBook Pro: You can use one of the standard settings, or you can customize the settings you use. Once your settings are configured, you can use the setting that is appropriate for what you are doing at any point in time.

Using a standard power setting

Mac OS X includes several default energy profiles that you can select to influence how the MacBook Pro operates and thus, the rate at which it uses energy. These profiles are made up of various time settings for putting the MacBook Pro to sleep, dimming the display, putting the hard disk to sleep, and putting the display to sleep.

1. **Open the Battery menu.**

2. **Select one of the following options (see figure 11.2):**

   - **Better Battery Life.** This shortens the time until various components go to sleep.

   - **Normal.** This includes mid-level power saving settings.

   - **Better Performance.** This maximizes performance at the expense of battery life.

   The MacBook Pro starts operating on the selected energy profile.

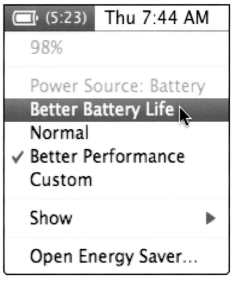

11.2 Choosing one of these standard energy profiles is an easy way to configure your MacBook Pro energy use.

Customizing power settings

Use the following steps to set up your MacBook Pro for minimum energy use and maximum working time:

1. **Open the System Preferences application.**

2. **Click the Energy Saver icon.** The Energy Saver pane appears.

3. **Click the Show Details button.** The pane expands and you see controls that you can use to configure the energy-saving settings in detail (see figure 11.3).

11.3 Use the Sleep tab to configure how and when your MacBook Pro sleeps.

4. **Choose either the power adapter or the battery as the power source for which you want to configure energy savings on the Settings for pop-up menu.**

5. **You can use the top slider to control the amount of inactive time before the entire system goes to sleep.**

6. **You can use the bottom slider to set the amount of inactive time before the screen goes dark.**

   There is also a dim function, which is different from sleep. Dimming causes the screen to go to a lower brightness setting before the display sleeps (when it goes totally dark). You configure this option on the Options tab.

219

7. **Leave the Put the hard disk(s) to sleep when possible check box checked.**

8. **Click the Options tab (see figure 11.4).**

Energy Saver

Show All

Settings for: Battery

Optimization: Custom

Your energy settings are optimized for long battery life.
Current battery charge: 91% Estimated time remaining: 4:27

Sleep   Options

☑ Slightly dim the display when using this power source
☑ Automatically reduce the brightness of the display before display sleep
☑ Show battery status in the menu bar

Hide Details   Schedule...

Click the lock to prevent further changes.

11.4 These options apply when your MacBook Pro is operating on battery power.

9. **Check the Slightly dim the display when using this power source check box if you want
   your display to have a lower brightness when operating on the battery.** In my experi-
   mentation, it appears that this function reduces screen brightness by about two ticks on the
   brightness indicator.

Genius

To maximize working time, use F1 to lower the brightness to the dimmest setting
that you can use comfortably.

10. **Check the Automatically reduce the brightness of the display before display sleep check box if you want your display's brightness to be reduced automatically before it goes to sleep.**

11. **Choose Power Adapter on the Settings for pop-up menu.** You see additional options in the pane, along with some of the same options for the battery.

12. **Check the Wake for Ethernet network administrator access check box if you want the MacBook Pro to wake up when an administrator tries to access it through an Ethernet network (see figure 11.5).** You aren't likely to need this option unless you access the MacBook Pro from another computer.

11.5 These options apply when your MacBook Pro is connected to the power adapter.

13. **Quit the System Preferences application.** Your energy settings take effect.

Automatically Starting or Stopping MacBook Pro

You can configure MacBook Pro to automatically start up, sleep, restart, or shut down according to a schedule. To do this, perform the following steps:

1. **Open the System Preferences application.**
2. **Click the Energy Saver icon.**
3. **Click the Schedule button.** The Schedule sheet appears.
4. **To set an automatic startup or wake time, check the Start up or wake check box.**
5. **To set an automatic sleep, restart, or shut down time, check the lower check box on the sheet and select Sleep, Restart, or Shut Down on the pop-up menu.**
6. **Click OK.** The sheet closes and the schedule you set takes effect.

Note If the MacBook Pro lid is shut, the schedule has no effect.

Adopting low energy habits

Although configuring the energy use of your MacBook Pro has some impact on how long you can operate it on its battery, you can also adopt low energy habits to maximize the amount of time your MacBook Pro operates on its battery. Here are some ideas to consider:

⊚ **Lower the brightness of your screen.** To dim your screen, use the Brightness slider on the Displays pane of the System Preferences application, or the F1 key.

Genius MacBook Pros have an ambient light sensor that can be used to automatically dim the display brightness, based on the ambient light conditions. This setting is enabled by default. This feature also determines when the keyboard backlight activates.

- **Avoid applications that constantly read from the hard drive.** While you probably won't have much choice on this, some applications have settings that impact their use, such as autosave features (you can increase the amount of time between automatic saves to reduce hard drive use).

- **Avoid applications that constantly read from a CD or DVD.** If you can copy files you need onto your hard drive and use them from there, you use power at a lower rate than if your MacBook Pro is constantly accessing its removable media drive. For example, when you want to listen to music, you can add the songs to your iTunes Music Library so you don't need to use the CD or DVD drive.

- **Use an iPod.** Playing content in iTunes requires a lot of hard disk activity and is a heavy user of battery power.

- **Configure sleep times on Energy Saver.**

- **Put your MacBook Pro to sleep whenever you aren't actively using it by closing the lid.** When you open the lid or press a key, the MacBook Pro wakes up quickly, so putting it to sleep frequently doesn't cause a lot of wasted time for you.

Powering MacBook Pro while Traveling

The odds are that you're going to run out of battery power, even if you have tweaked your MacBook Pro for maximum operating time and you practice low energy habits. You can reduce the chances of running out of power by being ready to power your MacBook Pro while you are on the move.

Genius

Most airports have power outlets available in the gate areas; as you move through an airport, keep an eye out for power outlets that you might be able to use.

Powering MacBook Pro with multiple batteries

One of the best ways to extend your operating time while working from a battery is to have more than one battery. Change the battery by following these steps:

1. **Save all open documents and quit all applications.**

2. **Choose Apple menu ⇨ Shut Down.**

3. **When the MacBook Pro powers down, turn it over.**

4. **Push the two slide switches toward the back of the computer.** The battery pops up.

5. **Insert the new battery until it clicks into place.**

6. **Power the MacBook Pro up again.**

Packing a power travel kit

The following are some recommended items that can help you manage your power on the move:

- **The standard power adapter.** Whenever there's a power outlet available, you can use the included adapter to run the MacBook Pro and to charge its battery.

- **Additional batteries.** Having an extra battery doubles the amount of working time.

Maintaining Battery Life

Over time, the accuracy of the battery charge indicator also decreases. However, you can make it more accurate again by calibrating it every so often. Here's how:

1. **Charge the battery so it's full.**

2. **Leave the battery in the fully charged state for at least two hours by leaving the power adapter connected.**

3. **Disconnect the power adapter.**

4. **Use the MacBook Pro on battery power until you see the second or third low power warning.**

5. **Save all your open documents and quit all applications.** Eventually, your MacBook Pro goes to sleep.

6. **Let the MacBook Pro sleep or shut it down for five hours.**

7. **Recharge the battery.**

● **MagSafe Airline Adapter.** With this adapter, you can connect your MacBook Pro to the power outlet that is available in some kinds of seats on airlines. The requirement is that the seat must have an EmPower or 20mm power port.

Caution

While the airline adapter looks like it might be compatible with the DC power port in automobiles, it isn't.

● **International Adapters.** If you travel internationally, get a set of power adapters so that you can connect the MacBook Pro power adapter to power outlets in a variety of countries.

How Can I Control MacBook Pro More Effectively?

To work with your MacBook Pro most effectively, you should understand how to tailor both the keyboard and trackpad so that they work according to your preferences. While the built-in keyboard and trackpad are very good, you might want to add a mouse or external keyboard to your toolkit, especially for those times when you are using the computer at a desk or other workstation. Bluetooth mice and keyboards enable you to do this without the hassle of dealing with wires.

Using the MacBook Pro Trackpad

A trackpad is an ideal input device for a mobile computer because it provides a similar degree of control that a mouse does, but doesn't require anything external to the computer. The MacBook Pro trackpad provides all the basic capabilities you need to enable you to point and click, but it certainly doesn't stop there. You can use it much more effectively by configuring its advanced options and tweaking all its options over time.

Note If you've used an iPhone, you experienced Apple multi-touch technology; you can control an iPhone using normal motions of your fingers on the screen, such as a pinching motion to zoom in and out. The MacBook Pro incorporates a similar interface on its trackpad. Apple has released software updates that add some of this capability to the trackpads of new MacBook Pros and MacBooks.

You can configure the trackpad to work according to your preferences with the Trackpad tab on the Keyboard & Mouse pane in the System Preferences application. Here's how:

1. **Choose Apple menu ⇨ System Preferences.**

2. **Click the Trackpad icon.** The trackpad's configuration options appear (see figure 12.1).

3. **Drag the Tracking Speed slider to the right to make the pointer move more with the same amount of finger movement, or to the left to cause it to move less.**

4. **Drag the Double-Click Speed slider to the right to reduce the time between presses of the trackpad button to register a double-click, or to the left to increase the time.**

5. **Drag the Scrolling Speed slider to the right to increase the amount of scrolling for the same amount of finger motion on the trackpad, or to the left to decrease the amount of scrolling for the same movement on the trackpad.**

6. **Select the Tap to Click gesture.** A video plays, showing you what the gesture is and what it does; at the top of the video window you see the desktop, while in the lower part, you see the gestures you make. With the Tap to Click gesture, you can press once on the trackpad to register a single click of the trackpad button.

7. **If you want to be able to use this gesture, check the Tap to Click check box.**

8. **Repeat Steps 7 and 8 for each of the gestures; select a gesture, watch the video to learn what it does, and then check its check box if you want to use it.**

12.1 Use the Trackpad tab to tweak the trackpad's behavior to your preferences.

9. **If you enable the Screen Zoom gesture, click the Options button.** The Options sheet appears (see figure 12.2).

10. **On the Zoom using pop-up menu, choose the key combination you want to press to activate zooming.**

11. **Click the Continuously with pointer radio button if you want the zoomed image to always move with the pointer.**

12. **Click Only when the pointer reaches an edge if you want the zoomed image to remain stationary until your pointer reaches the edge of the screen.**

12.2 Use the Trackpad pane to tweak the trackpad's behavior to your preferences.

13. **Click So the pointer is at or near the center of the image if you want the zoomed image to remain centered around the pointer.**

14. **If movement seems sluggish when zoomed, uncheck the Smooth images check box.**

15. **Click Done.** The sheet closes.

16. **Quit the System Preferences application.** The trackpad behaves according to your preferences.

Using the MacBook Pro Keyboard

Don't just think of your MacBook Pro keyboard as something you type on, because it's also an important way that you can control your MacBook Pro, from issuing commands to changing what appears on the desktop. In this section, you first learn how to configure the basic functions of the keyboard and then how to control the language it uses. In the latter parts, you learn how to use the keyboard to efficiently control your MacBook Pro.

Configuring the keyboard

Start with the Keyboard & Mouse pane of the System Preferences application, as shown in the following steps:

1. **Open the System Preferences application.**

2. **Click the Keyboard & Mouse icon.**

3. **Click the Keyboard tab (see figure 12.3).**

4. **Use the Key Repeat Rate slider to set how fast a key repeats itself.**

5. **Use the Delay Until Repeat slider to set the amount of time it takes for a key to repeat itself.**

6. **If you want the function keys to behave as standard function keys instead of the default actions they are programmed to perform, check the Use all F1, F2, etc. keys as standard function keys check box.** If you check this option, you must hold the fn key down and press the appropriate key to perform its action (such as F3 to mute your MacBook Pro sound).

7. **To enable the keyboard's backlighting, check the Illuminate keyboard in low light conditions check box.**

12.3 Use the Keyboard tab to tune your MacBook Pro keyboard.

8. **Use the slider to set the amount of time backlighting remains on when the computer is not being used.**

9. **Click the Modifier Keys button.** The Modifier Keys sheet appears.

10. **For each of the four modifier keys, select the action that you want to occur when you press that key.** If your keyboard preference is such that the Control key is more convenient for you, you might want to set it to be the Command key, because you use that key more frequently. You can select No Action to disable a key.

11. **Click OK to set your preferences and close the sheet.**

Configuring the keyboard's language settings and the Input menu

You can configure the languages you use for the keyboard, along with other input preferences, using the International pane of the System Preferences application. You can also configure the Input menu, which enables you to quickly choose among languages and select some other handy keyboard tools. Here's how:

Genius

I have never discovered a real use for the caps lock key, but I have accidentally turned it on thousands of times and found myself TYPING IN ALL CAPS, which is very annoying. You can disable this key by choosing No Action on its pop-up menu. Ah, now you don't have to see caps screaming as you type just because you accidentally hit the key.

1. **Open the International pane of the System Preferences application.**

2. **Click the Language tab (see figure 12.4).**

3. **Drag the language you want to be the default to the top of the list.**

![International preferences pane]

○ ○ ○	International	

◀ ▶ Show All   🔍

     Language   Formats   Input Menu

Languages:

English
Deutsch
Español
Português
Dansk
Suomi

Drag languages into the order you prefer for use in application menus, dialogs, and sorting.

(Edit List...)

⚠ Changes take effect in the Finder the next time you log in. Changes take effect in applications the next time you open them.

Order for sorted lists:

| English | ⬍ |

Word Break:

| English (United States, Computer) | ⬍ |

(?)

12.4 I only wish I could understand all these languages!

4. **On the Word Break pop-up menu, choose how you want word breaks to be applied.**

5. **Click the Formats tab.** You use this tab to select formats that you want to be used for various kinds of information, such as dates, times, and currency.

6. **Click OK.** Any changes you made are saved and you return to the Formats tab.

7. **On the Calendar pop-up menu, choose the calendar you want to use.**

8. **To customize the time formats, click the lower Customize button.** The Time Customization sheet appears.

9. **On the Currency pop-up menu, choose the currency you want to use.**

10. **On the Measurement Units pop-up menu, choose the measurement unit system you want to use.**

11. **Click the Input Menu tab (see figure 12.5).** You use this area to show the Keyboard Input menu on the Finder menu bar and to configure the items you see on it.

12.5 Use the Input Menu tab to configure the Input menu on which you can select languages and other options.

12. **Check the Show input menu in menu bar check box.** The Input menu appears on the menu bar; its icon is the flag for the currently selected region or language.

13. **Check the Character Palette check box to add that to the menu.** You can use this option to select, configure, and use special characters such as accent marks.

Using keyboard tricks

It's worth taking some time to learn some of the ways you can control your MacBook Pro using its keyboard; there's a lot of power hidden behind those mild-mannered keys.

Controlling the keyboard's backlight

If you ever tried to use a computer in a darkened environment (such as an airplane on a night flight), you'll really appreciate the MacBook Pro backlit keyboard. When enabled, backlighting works automatically. When your MacBook Pro senses the environment is darkened, the backlight comes on. When things brighten up, backlighting turns off.

You can also manually control backlighting by using the following function keys:

- **F8.** This key disables backlighting. Press it again to re-enable backlighting.
- **F9.** This key decreases the brightness of backlighting.
- **F10.** This key increases the brightness of backlighting.

These keys work only when backlighting is on, which means when you are in a darkened environment and you haven't disabled it.

Controlling your MacBook Pro with function keys

The MacBook Pro includes a number of built-in functions on the function keys that are quite useful (see Table 12.1).

Table 12.1 MacBook Pro Function Keys

Function Key	What It Does
F1	Decreases display brightness.
F2	Increases display brightness.
F3	Mutes volume.
F4	Decreases volume.
F5	Increases volume.
F6	Locks the keyboard so that a set of letters (6 to -, U to P, J to ;, M to /) acts like a numeric keypad. To return the keys to their defaults, press F6 again.
F7	Turns video mirroring on or off (more about that in Chapter 13).
F8	When in a darkened environment, turns keyboard backlighting on or off.
F9	When in a darkened environment, decreases the brightness of keyboard backlighting.
F10	When in a darkened environment, increases the brightness of keyboard backlighting.
F11	Uses Exposé to hide all open windows.
F12	Opens or closes the Dashboard.

Controlling your MacBook Pro with default keyboard shortcuts

Mac OS X includes support for many keyboard shortcuts by default. For example, you've probably used ⌘+Q to quit applications. There are many more keyboard shortcuts available to you. The only challenge to using keyboard shortcuts is learning which ones are available to you. Fortunately, there are a number of ways to discover keyboard shortcuts, as described in the following list:

● **The Keyboard Shortcuts tab of the Keyboard & Mouse pane of the System Preferences application.** If you open this tab, you see a list of Mac OS X keyboard shortcuts (see figure 12.6). You can also use this pane to change shortcuts and to create new ones.

12.6 You can get familiar with the keyboard shortcuts for the commands you use most frequently.

● **Menus.** When you open menus, keyboard shortcuts are shown next to the commands for which they are available.

● **Mac Help.** Open the Help menu and search for shortcuts.

Configuring keyboard shortcuts

Using the Keyboard Shortcuts tab of the Keyboard & Mouse pane, you can configure many of the available keyboard shortcuts. You can enable or disable some of the standard keyboard shortcuts and add keyboard shortcuts for commands in applications that you use. Using the Full Keyboard Access feature, you can access the interface elements with the designated keys.

To configure keyboard shortcuts, perform the following steps:

1. **Open the Keyboard & Mouse pane of the System Preferences application.**

2. **Click the Keyboard Shortcuts tab.** You see a list of standard OS keyboard shortcuts in a number of areas, such as Screen Shots, Universal Access, and Keyboard Navigation.

3. **To see all the available commands in a section, expand it by clicking the right-facing triangle next to the section's title.** The section expands.

4. **Disable any of the listed shortcuts by unchecking the shortcut's On check box.**

5. **To change the key combination for a shortcut, click the command and then click the shortcut.** It becomes highlighted to indicate that you can edit it.

6. **Press the key combination you want to use for that command.**

Creating your own application keyboard shortcuts

You can create your own keyboard shortcut for any menu command in any application. To add your own keyboard shortcuts, perform the following steps:

1. **Identify the specific command for which you want to create a keyboard shortcut.** If it is a command specific to an application, note the exact name of the command, including whether or not it includes an ellipsis.

2. **Open the Keyboard Shortcuts tab of the Keyboard & Mouse pane in the System Preferences application.**

3. **Click the Add Shortcut button (+) at the bottom of the list of shortcuts.** The Add Shortcut sheet appears (see figure 12.7).

4. **On the Application pop-up menu, choose All Applications if you want the shortcut to be available for all applications, or choose a specific application to create the shortcut within it.**

| Application: | Microsoft Excel |
| Menu Title: | Down |

Enter the exact name of the menu command you want to add.

| Keyboard Shortcut: | ⌥⇧⌘D |

Cancel   Add

12.7 You can use this sheet to create your own keyboard shortcuts in any application.

5. **In the Menu Title box, type the name of the command for which you want to create a shortcut, exactly as it appears on its menu.** If the command contains an ellipsis, you also need to include that.

Genius

To type an ellipsis, press Option+;.

6. **In the Keyboard Shortcut field, press the key combination for the shortcut that you want to use to access the command.**

7. **Click Add.** The sheet closes and when you return to the Keyboard Shortcuts tab, the short-cut you added is shown under the related application located in the Application Keyboard Shortcuts section.

8. **Open the application in which you created the shortcut.** The keyboard command you created is shown next to the command on the application's menu.

Navigating with the keyboard

One of the least used, but most useful, aspects of using keyboard shortcuts is keyboard navigation. You can use the keyboard to access almost any area on your MacBook Pro in any application, including the Finder. For example, you can open any menu item by using only keys, even if that item does not have a keyboard shortcut assigned to it.

To see what the default keyboard navigation tools are, open the Keyboard Shortcuts tab of the Keyboard & Mouse pane in the System Preferences application and expand the Keyboard Navigation section. You see the commands explained in Table 12.2.

Using the Input menu

The Input menu enables you to change the current language you are using or to activate specific tools, such as the Character Palette. A flag representing the language you have made the default is shown at the top of this menu on the menu bar. When you open it, you see the items you configured there (see figure 12.8).

You can change the current language, which is indicated by the check mark, to a different one by selecting a different source on the menu. When you do this, the keyboard is con-verted to the layout appropriate to the lan-guage you selected.

12.8 Here, you can see that I've enabled two languages on the Input menu.

Using the Character Palette

The Character Palette is a tool to help you find special characters in various languages and quickly apply those characters to your documents.

The Character Palette opens and has two tabs (see figure 12.9). The by Category tab enables you to select and insert characters you need. When you find a character you use regularly, you can add it to the Favorites tab, so you can grab it easily and quickly.

Table 12.2 Keyboard Navigation

Description	What It Does	Default Shortcut
Turn full keyboard access on or off	Enables or disables the use of certain keys, to navigate.	Ctrl+F1
Move focus to the menu bar	Opens the first menu on the current menu bar; use the Tab or arrow keys to move to other menu items.	Ctrl+F2
Move focus to the Dock	Makes the Dock active; use the Tab or arrow keys to move to icons on the Dock.	Ctrl+F3
Move focus to the active window or next window	Moves into the currently active window or takes you to the next window if you are already in a window.	Ctrl+F4
Move focus to the window toolbar	If you are using an application with a toolbar, this makes the toolbar active. Use the Tab or arrow keys to select a button on the toolbar.	Ctrl+F5
Move focus to the floating window	If you are using an application that has a floating window, this takes you into the floating window.	Ctrl+F6
Move focus to the next window in the active application	Moves you among the open windows in any application.	⌘+`
Move between controls or text boxes and lists	If the Text boxes and lists only option is selected at the bottom of the window, then when you are viewing windows or dialogs with controls, pressing the Tab key moves you among only the text boxes and lists in that open window or dialog.	Ctrl+F7
	If the All controls option is selected, then pressing Tab moves you among all the elements of the window.	
Move focus to the window drawer	If the application you are using has a drawer, such as iDVD, this moves you into that drawer so you can use its tools.	⌘+Option+`
Move focus to the status menus in the menu bar	If you have enabled additional menus in the Mac OS X menu bar, this command enables you to open them.	Ctrl+F8
Show or hide the Character Palette	Shows or hides the Character Palette.	⌘+Option+T

To find and use a special character, perform the following steps:

1. **Open the Character Palette.**

2. **On the View pop-up menu, select the language sets you want to access.**

3. **Click the by Category tab.**

4. **Select the category of character you want to view in the left pane.**

5. **Select a character by clicking it.**

6. **Expand the Character Info section by clicking its expansion triangle at the bottom of the window.** You see a large version of the selected character along with its name.

7. **To apply different fonts to the character, click the expansion triangle next to the Font Variation tab.**

12.9 The Character Palette enables you to configure and select special characters.

8. **Select the font collection you want to use on the Collections pop-up menu.**

9. **Click the version of the character you want to use.**

10. **Click Insert with Font.** The character is pasted into the active document at the insertion point.

11. **Close the palette.** Because it remains on top of all other windows, you'll probably want to keep it closed whenever you aren't using it.

Using the Keyboard Viewer

The Keyboard Viewer is a simple tool that shows you the layout of the keyboard in specific situations. To use it, select Show Keyboard Viewer on the Input menu. The Keyboard Viewer appears (see figure 12.10). You see what each key on the keyboard represents. Hold down the modifier keys to see the impact they have.

12.10 If you want to see what pressing a key does, check out the Keyboard Viewer.

Playing Favorites

You can create a set of favorite characters on the Character Palette to let you quickly choose a special character to insert into a document. Follow these steps:

1. Open the Character Palette.

2. Select and configure the character that you want to save as a favorite.

3. Open the Action menu at the bottom of the window and select Add to Favorites. This copies the character onto the Favorites tab.

Genius

You can search for special characters by description or code using the Search tool that appears at the bottom of the Character Palette window.

Configuring Bluetooth on a MacBook Pro

Bluetooth support is built into your MacBook Pro, so you can wirelessly connect to and use any Bluetooth device.

Bluetooth communication is set up between two devices through a process called pairing, where each device recognizes the other and they are paired so that they can communicate with each other. A single device can communicate with more than one other Bluetooth device at the same time. Each device with which your MacBook Pro communicates over Bluetooth must be paired separately.

To be able to pair two devices together, the devices must be discoverable, meaning that they are broadcasting their Bluetooth signals to other devices in the area so that those devices can find and pair with the discoverable device.

Bluetooth communication requires hardware (transmitter/receiver) and software. Both of these are part of your MacBook Pro, but you need to configure Bluetooth services on your MacBook Pro before you try to connect Bluetooth devices to it. Here's what to do:

1. **Open the System Preferences application.**

2. **Click the Bluetooth icon.** The Bluetooth pane appears (see figure 12.11). In the center part of the pane, you see the devices with which your MacBook Pro is currently communicating, or the "No Devices" message if you haven't paired it with any devices yet.

3. **Check the On check box.** Bluetooth services start.

4. **Check the Discoverable check box.** This makes your MacBook Pro discoverable by other devices because your MacBook Pro transmits signals that other devices can detect. You can still connect to your configured Bluetooth devices when this box is unchecked; your MacBook Pro just won't be able to be detected by other devices automatically.

12.11 Use the Bluetooth pane to configure Bluetooth services on your MacBook Pro.

5. **Check the Show Bluetooth status in the menu bar check box.**

6. **Click the Advanced button.** The Advanced sheet appears.

7. **Leave the Open Bluetooth Setup Assistant at startup when no input device is present check box unchecked.** This is for desktop computers that might only have Bluetooth input devices; because your MacBook Pro has a built-in keyboard and trackpad, it always has input devices.

8. **Check the Allow Bluetooth devices to wake this computer check box.** When you use a Bluetooth mouse or keyboard, you'll be able to wake your MacBook Pro with one of those devices.

9. **Check the Prompt for all incoming audio requests check box if you want to be warned when Bluetooth audio devices attempt to communicate with your MacBook Pro.**

10. **To share your MacBook Pro Internet connection using Bluetooth, check the Share my Internet connection with other Bluetooth devices check box.** Because it's slower than Wi-Fi, you should use AirPort or Ethernet instead of Bluetooth to share an Internet connection with other computers. However, sharing through Bluetooth can be useful for PDAs or other handheld Internet devices.

11. **Click OK.** The sheet closes. Your MacBook Pro is ready to connect to Bluetooth devices.

Adding a Bluetooth Mouse

Using Bluetooth, you can easily connect a mouse to your MacBook Pro.

The rest of this section focuses on Bluetooth mice, but using a wireless USB mouse is similar in many respects. The biggest difference is that you have to connect the USB transmitter, but you don't have to go through the pairing process.

Pairing a Bluetooth mouse with MacBook Pro

To set up a new Bluetooth device by pairing it with your MacBook Pro, you use the Bluetooth Setup Assistant. Follow these steps to do this:

1. **If the mouse is not auto-discoverable, and most mice are not, then press its discoverable button.** These are usually small buttons located on the bottom of the mouse. When you push this button, the mouse goes into Discoverable mode, which causes the device to start broadcasting a Bluetooth signal that your MacBook Pro can detect.

2. **Open the Bluetooth Setup Assistant by clicking the Set Up New Device button on the Bluetooth pane of the System Preferences application.** The Bluetooth Setup Assistant opens.

3. **Click Continue.**

4. **Click Mouse.**

5. **Click Continue.** Your MacBook Pro searches for available Bluetooth mice and presents all the mice it finds on the list (see figure 12.12).

12.12 My MacBook Pro has found a Kensington PocketMouse for Bluetooth.

6. **Select the mouse you want to pair.**

7. **Click Continue.** When the pairing is successful, you see the Conclusion screen.

8. **Click Quit.** The Bluetooth mouse is ready to configure.

Configuring a Bluetooth mouse

Following are the steps to configure a Kensington PocketMouse for Bluetooth (mice that have other features are configured for those specific features, but the general process is the same):

1. **Open the Keyboard & Mouse pane of the System Preferences application.**

2. **Click the Mouse tab** (see figure 12.13). Use the features there to determine tracking, scrolling, and double-clicking speeds.

12.13 The controls you see on the Mouse tab depend upon the type of mouse you are using.

3. **Choose which button you want to be the primary button by clicking Left or Right.** The primary button is the one you click to select something, while the secondary button is the one you use to Ctrl+click.

4. **Click the Options button.** The Options sheet appears, and you can configure zooming options.

5. **Click Done.** Your changes are saved and the sheet closes. Your mouse is ready to use.

Adding a Bluetooth Keyboard

Like a mouse, there may be times when you prefer to use an external keyboard instead of the MacBook Pro built-in version. Just like a mouse, it is easy and convenient to add a Bluetooth keyboard.

Pairing a Bluetooth keyboard with MacBook Pro

1. **If the keyboard is not auto-discoverable, press its discoverable button.** These are usually small buttons located on the bottom of the keyboard. When you push this button, the keyboard goes into Discoverable mode, which causes it to start broadcasting a Bluetooth signal that your MacBook Pro can detect.

Note Some keyboards, such as the Apple Wireless Keyboard, have a power button. Of course, you need to press this button to turn on the keyboard before you can pair it. In most cases, this also puts the keyboard into Discoverable mode.

2. **Open the Bluetooth Setup Assistant by clicking the Set Up New Device button on the Bluetooth pane of the System Preferences application.** The Bluetooth Setup Assistant opens.

3. **Click Continue.**

4. **Click Keyboard.**

5. **Click Continue.** Your MacBook Pro searches for available Bluetooth keyboards and presents all those it finds on the list (see figure 12.14). Each keyboard is indicated by its name or a series of numbers, depending on whether your MacBook Pro can decipher the keyboard's signal to include its name.

6. **Select the keyboard you want to pair.**

7. **Click Continue.** The pairing process starts and you see the Keyboard setup screen. Here, you type the passkey shown on the keyboard to complete the pairing process.

8. **On the Bluetooth keyboard, type the passkey shown in the Assistant's window.**

9. **Press Return.** If the pairing is successful, you see the Conclusion screen.

10. **Click Quit.** The Bluetooth keyboard is ready to configure.

12.14 The keyboard called bradm's keyboard is actually an Apple Wireless Keyboard.

Configuring a Bluetooth keyboard

After you've paired a Bluetooth keyboard with your MacBook Pro, configure it using the Keyboard tab of the Keyboard & Mouse pane in the System Preferences application. You see controls for the specific keyboard you are using. These might or might not be the same as the MacBook Pro internal keyboard, but in most cases, they are the same. See the section, Configuring the keyboard, earlier in this chapter for the steps to configure a typical keyboard (without the backlight configuration, of course).

Note If you use different preferences for the Bluetooth keyboard than what you prefer with the MacBook Pro internal keyboard, you need to reconfigure the Keyboard preferences each time you change keyboards.

Color LCD

◄ ► | Show All

Display | Arrangement | Color

Resolutions:

640 × 480
640 × 480 (stretched)
720 × 480
720 × 480 (stretched)
800 × 500
800 × 600
800 × 600 (stretched)
1024 × 640
1024 × 768
1024 × 768 (stretched)

Colors: Millions

Refresh Rate: n/a

Detect Displays

Gather Windows

☑ Show displays in menu bar | (?)

Brightness:

☑ Automatically adjust brightness as ambi

VX900-2

Display | Color

Resolutions:

640 × 512
800 × 600
800 × 600 (stretched)
800 × 640
832 × 624
1024 × 768
1024 × 768 (stretched)
1024 × 820
1280 × 960
1280 × 1024

Colors: Millions

Refresh Rate: 75 Hertz

Detect Displays

Gather Windows

Rotate: Standard

(?)

MacBook Pros have large (15- or 17-inch) displays. Even so, more display space is always better. You can maximize the amount of information you see on your MacBook Pro screen by configuring its display. For more working room, you can attach and use an external display. For the ultimate in screen size, you can connect your MacBook Pro to a projector. When you are using an external display or projector, you can have the same image displayed on the MacBook Pro display and the external device, or you can expand your desktop over both displays to maximize your desktop space.

Configuring the MacBook Pro Display

While the physical size of the MacBook screen is fixed, the amount of information that can be displayed on it (its resolution) is not. Setting the appropriate resolution, which determines the amount of information that is displayed on the screen, is a matter of choosing the largest resolution that you can view comfortably with no eyestrain.

There are resolutions that are more common to use, but those that are available to you depend on the specific MacBook Pro you are using. The 15-inch model has a different set of resolutions than does the 17-inch model, which has a different set than the 17-inch model with the high-resolution screen. Here's how to find your maximum resolution:

1. **Open the System Preferences application.**

2. **Click the Displays icon.** The Displays pane appears (see figure 13.1).

```
                          Color LCD
  ◀ ▶   Show All                              🔍

              ┌─ Display ─┬─ Color ─┐

  Resolutions:
  ┌──────────────────────┐         Colors:  Millions  ▼
  │ 640 x 480            │
  │ 640 x 480 (stretched)│    Refresh Rate:  n/a       ▼
  │ 720 x 480            │
  │ 720 x 480 (stretched)│              Detect Displays
  │ 800 x 500            │
  │ 800 x 600            │
  │ 800 x 600 (stretched)│
  │ 1024 x 640           │
  │ 1024 x 768           │    ☑ Show displays in menu bar    ?
  │ 1024 x 768 (stretched)│
  └──────────────────────┘

  Brightness:  ═══════════●══════════
               ☑ Automatically adjust brightness as ambient light changes
```

13.1 Use the Displays pane to maximize the amount of room you have on your desktop that's comfortable to view.

3. **Click the Display tab if it's not selected already.** In the Resolutions pane, you see all the resolutions that are supported by your MacBook Pro display. Resolutions are shown as the number of horizontal pixels by the number of vertical pixels, as in 1024 x 768. Larger values have a higher resolution. Some resolutions are stretched so that they fill the screen (the MacBook Pro has a widescreen format display).

4. **Click a resolution.** The screen updates to use the resolution you selected.

5. **Drag the Brightness slider to the right to make the screen brighter, or to the left to make it dimmer.**

6. **To have MacBook Pro automatically adjust the brightness based on the ambient light, check the Automatically adjust brightness as ambient light changes check box.**

7. **Hide the System Preferences application by pressing ⌘+H.**

8. **Open several windows on the desktop.**

9. **If the information in the windows is too small to read comfortably, move back to a lower resolution.**

Adding an External Display

One truth of working with computers is that you can never have too much screen space to work with.

As you learned in the previous section, one way to gain more display space is to make the resolution as large as you can comfortably view to maximize the number of pixels on the screen and thus, the amount of information displayed there. At some point you'll reach a maximum amount of information on the screen due to the maximum resolution of the MacBook Pro (currently 1440 x 900 for the 15-inch model, 1920 x 1200 for the 17-inch model, or 2560 x 1600 for the 17-inch model with the high-resolution display).

To add more screen space to your MacBook Pro (which can support many different displays and resolutions), you can connect an external display. You can use this display in two ways. It can become an extension of your desktop so that you can open additional windows on it just as if it was part of your MacBook Pro built-in display. Or, you can use video mirroring, which means the same information appears on both displays.

Connecting an external display

Attaching an external display to a MacBook Pro is easy:

1. **Connect one end of the video cable to the Mini DisplayPort on the MacBook Pro, and the other end to the display.**

2. **Connect the display to a power source.**

3. **Power up the display.**

Configuring an external display

Once an external display is connected to your MacBook Pro, you can configure it with the following steps:

1. **Open the System Preferences application.**

2. **Click the Displays icon.** A Displays pane opens on the MacBook Pro display and on the external display. The name of the pane on the MacBook Pro internal display is Color LCD, while the name of the pane on the external display is the name of the display. Also notice that the Displays pane on the primary display (by default, the MacBook Pro display) contains the Arrangement tab.

Genius

If the second display doesn't become active, click the Detect Displays button in the Displays pane. This should activate it.

3. **Click the Arrangement tab on the Displays pane on the MacBook Pro screen (see figure 13.2).** You see an icon representation of each display. The display marked with the menu bar at the top is the primary display, which by definition is the one on which the menu bar appears. The Dock also appears on the primary display.

```
Color LCD
◀ ▶   Show All                                    Q

        Display   Arrangement   Color

To rearrange the displays, drag them to the desired position.
To relocate the menu bar, drag it to a different display.




☐ Mirror Displays                                  ?
```

13.2 On the left is the MacBook Pro display, while on the right is the external display; the menu bar is on the primary (MacBook Pro) display.

4. **Drag the external display's icon so it is on the left or right side of the MacBook Pro display's icon, to match the physical location of the display compared to MacBook Pro.**

5. **If you want the external display to be the primary display, drag the menu bar from the MacBook Pro display's icon onto the external display's icon.** When you release the trackpad button, the menu bar jumps to the external display. Windows that were open on the MacBook Pro display move onto the external display.

6. **Select the Displays pane for the external display.**

7. **Choose the resolution for the external display by selecting it on the list of available resolutions.**

8. **If the Refresh rate menu appears, choose the highest rate available (see figure 13.3).**

13.3 Here's the Displays pane for a ViewSonic VX900 display.

9. **Quit the System Preferences application.**

Using an external display

You can now use the space on the external display like you use the internal display. To place a window on the external display, drag it from the MacBook Pro display onto the external display. You can move windows, the pointer, and other items from one display to the other. You configure windows on each display so that you can see several windows at the same time.

The menu bar remains on the primary display, so if you do most of your work on the external display, you might want to make it the primary display to make menu access easier.

Running with the Lid Closed

If you use Bluetooth devices, configure the MacBook Pro so that those devices can wake the computer. Close the MacBook Pro lid so that it goes to sleep. Use the keyboard or mouse to wake it up. The internal display remains off, but the external display wakes up when the computer does.

To restore the internal display, disconnect the external display, or open the MacBook Pro, open the Displays menu, and choose Detect Displays. The internal display becomes active again.

Genius

If you click the Gather Windows button on the Displays pane, each pane is moved onto the primary monitor.

If the resolutions are significantly different between the two displays, you see a big change in appearance when you move a window between them. You might have to resize a window on one display that was the right size on the other.

Using a Projector

With a projector, you can broadcast your MacBook Pro display to very large sizes for easy viewing by an audience. Using a projector is similar to using an external display, so if you can work with one of them, you can work with the other.

Obtaining a projector is a bit more complicated than a display and is usually more expensive. Among the many things to consider when obtaining a projector are the following:

- **Resolution.** There is more variability in the resolution of projectors than of displays. At the lower end of the price range, you'll find projectors that are capable of only 800 x 600 resolution. Many Mac applications can't even run at this low a resolution. The lowest resolution you should consider for a projector is 1024 x 768 (also called XGA).

- **Brightness.** The brightness of a projector is specified in lumens. Projectors with higher lumen ratings are generally able to throw larger images farther.

- **Throw range.** This measures the closest and farthest distances at which the projector can be used.

- **Video interface.** Like displays, the options for projectors include DVI or VGA. However, most projectors provide a number of other input options, such as component, composite, and S-video. These are important if you will also be using the projector with other sources, such as a DVD player.

- **Bulb life.** Projectors use a bulb to project an image. Like all other bulbs, these will eventually fail and need to be replaced. Unlike bulbs for lights, you can expect to pay hundreds of dollars for a replacement bulb for a projector, so you should try to get one with a long bulb life.

Genius If you are using an unfamiliar projector, set the MacBook Pro resolution to a relatively low value, such as 1024 x 768. If the projector doesn't display, reduce the resolution to see whether it starts displaying. Once it displays, increase the resolution until the projector is no longer capable of displaying the image.

Using a projector is very similar to using an external display. You connect a projector to the MacBook Pro using DVI or VGA and then use the Displays pane to set its resolution.

However, in most cases, you want to use video mirroring so that the image being projected is the same as you see on the MacBook Pro desktop; this is the usual arrangement for presentations and such, because you can stand in front of and face the audience, and view the MacBook Pro display while the audience sees the same image through the projector.

You can activate video mirroring in several ways:

- Open the Displays pane of the System Preferences application, click the Arrangement tab, and check the Mirror Displays check box.

- Open the Displays menu and select Turn On Mirroring (see figure 13.4).

- Press F7.

When you turn video mirroring on, the projector takes on the same resolution as the MacBook Pro internal display.

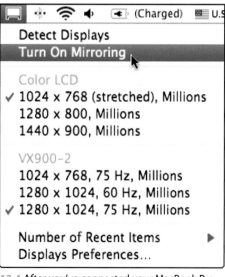

13.4 After you've connected your MacBook Pro to a projector, use the Turn On Mirroring command to have it display the same content that you see on the internal display.

How Do I Make Better Use of MacBook Pro Audio?

Sound is an important part of the MacBook Pro experience. If you use iTunes, iDVD, Front Row, GarageBand, or any other Mac digital media application, audio is sometimes the entire point. Understanding how to get the most from your MacBook Pro audio capabilities is fundamental to enjoying your MacBook Pro to the fullest. On its own, a MacBook Pro has reasonable audio capabilities. If you want to invest in a bit of hardware and some additional software, you can transform your MacBook Pro into an audio powerhouse.

Getting Sound Out of a MacBook Pro

Many applications that you use, including iTunes, iDVD, iPhoto, DVD Player, QuickTime, and iChat, involve the use of sound. In this section, you can learn about sound output options that are available to you, and how to choose and use those options to ensure that you have a great audio experience as you work with your MacBook Pro.

Understanding sound output options

When it comes to audio, there are two fundamental options: analog or digital. Like seemingly everything else, digital is better than analog from the quality perspective, but taking advantage of digital sound is more expensive and requires a bit more work than does analog sound. With your MacBook Pro, you can use both options in different situations.

On the analog side, you have the following methods for getting sound out of your MacBook Pro:

- **Built-in speakers.** MacBook Pros include built-in stereo speakers. They actually do a decent job considering their small size and basic capabilities. However, if the quality of sound is important to you when you listen to music or watch movies or television shows, it's unlikely that the internal speakers will satisfy you. They are a bit on the tinny side and their bass certainly isn't impressive (or even noticeable).

- **Headphones.** You can connect any analog headphones to the MacBook Pro digital out/headphone minijack located on the left side of the computer (it's marked with the headphones icon).

- **External speakers.** You can connect any set of powered (also called computer) speakers to your MacBook Pro digital out/headphone minijack.

When it comes to digital music, you need to add an external speaker system, such as a 5.1 surround sound speaker system, to be able to experience the best in sound quality for movies, television shows, and music. Fortunately, your MacBook Pro has the internal hardware required to support digital speaker systems so that all you need to add is the system itself.

Using external speakers

To be compatible with your MacBook Pro, you must use a powered set because the MacBook Pro headphones minijack doesn't provide enough power to drive a speaker, so you can't just use standard audio speakers. The good news is that there are many kinds of powered speaker sets available.

Genius Many speaker systems that are designed for iPods work great with a MacBook Pro. As long as a speaker system has a jack for external input, you can connect that system to your MacBook Pro.

Connecting an analog speaker system

Analog speakers are the simplest to install. If you have a two-speaker set, place one speaker on your right and one on your left. If you have a three-speaker system, place the bass unit on the ground or on your desktop. Connect the input line for the speaker set (which is usually connected to one of the satellite speakers or to the bass unit) to the headphones minijack on the MacBook Pro. Connect the speakers to the bass and power the system. That's all there is to it, and you're ready to control the sound (see "Controlling sound output" later in this section for details).

Connecting a digital speaker system

Your MacBook Pro has only one sound out port, which is the headphones/digital audio out port. While this looks like a typical stereo minijack port, its appearance is deceiving. When you connect a typical stereo minijack plug, it behaves like a regular stereo minijack, such as the headphones port on an iPod, and you get stereo sound output. To access the digital output from the port, you need a special adapter that connects to a digital audio cable and fits into the port in order to make the correct connections for digital audio. This is called a Mini Toslink adapter; when you are buying a digital audio cable, look for one that includes this adapter (see figure 14.1). You can also purchase the cable and adapter separately.

14.1 To connect to a digital sound system, you use a digital cable with a Mini Toslink adapter, such as this example from Belkin.

The input connectors on your speaker system determine the specific type of audio cable you need. There are two basic options: digital coax or Toslink (which is more commonly called optical digital). If you use a 5.1 system, it probably includes a central control unit with the input jacks; the jacks available on this control unit determine the cable you need. It probably has more than one input, including a digital optical input, digital coax input, and analog stereo input.

After you've placed the speakers, you need to connect their wires together at a central point; typically, you connect them to the bass speaker along with power. Then you connect the bass input wire to the control unit and use the cable you purchased to connect the control unit's input jack to your MacBook Pro headphones/digital audio out minijack.

Controlling sound output

When it comes to sound output, you need to realize that there are up to three types of volume levels.

The first is the system volume level, which sets the base level of volume output for the MacBook Pro.

The second is the relative volume of applications, such as iTunes and DVD Player. When you adjust volume levels within applications, you change their volume relative to the system volume level.

The third level is the physical volume level of an external speaker system, which you control with the system's volume controls. Like the system volume level, changes you make impact all of the audio coming from your MacBook Pro.

To configure your MacBook Pro output sound, perform the following steps:

1. **If you are using headphones or an external speaker system, connect them to the MacBook Pro headphones/digital audio out minijack.**

2. **Open the System Preferences application.**

3. **Click the Sound icon.** The Sound pane appears.

4. **Click the Output tab (see figure 14.2).** On this tab, you see the available output devices on the list at the top of the pane. When you select an output device, you see controls for the selected device below the list.

5. **Select the output device over which you want your MacBook Pro to play sound.** The most common options are:

   - Internal Speakers.

   - Headphones, which is used for headphones or for external, analog speaker systems.

   - Digital Out, which is used for an external, digital speaker system.

6. **Use the controls that appear for the selected device to adjust its sound.**

```
●○○                          Sound
◀ ▶   Show All                                    Q|

            ┌─ Sound Effects   Output   Input ─┐

        Choose a device for sound output

        Name                        Type
        Digital Out                 Built-in Output



        Settings for the selected device:

                    The selected device has no output controls


                                                        ?


        Output volume:   ◀ ──────────────○ ◀))  ☐ Mute
                         ☑ Show volume in menu bar
```

14.2 Use the Output tab of the Sound pane of the System Preferences application to configure how you hear audio.

Genius

7. **Drag the Output volume slider to near its center point.** This sets the system volume level at mid-level.

To mute all sound, check the Mute check box or press F3. To unmute the sound, uncheck the Mute check box or press F3. (Remember, when you are using a digital speaker system, these controls are disabled.)

Genius

8. **Check the Show volume in menu bar check box.**

9. **If you are using an external speaker system, set its volume at a relatively low level.**

10. **Open an application that you use to play audio, such as iTunes.** Use that application's volume slider to set its relative volume level to a mid-level (see figure 14.3).

11. **Play the audio and adjust the system volume level accordingly.**

14.3 Use the volume slider on iTunes to set the application's volume to mid-level.

Working with Sound Effects

Mac OS X includes a number of sound effects that the system uses to alert you or to provide audible feedback for specific events. You control these effects on the Sound Effects tab of the Sound pane of the System Preferences application.

Configuring sound effects

To configure sound effects, perform the following steps:

1. **Open the System Preferences application.**

2. **Click the Sound icon.** The Sound pane appears.

3. **Click the Sound Effects tab (see figure 14.4).**

14.4 Use the Sound Effects pane to configure the alert and other interface sounds.

4. **Click a sound on the alert sound list.** The sound plays and becomes the current alert sound.

5. **If your MacBook Pro can output sound through different devices simultaneously, such as through internal speakers and a sound system connected to a USB port, then select the system on which you want the sounds to be played on the Play alerts and sound effects through pop-up menu.**

6. **Drag the Alert volume slider to the right to make it louder, or to the left to make it quieter.**

7. **If you don't want to hear sound effects for system actions, such as when you empty the trash, uncheck the Play user interface sound effects check box.**

8. **If you don't want audio feedback when you change the volume level, uncheck the Play feedback when volume is changed check box.**

9. **If you don't want to want to hear Front Row's sound effects, uncheck the Play Front Row sound effects check box.**

Using your own alert sounds

You can also create and use your own alert sounds if you want your MacBook Pro to sport a unique way of communicating with you.

Under Mac OS X, system alert sounds are in the Audio Interchange File Format (AIFF). Using iTunes, you can convert or record almost any sound into the AIFF format and use that sound as a custom alert sound.

There are two basic ways in which you can add custom alert sounds. You can add them to specific user accounts so only that user can access them, or you can add them to the system so they are accessible to everyone who uses your MacBook Pro. The steps to add alert sounds are slightly different for each option.

Creating an alert sound

There are many ways to create a custom alert sound, including the following:

● **iMovie.** Use iMovie to create an audio track and save it as an AIFF file. Or, you can save part of a movie's audio track as an AIFF file. You can also record narration or other sounds to use as an alert sound. (You'll learn about getting sound into your MacBook Pro in a later section of this chapter.)

- **iTunes.** You can use iTunes to convert any sound in your Library to the AIFF format.

- **GarageBand.** Create a music snippet.

- **Record audio playing on your MacBook Pro.** Using an application like WireTap Pro from Ambrosia Software, you can record any audio playing on your MacBook Pro and use what you record as an alert sound.

I have included an example showing how to use iMovie to create and save a sound as an alert sound from audio stored in your iTunes Library. This technique enables you to add just about any sound as an alert sound. Here's how:

1. **Move the audio you want to use as an alert sound into your iTunes Library.** You can add it from the iTunes Store, download it from the Internet or record it in another application.

2. **Launch iMovie.**

3. **Choose File ⇨ New Project.** The New Project sheet appears.

4. **Name your project.**

5. **Click Create.** The new project is created and appears on the project list.

6. **Click the Titles button (the button with the capital 'T').** The Titles Browser appears in the lower-right corner of the window.

7. **Drag a title into the project window (shown with the words *Dummy Title* in figure 14.5).** It doesn't matter which title you choose because it's not going to be seen anyway. You should do this step because iMovie needs some video in a project to be able to work with audio content.

8. **Select the title in the project window.**

9. **Click the duration icon (the clock) in the lower-left corner of the title's clip.** The Duration sheet appears.

10. **Enter a duration for the title clip.** The default is four seconds. You want the clip to be the length of your alert sound; choosing a long duration makes the alert sound annoying because it lasts too long.

11. **Click OK.** The sheet closes and the duration of the clip is adjusted accordingly.

12. **Click the Music and Sound Effects button (the musical note icon).** The Music and Sound Effects Browser appears in the lower-right corner of the window.

13. **Choose iTunes on the pop-up menu.** The content of your iTunes Library appears.

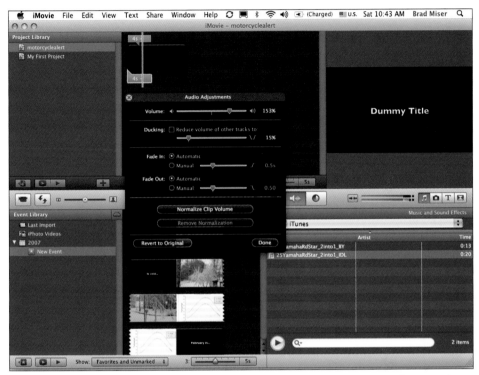

14.5 I've added the motorcycle sound to the dummy title clip and am adjusting its audio properties.

14. **Search or browse for the audio you want to use as the alert sound.**

15. **Select the audio and click the Play button to preview it.**

16. **Drag the audio from the Music and Sound Effects Browser and drop it onto the title clip in the Project window.** Make sure you drop the audio clip on the title clip and not just into the Project window. If you don't place it on the title clip, it's harder to edit.

17. **Preview the audio clip by pressing the Space bar.**

18. **Decide which part of the clip you want to use as the alert sound.**

19. **Drag the left end of the audio clip (the green bar underneath the title) to crop the front of it until it starts where you want the alert sound to start.**

20. **Drag the right end of the audio clip to crop the end of it until it stops where you want the alert sound to end.**

21. **Drag the audio clip to line up with the title clip so they start at the same point.** When you get to the beginning of the title clip, the audio clip snaps to it.

22. **Select the audio clip and click the Audio Adjustments button.** The Audio Adjustments dialog appears (see figure 14.5).

23. **Use the tools in the Audio Adjustments dialog to make changes to the audio clip.** For example, you can increase its volume or make it fade in or out.

24. **Click Done.** The Audio Adjustments dialog closes.

25. **Select Share ⇨ Export using QuickTime.** The Save exported file as dialog appears.

26. **On the Export pop-up menu, choose Sound to AIFF.**

27. **Name the sound file.**

28. **Append an *f* to the existing filename extension so it is .aiff (it is .aif by default).**

29. **Choose a location in which to save the alert sound.**

30. **Click Save.** The file is exported from iMovie and is ready to use as an alert sound.

Adding an alert sound for a specific user

To add a custom alert sound to a specific user account, perform the following steps:

1. **Log in to the user account under which you want to make the alert sound available.**

2. **Place the alert sound file in the user's Sounds folder that is located in the Library folder within the Home folder.**

3. **If the System Preferences application is open, quit it, then open it.**

4. **Click the Sound Effects tab.**

5. **Select and configure the custom alert sound just like one of the default sounds (see figure 14.6).** Note that the type of alert sounds you create is Custom to differentiate them from default sounds, which have Built-in as the type.

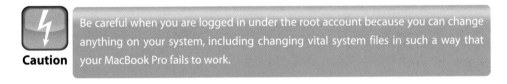

14.6 If this book had a soundtrack, you'd hear a deep, rumbling motorcycle sound that is now the MacBook Pro alert sound.

Adding an alert sound for all users

You can also add alert sounds to the system so they are available to all of the user accounts on your computer. However, to do this, you must log in under the root account.

Caution Be careful when you are logged in under the root account because you can change anything on your system, including changing vital system files in such a way that your MacBook Pro fails to work.

To add alert sounds to your system, follow these steps:

1. **Log in under the root account (see Chapter 2).**

2. **Drag the AIFF file into the folder *startupvolume*/System/Library/Sounds, where *star-tupvolume* is the name of your Mac OS X startup volume.**

3. **Log out of the root account.**

4. **Log in under another user account.**

5. **If the System Preferences application is open, quit it, then open it.**

6. **Click the Sound Effects tab.**

7. **Select and configure the custom alert sound just like one of the default sounds.** Alert sounds that you add to the system have the type Built-in and also behave the same as the default alert sounds, and so any user can access them.

Getting Sound into a MacBook Pro

There are many situations in which you may want to put sound into your MacBook Pro. For example, you might want to add narration to iMovie projects; you need to have audio input for audio and video chats in iChat; if you use GarageBand, you'll want to record instruments and vocals; or, you might want to add narration to a slide show you create in iPhoto.

On the simplest side, you can use the MacBook Pro built-in microphone to record voice narration or other sounds, and it is certainly good enough for most audio and video chats. Toward the more complex, you can add an external MIDI (Musical Instrument Digital Interface) keyboard or other device that enables you to record sound from musical instruments and other sources.

Caution

The MacBook Pro audio line in/optical digital audio in minijack is not powered. This means that you can't just plug a standard analog microphone into it and record sound. Whatever you connect to the minijack must provide amplification to be able to record sound from it. To be able to connect a microphone to it, there must be a power source for the microphone.

Recording sound with the MacBook Pro internal microphone

Using the MacBook Pro internal microphone is easy and is probably good enough for a number of purposes, such as audio and video chats, recording narration for iMovie and iPhoto projects, and other relatively simple projects.

Configuring the internal microphone

To record audio with the built-in microphone, first configure the internal microphone by performing the following steps:

1. **Open the System Preferences application.**

2. **Click the Sound icon.** The Sound pane appears.

3. **Click the Input tab.** On the Input tab, there are two default options: Internal microphone or Line In. Under the device list, you see the controls you use to configure the device selected on the list.

4. **Select Internal microphone.** As your MacBook Pro receives audio input through the microphone, the relative volume of the input is shown on the Input level gauge (see figure 14.7).

14.7 Use the Input level gauge to assess the input level of sound coming in to the MacBook Pro.

5. **As you speak or play the sound, monitor the input on the level gauge.** The maximum level freezes briefly so that you can see where it is.

6. **If the gauge shows input when you aren't speaking or playing a sound, check the Use ambient noise reduction check box.** This applies a filter that screens out background sound.

7. **Drag the Input volume slider to the left to reduce the level of input sound, or to the right to increase it.** The microphone should be ready to use to record sound in an application.

Recording sound with the internal microphone in iMovie

A common use of recorded sound is as narration in iMovie projects. Here's how to add your own narration to an iMovie project:

1. **Launch iMovie.**

2. **Select the project in which you want to record sound using the internal microphone.**

3. **Click the Voiceover button (the microphone).** The Voiceover dialog appears (see figure 14.8).

Voiceover

Record From: Built-in Microphone

Input Volume: 70%

Left:

Right:

Noise Reduction: −20dB

☑ Voice Enhancement

☐ Play project audio while recording

14.8 Here, I'm recording narration for an iMovie project.

4. **On the Record From pop-up menu, choose Built-In Microphone.**

5. **Speak in a normal conversational voice.**

6. **As you speak, monitor the sound levels using the two input gauges under the Input Volume slider.** You want the sound level to be as high as possible without going into the red.

7. **To increase the sound level, move the Input Volume slider to the right; move it to the left to decrease the sound input level.**

8. **To reduce the amount of background noise in the recording, slide the Noise Reduction slider.**

9. **Check the Voice Enhancement check box.**

10. **Select the clip over which you want to record narration.** As you point to a clip, you see the microphone icon attached to the pointer to indicate that you are in recording mode.

11. **When the pointer is at the location at which you want to start recording, click the trackpad button.** You see a countdown (from 3) in the Preview pane, and you hear three pings as the countdown proceeds.

12. **When the countdown finishes, start speaking.** A red bar fills the clip you are recording over, and you see a large red dot and the "Recording" message in the Preview pane.

13. **When you are done speaking, press the Space bar.** The recording stops, and an audio clip appears under the clip on which you recorded sound.

14. **Edit the recorded audio clip just like other audio clips.** For example, you can make it fade in, adjust its volume, and move it earlier or later in the project.

Recording sound with a USB headset

If you are going to be recording a lot of narration or you want better quality when you have video or audio chats, a USB headset is a good option. Like other audio input devices, you configure the USB headset to record its input and then use it to record sound in applications.

Configuring a USB headset

Configuring a USB headset is similar to configuring the internal microphone, as you will see in the following steps:

1. **Connect the headset to a USB port.**

2. **Open the System Preferences application.**

3. **Click the Sound icon.**

4. **Click the Input tab (see figure 14.9).** You should see the USB headset on the list of devices.

5. **Select the USB headset.** As the MacBook Pro receives audio input through the headset, the relative volume of the input is shown on the Input level gauge.

6. **As you speak or play the sound, monitor the input on the level gauge.** The maximum level freezes briefly so that you can see where it is.

7. **Drag the Input volume slider to the left to reduce the level of input sound, or to the right to increase it.** The USB headset should be ready to use to record sound in an application.

14.9 Configuring a USB headset improves the quality of its sound in applications.

Using a USB headset

Recording sound from a USB headset is similar to recording sound with other input sources. For example, the steps to record sound in iMovie are the same as the steps described earlier for the internal microphone, except that you select the USB headset instead of Built-in Microphone.

Recording sound with a video camera

While it might not be obvious, a video camera can be a great way to record sound for your projects and other purposes. You can then use iMovie to save that sound as a file to use in projects, to add to your iTunes Library, and for other purposes. Here's how to move sound that you've recorded using a video camera into your iTunes Library:

1. **Use the video camera to capture the sound you want to use in an application.**

2. **Connect the camera to your MacBook Pro.**

3. **Launch iMovie.**

4. **Add the clips containing the audio to the Event Library.**

5. **Choose File ⇨ New Project.** The New Project sheet appears.

6. **Name your project.**

7. **Click Create.** The new project is created and appears on the project list.

8. **Add the clips with audio you want to save to the new project.**

9. **Edit the clips until the audio track is what you want to use.**

10. **Choose Share ⇨ Export using QuickTime.** The Save exported file as dialog appears.

11. **On the Export pop-up menu, choose Sound to AIFF.**

12. **Choose a location in which to save the alert sound.**

13. **Name the sound file.**

14. **Click Save.** The file is exported from iMovie.

15. **Launch iTunes.**

16. **Choose File ⇨ Add to Library.** The Add To Library dialog appears.

17. **Move to and select the sound file you created in iMovie.**

18. **Click Open.** The sound is added to your iTunes Library where you can listen to it, or you can select it from other applications using the Media Browser (for example, you can select it as a soundtrack for an iPhoto slide show).

Recording sound from external microphones and musical instruments

If you want to record sound from external microphones and musical instruments, you need an interface between the devices and the MacBook Pro. These devices can use either the audio line in/optical digital audio in minijack or USB port to connect to your MacBook Pro, but USB is a more common interface that is easier to work with in most situations.

There are a variety of USB audio devices that you can use for this purpose. Some devices include a MIDI instrument, such as a keyboard, as part of the interface device; these are convenient because you get an input source (the instrument) and the interface in one unit.

To use devices like these, connect the device to a USB port on your MacBook Pro. You then connect microphones or instruments from which you want to record sound into the various ports.

Once the device is configured, you can choose it as the input device in audio applications, such as GarageBand, so that you can record the output of the microphones and instruments in those applications.

How Do I Print with MacBook Pro?

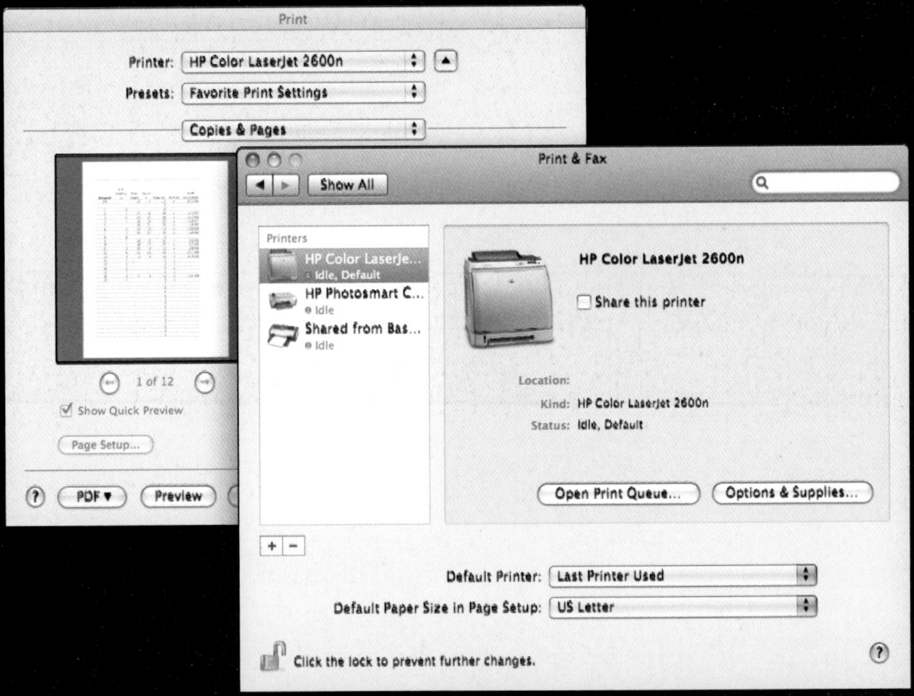

While the world has gone digital, there are still occasions when you need to print documents using good old-fashioned paper. There are many kinds of printers that you can use with your MacBook Pro, and there are several common ways to connect to those printers: through a USB port, a wired network, or a wireless connection. Once a printer is ready to work for you, Mac OS X includes a couple of tools you can use to manage your print jobs. Because it really is a digital world, you can print electronically by creating PDF documents.

Connecting to USB Printers

The benefits of a USB connection are that all modern computers have at least one USB port, the speed of USB is perfectly capable for printing, and USB cables are inexpensive. As long as it offers Mac OS X-compatible drivers, you can install and use any USB printer with your MacBook Pro.

Because USB is hot swappable, you can disconnect a USB cable at any time, making it simple to connect to the printer, print, and then disconnect again.

Installing a USB printer

Installing a USB printer is a simple process, as you can see in the following steps:

1. **Connect the printer to a power supply.**

2. **Use a USB cable to connect the printer to the USB port on your MacBook Pro.**

3. **Install the printer driver software, if necessary.** If the printer you are using is an inkjet from HP, Lexmark, Canon, or Epson, the drivers are probably already built into Mac OS X. The printer is ready to be configured on your MacBook Pro.

Configuring a USB printer

Once your MacBook Pro can communicate with the printer through the USB connection, you can configure using steps that are similar to the following (these show detailed steps for an HP Photosmart printer, but the steps to configure any USB printer are similar):

1. **Open the System Preferences application.**

2. **Click the Print & Fax icon.**

Genius

If you see the USB printer on the printer list already, it has been configured for you automatically. When you connect a USB printer to a MacBook Pro, Mac OS X attempts to recognize and configure the printer for you. If this is successful, the printer appears on the printer list and is ready to be used.

3. **Click the Add button (+) located at the bottom of the printer list.**

4. **Click Default on the Printer Browser.** You see a list of each printer with which the MacBook Pro can communicate and the type of connection it uses.

5. **Select the USB printer you want to configure by clicking its name in the list (see figure 15.1).**

15.1 The HP Photosmart printer to which this MacBook Pro is connected has been found.

6. **If Mac OS X doesn't find a driver, open the Print Using pop-up menu and choose the appropriate driver.**

7. **Click Add.** You return to the Printer List on the Print & Fax pane, and the printer you selected and configured appears on the list.

8. **Click the Options & Supplies button.** The printer's Options sheet appears.

9. **Click the General tab.** You can edit the name and location of the printer here if you want to change it.

10. **Click the Supply Levels tab.** On this tab, you see the current state of the ink cartridges if Mac OS X can read that information from the printer (not all printers are supported).

11. **Click OK.** Any changes you made are saved and the sheet closes.

12. **On the Default Paper Size in Page Setup pop-up menu, choose your default paper size.** You can change it for specific documents to override the default setting. The printer is ready to print your documents.

Connecting to Network Printers

Adding a printer to your network is a great way to provide printing services to all the computers on that network. Configuring a network printer is no harder than configuring one that is connected directly to a computer; in most cases, Bonjour identifies the networked printer and all you have to do is select it on the list of available printers.

Many printers offer network connections, the most common type of which is Ethernet. Some printers offer wireless networking directly, but if you have an AirPort Base Station or an Ethernet hub on your network, it's just as easy to connect it through Ethernet.

Installing a network printer

Installing a network printer isn't difficult, as you can see in the following steps:

1. **Connect the printer to a power source.**
2. **Connect the printer to the network in one of the following ways:**
   - Use an Ethernet cable to connect the printer to an available port on an AirPort Extreme or Express Base Station.
   - Use an Ethernet cable to connect the printer to an available port on a hub that's part of the network.
   - Configure a wireless connection between the printer and your wireless network.
3. **Install the printer driver software, if necessary.** If the printer you are using is from HP, Lexmark, Canon, Epson, or many others, the drivers are probably already built into Mac OS X. The printer is ready to be configured on your MacBook Pro.

Configuring a network printer

Configuring your MacBook Pro to access a networked printer is quite similar to configuring it to access a printer connected through USB. The following steps show how to configure an HP 2600dn that is connected to an Ethernet hub on the local network:

1. **Open the System Preferences application.**
2. **Click the Print & Fax icon.** The Print & Fax pane appears (see figure 15.2).
3. **Click the Add button (+) located at the bottom of the printer list.**
4. **Click Default in the Printer Browser.** You see a list of each printer with which the MacBook Pro can communicate, and the type of connection it uses.
5. **Select the network printer you want to configure by clicking its name in the list.**

15.2 This MacBook Pro currently has access to two printers.

6. **If Mac OS X didn't find a driver, open the pop-up menu and choose the appropriate driver.**

7. **Click Add.** You return to the Printer List on the Print & Fax pane, and the printer you selected and configured appears on the list.

8. **Click the Options & Supplies button.** The printer's Options sheet appears.

9. **Click the General tab.** You can edit the name and location of the printer here if you want to change it.

10. **Click the Driver tab.**

11. **Click the Supply Levels tab.** On this tab, you see the current state of the toner cartridges if Mac OS X can read that information from the printer (see figure 15.3).

12. **Click OK.** Any changes you made are saved and the sheet closes.

13. **On the Default Paper Size in Page Setup pop-up menu, choose your default paper size.** You can change it for specific documents to override the default setting. The printer is ready to print your documents.

15.3 Looks like the black cartridge is getting a bit low.

Printing Wirelessly

Because you'll be moving your MacBook Pro around a lot, you probably want to be able to print wirelessly. You can print to a USB printer wirelessly by connecting it to an AirPort Extreme (or Express) Base Station. In effect, the base station shares the printer with the network and it behaves pretty much like a networked printer.

> **Note** It's better to share a printer from a base station than from a Mac because you'll leave the base station running at all times so that your network is available at all times (unlike a Mac, which probably sleeps from time to time, or that you'll probably shut off once in a while).

To print to a USB printer connected to an AirPort Base Station requires two general steps. First, connect the printer to the base station and configure the base station to share it with the network. Second, configure your MacBook Pro to access the printer.

The following sections show how to accomplish both these steps for an AirPort Extreme Base Station and an HP Photosmart printer. Installing and configuring an AirPort Express Base Station or a different type of printer is similar.

Configuring AirPort Extreme Base Station to share a printer

To configure an AirPort Extreme Base Station to share a USB printer, perform the following steps:

1. **Configure the AirPort Extreme Base Station to create a network (see Chapter 3).**

2. **Connect the printer to the USB port on the AirPort Extreme Base Station.**

3. **Open the AirPort Utility application, which is located with the Utilities folder in the Applications folder.**

4. **Select the Base Station to which the printer is connected.**

5. **Click Manual Setup.**

6. **If prompted, enter the Base Station's password and click OK.** The Manual Configuration window appears.

7. **Click the Printers tab (see figure 15.4).**

AirPort Utility – Base Station Alpha

AirPort   Internet   Printers   Advanced

Q Setting Name

Find a setting

Base Station Alpha

Base Station eaaa6d

This pane shows USB printers connected to your base station.

USB Printers: Shared from Base Station

hp photosmart 7700 series

☐ Share printers over Ethernet WAN port

Revert   Update

15.4 Use the Printers tab of the AirPort Utility to name a printer connected to the USB port on an AirPort Extreme Base Station.

8. **Enter a name for the printer in the USB Printers box.**

9. **Click Update.** The AirPort Utility updates the base station and restarts it.

10. **Quit the AirPort Utility.** The printer is accessible wirelessly through AirPort and on a wired network connected to the base station.

Connecting to a USB printer connected to an AirPort Extreme Base Station

Connecting to a USB printer that is connected to an AirPort Extreme Base Station is very simple:

1. **Open the System Preferences application.**

2. **Click the Print & Fax icon.** The Print & Fax pane appears.

3. **Click the Add button (+) located at the bottom of the printer list.**

4. **Click Default in the Printer Browser.**

5. **Select the printer connected to the AirPort Base Station that you want to configure by clicking its name in the list.**

6. **If Mac OS X didn't find a driver, open the Print Using pop-up menu and choose the appropriate driver.** If you can't find a driver for the printer, you need to install one from the printer's manufacturer.

7. **Click Add.** You return to the Printer List on the Print & Fax pane, and the printer you selected and configured appears on the list.

8. **Click the Options & Supplies button.** The printer's Options sheet appears.

9. **Click the General tab.** You can edit the name and location of the printer here if you want to change it.

10. **Click the Driver tab.**

11. **Click the Supply Levels tab.** On this tab, you see the current state of the toner cartridges if Mac OS X can read that information from the printer.

12. **Click OK.** Any changes you made are saved and the sheet closes.

13. **On the Default Paper Size in Page Setup pop-up menu, choose your default paper size.** You can change it for specific documents to override the default setting. The printer is ready to print your documents.

Managing Print Jobs

While you can just press ⌘+P and then press Return from almost any application to print, there's more to printing to customize your print jobs and manage them while they are in process. In this section, you learn about some of the more advanced capabilities of the Print dialog and the Print Queue application.

Configuring print jobs with the Print dialog

While the Print command is the same for all applications, the Print dialog that results from that command is definitely not. This dialog contains configuration controls that are determined by the application from whence it came and the selected printer.

There are two versions of the Print dialog: one is collapsed so that you only see basic print controls (see figure 15.5).

When you expand the Print dialog, you see additional menus and commands (see figure 15.6).

Print

Printer: HP Color LaserJet 2600n

Presets: Standard

PDF ▼   Preview   Cancel   Print

15.5 The collapsed Print dialog is basic but functional.

15.6 The expanded Print dialog is packed with controls that depend on the printer you use and the application you're printing from.

You select the group of settings you want to configure on the pop-up menu in the center of the dialog and then configure those settings with the resulting controls that appear in the lower part of the dialog. In addition to the tools in the collapsed Print dialog, and depending on the printer and application you are using, the options you have can include the following:

- **Application, where *Application* is the name of the application from which you are printing.** When you select this setting on the menu, you see the application's print configuration controls in the lower part of the dialog.

- **Copies & Pages.** These controls enable you to set the number of copies you want to print, collation, the part of a document you want to print, and scaling options. You can change the Page Setup options by clicking the Page Setup button.

- **Layout.** These commands enable you to control how many pages print per sheet of paper, the direction in which your document layout prints, whether a border is printed, and whether the document will be printed on both sides of the paper (for printers that support that functionality).

- **Paper Handling.** With these options, you can select which pages to print, the destination paper size, scaling, and page order.

- **Scheduler.** This pane of controls enables you to schedule a print job for a specific time and also to set its priority in the print queue.

- **Paper or Paper Type/Quality.** You use these controls to select a paper type and source. For printers that support different quality levels of printing (for example, Draft mode), you can select the quality of the job.

- **Color Options.** As you might suspect, you use these controls to configure the color settings for the print job.

- **Print Options.** Here you can set the resolution of a print job.

- **Supply Levels.** This command shows you the current levels of the ink or toner cartridges.

Printing Presets

Presets are collections of print settings that you configure and save. When you want to print with a preset, you choose it on the Presets menu, and the settings contained within that preset are configured for you.

To create a preset, do the following:

1. **Configure the print options that you want to save as a preset.**
2. **Open the Presets pop-up menu.**
3. **Select Save As.**
4. **Name the preset.**
5. **Click OK.**

You can print with the same collections of settings by choosing the preset (by name) on the Presets pop-up menu before you click the Print button.

Managing print jobs with the Print Queue

After you have sent a document to a printer, the Print Queue application opens; its icon on the Dock looks like the printer to which you sent the print job. When you click the icon to open that application (which has the same name as the printer), you see a window showing the print jobs currently being processed by the printer and providing commands you can use to manage those jobs (see figure 15.7).

15.7 Here's the Print Queue application for an HP Color LaserJet 2600n printer.

In the upper part of the window, you see the document currently printing and the status of the printer. With this application, you can perform the following tasks:

- Select a print job on the list and click Delete to remove the job from the queue.

- Click a print job and click Hold. The printing process for that job stops, and its status becomes On Hold.

- Select an On Hold job and click Resume to start printing again.

- Click Pause Printer to pause the printer, which stops all print jobs.

- Click Resume Printer to start the printer again.

- Click Supply Levels to view the current state of the printer's ink or toner cartridges.

Printing to PDF

PDF files are one of the most useful ways to output documents for electronic viewing and for transmitting to other people through e-mail or other means. Any PDF document can be easily read by anyone using any computer platform.

Under Mac OS X, PDF is a native file format. This means that you can create PDFs from within any Mac OS X application, and you can read any PDF file with the Preview application.

Creating PDF Files

Creating PDF files is a simple task:

1. **Open the document for which you want to create a PDF.**

2. **Choose File ⇨ Print.** The Print dialog appears.

3. **Open the PDF pop-up menu and select Save as PDF.** The Save dialog appears (see figure 15.8).

15.8 Use the Save dialog to configure and save a PDF version of a document.

4. **Name the document.**

5. **Replace the existing filename extension with .pdf.** This step is optional as the correct extension is added automatically; however, it is added at the end of the current extension, and so if you are working with an Excel document, its PDF has the extension, .xls.pdf, which can be confusing.

6. **Choose a location in which to save the PDF.**

7. **Enter keywords for the PDF in the Keywords field.** These are useful for searches, such as Spotlight searches.

8. **Click Security Options.** The Security Options dialog appears.

9. **To require that the viewer enter a password to be able to view the PDF, check the Require password to open document check box.**

10. **Enter a password in the Password and Verify boxes.**

11. **Click OK.** Any options you selected are set, and the dialog closes. You return to the Save dialog.

12. **Click Save.** The PDF is created in the location you specified with the settings and other information you configured.

Note

Creating a standard PDF does not create or preserve any hyperlinks in a document. For example, if you create a PDF of a Web page, the links on that page are not functional. To create a PDF that does contain active links requires a more sophisticated application.

More PDF Commands

In addition to saving a standard PDF document, there are a number of other options on the Save As PDF pop-up menu, including the following:

- **Save as PostScript.** This creates a PostScript file for the document.
- **Fax PDF.** If you configured your MacBook Pro to fax documents, use this command to fax the PDF.
- **Mail PDF.** This creates a PDF of the document and attaches it to an e-mail message in your default e-mail application.
- **Save as PDF-X.** This command saves the document in the PDF/X format that adds information intended to improve the reliability of printing the document.
- **Save PDF to iPhoto.** This creates a PDF version of the document and adds it to iPhoto.
- **Save PDF to Web Receipts Folder.** This is ideal for saving various kinds of receipts you see on the Web, such as when you buy something, so you don't have to print them and deal with the resulting paper.

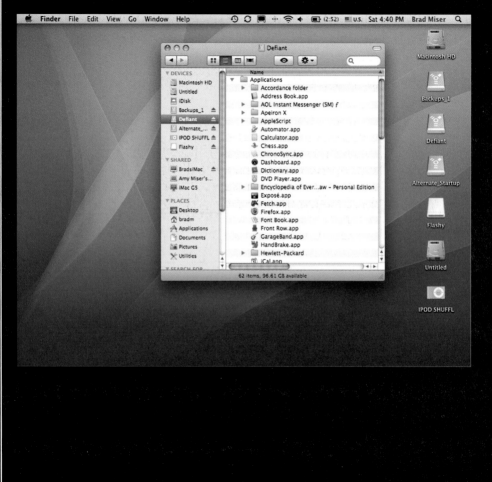

There are two primary reasons to add more data storage space to your MacBook Pro, and both of them are important. One is to back up data on your MacBook Pro; one of the easiest ways to do this is to use Time Machine, which requires that you use an external hard drive. The other is that over time, you'll end up with a lot of data, especially if you create iMovie projects or you download movies or other video. Your MacBook Pro hard drive is only so big; adding more storage space enables you to work with more information.

Using External Hard Drives

Adding an external hard drive to your MacBook Pro system is an easy and relatively inexpensive way of making more storage space available; it is also a requirement if you want to use Time Machine for backing up your MacBook Pro. In this section, you'll learn how to add more space to your MacBook Pro by adding, configuring, and using an external hard drive.

Installing an external hard drive

Installing an external hard drive is about as simple as it gets.

1. **Connect the power supply to the drive and to an electrical outlet.**

2. **Connect the FireWire, USB 2, or FireWire 800 cable to the drive and to the appropriate port on your MacBook Pro.**

3. **Power up the drive.** If the drive is formatted so that it is compatible with your MacBook Pro, it mounts on your desktop and you see it on the Sidebar in a Finder window (see figure 16.1). If not, you won't see the device. In either case, you should reformat and initialize the drive before you start using it.

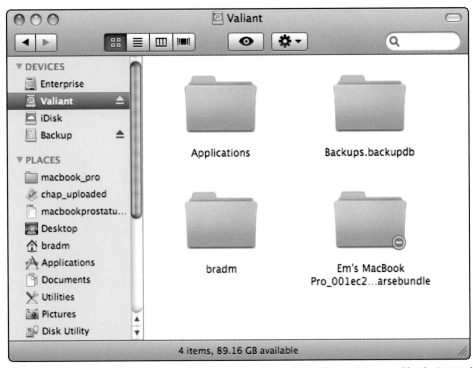

16.1 A mounted external hard drive appears in the DEVICES section of the Sidebar, just like the internal hard drive does.

Using Disk Utility to prepare an external hard drive

Before you use a hard drive, you should initialize and format it. You can also partition a hard drive to create multiple volumes on a single drive so that it behaves as if it is more than one drive.

Genius

I recommend that you reformat your external drive to ensure that you have the most storage space available and that the drive is formatted in the best way for your MacBook Pro. Some drives include software, especially if the drive is intended for Windows computers, in which case that software is a waste of space and you should get rid of it.

Documents you store on a separate volume aren't secured using the Mac OS X default permissions, like documents you store within your Home folder are. If you want to provide broader access to files, this is a good thing. If you don't want people to be able to access these documents outside the control of the Mac OS X security, it isn't.

Generally, you should keep your partitions pretty large, unless you create one for a very specific purpose, such as to install Mac OS X for an alternate startup drive. If you run out of space on a partition, you have to delete files from it or re-partition the disk, which means that you must start over and reformat the disk (resulting in all files being erased). Unless you have a very specific reason to do so, you typically shouldn't partition a drive into more than two volumes. In many cases, especially if you are only using the disk for backups, one partition is the best option.

To initialize, format, and partition a disk, perform the following steps:

1. **Launch the Disk Utility application, which is located in the Utilities folder within the Applications folder.** In the Disk Utility window, you see two panes. In the upper part of the left pane, you see the drives with which your MacBook Pro can communicate, along with the MacBook Pro internal optical drive. Under each disk, you see the volumes into which that disk has been partitioned. Below the drives, you see any disk images that are currently mounted on your MacBook Pro. In the right pane, you see information and tools for the drive or volume that is selected in the left pane.

Caution

When you follow these steps, all the information currently on the disk is erased.

2. **Select the drive you want to format.**

3. **Click the Partition tab (see figure 16.2).** In the left part of this tab, you see a graphical representation of the partitions on the disk.

4. **Select the number of partitions you want to have on the drive using the Volume Scheme pop-up menu.**

5. **Select a partition by clicking its box in the graphical representation of the drive.**

LaCie Group SA		

Verify Info Burn Mount Eject Enable Journaling New Image Convert Resize Image Log

First Aid   Erase   **Partition**   RAID   Restore

149.1 GB FUJITSU MHW216
  Macintosh HD
  disk0s3
232.9 GB LaCie Group SA
  Backup
232.9 GB LaCie Group SA
  Defiant
HL-DT-ST DVDRW GSA-S1(

en_dinerdashfloontheg .dm
  Diner Dash – Flo on the (
Messenger603.dmg
  Microsoft Messenger
disk4
  disk4

Volume Scheme:

2 Partitions

Backups_1

Alternate_Startup

Volume Information

Name: Alternate_Startup

Format: Mac OS Extended (Journaled)

Size: 32.89   GB

To partition the selected disk, choose a volume scheme. Set the name, format, and size for each volume. Then click Apply.

A new volume will be created.
Size: 32.9 GB

＋ −   Options...   Revert   Apply

Disk Description : LaCie Group SA
Connection Bus : FireWire
Connection Type : External
Connection ID : 58629494784962638

Total Capacity : 232.9 GB (250,059,350,016 Bytes)
Write Status : Read/Write
S.M.A.R.T. Status : Not Supported
Partition Map Scheme : GUID Partition Table

16.2 This disk will have two partitions: one called "Backups_1" with 200GB, and one called "Alternate_Startup" with 32.89GB.

Genius

Instead of a space in a partition name, use an underscore or just run the words together so the space isn't replaced by 20% in a path name.

6. **Name the selected volume by typing a name in the Name box.** As you type the name, it is shown in the partition's box.

7. **Select the format for the partition on the Format pop-up menu.** In most cases, you should choose Mac OS Extended (Case-sensitive, Journaled) to take advantage of the most sophisticated format option.

8. **Enter the size of the partition in the Size box.** You can enter a size up to the maximum capacity of the drive, but it also depends on the number of other partitions on the drive and how much space is allocated to each.

9. **Once you've configured all the partitions on the disk, click Options.** The Options sheet appears.

10. **If it isn't selected already, click the GUID Partition Table radio button.** The other options don't apply when you are using the disk with a MacBook Pro.

Caution If you purchase a drive that's been formatted for Windows computers using the Master Boot Record format option, it won't mount on your MacBook Pro and will be unusable. You must format the disk with the GUID Partition Table format before you'll be able to use it.

11. **Click OK.** The format option is set and the sheet closes.

Caution Before proceeding, make sure that the drive doesn't contain any data you need. Performing the next step erases all the data from the disk.

12. **Click Apply.**

13. **If you are sure that you want to initialize and partition the drive, click Partition in the Warning sheet.** Once this process is completed, you should see the partitions you created under the drive's icon.

Working with external hard drives

After you've configured an external hard drive, you can use it in the following ways:

- **Store files on the drive.**
- **Backing up to the drive with Time Machine.** I discuss Time Machine in Chapter 17.

- **Stop using the drive.** Before you stop using a hard drive and any of its partitions, you need to eject the drive. This makes sure that all data has been written to the drive and all processes impacting it are stopped so that when you disconnect the drive, the data isn't damaged.

- **Start using the drive again.** To start using the drive again, simply reconnect the drive to your MacBook Pro. After a few moments, the drive is mounted, you see all of its partitions in the Sidebar, and it is ready to use.

Sharing an External Hard Drive

An external hard drive is a great way to share files among multiple computers. You can do this in a number of ways:

- **Physically connect the drive to different computers.**
- **Share the drive over a network.**
- **Share the drive from an AirPort Base Station.** If you connect a USB external hard drive to an AirPort Base Station, any computer that can access the Base Station's network can also access the drive.

Maintaining hard drives

Keeping your hard drives, whether internal or external, in good working condition goes a long way to making your MacBook Pro reliable. In this section, you'll learn about some of the more important disk maintenance habits you should practice to keep your disks in top form.

Managing a hard drive's free space

If your disks get too full, their performance slows down significantly. You can also run into all kinds of problems if you try to save files to disks that are full to the brim; how full this is depends on the size of the files with which you are working.

As you use your hard drives, keep an eye on their available space by selecting the drive in the Sidebar and looking at the space available shown at the bottom of the Finder window (see figure 16.3). If the space available gets below 10GB, you can start running into problems when you try to save files or perform other tasks.

Genius One of the biggest wastes of disk space is application installers that you download from the Internet. After you have successfully installed an application, remove the installer files from your hard disks.

Learn and practice good work habits such as deleting files you don't need, uninstalling software you don't use, keeping your files organized (no duplicates), and archiving files you are done with (such as on a DVD). Regularly removing files that you no longer need from your hard drives will go a long way toward keeping them performing well for you, not to mention maximizing the room you have to store files you do need.

Using Activity Monitor to check a drive's available space

You can use Activity Monitor to get more information about how you are using a specific disk:

1. **Launch the Activity Monitor application located in the Utilities folder within the Applications folder.**

2. **Click the Disk Usage tab located at the bottom of the window.**

3. **On the pop-up menu, choose the disk or partition whose information you want to view.** You see a pie chart showing the amount of free space (in green) versus the amount of space used (in blue), along with the specific values within each category (see figure 16.4).

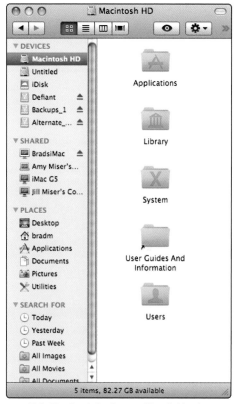

16.3 This MacBook Pro internal hard drive has more than 80GB available, so it is in good shape.

 Note

Each partition and disk has its own Trash. If you empty the Trash while an external drive that has files in its Trash is disconnected, the Trash icon becomes full again when you reconnect the drive because the Trash associated with that disk still has files in it. Just empty the Trash again once you've reconnected the drive to get rid of the trashed files.

 Genius

If you want to change the colors associated with free or used space, click the color button next to the number of bytes in each category.

PID	Process Name	User	CPU	Thr	RSIZE	VSIZE	Kind
8285	Activity Monitor	bradm	20.8	5	22.30 MB	875.42 MB	Intel
7554	AppleVNCServer	bradm	0.0	2	2.33 MB	721.52 MB	Intel
7564	ATSServer	bradm	0.0	2	3.23 MB	631.07 MB	Intel
8227	Disk Utility	bradm	0.0	5	18.05 MB	841.13 MB	Intel
7561	Dock	bradm	0.2	3	14.98 MB	816.92 MB	Intel
7566	Finder	bradm	0.1	9	31.30 MB	877.48 MB	Intel
7573	iTunes Helper	bradm	0.0	2	2.44 MB	730.95 MB	Intel
119	launchd	bradm	0.0	3	576.00 KB	585.73 MB	Intel
3919	LKDCHelper	bradm	0.0	1	860.00 KB	586.62 MB	Intel
7539	loginwindow	bradm	0.0	3	5.13 MB	737.71 MB	Intel
8281	mdworker	bradm	0.0	4	3.08 MB	599.95 MB	Intel
7574	Microsoft AU Dae...	bradm	0.0	2	9.84 MB	796.12 MB	PowerPC
7560	pboard	bradm	0.0	1	584.00 KB	586.63 MB	Intel
7572	Snapz Pro X	bradm	0.4	6	20.12 MB	838.77 MB	Intel
7556	Spotlight	bradm	0.0	2	4.35 MB	732.91 MB	Intel
7580	SystemUIServer	bradm	0.1	8	11.25 MB	800.69 MB	Intel

CPU   System Memory   Disk Activity   Disk Usage   Network

Defiant

Space utilized: 136.15 GB   146,186,899,456 bytes
Space free: 96.61 GB   103,738,191,872 bytes   232.76 GB

16.4 The disk called Defiant has about 136GB of files stored on it.

Using Disk Utility to check or repair an external drive

Two of the tasks for which you can use Disk Utility are to check or repair an external disk drive. If you start having problems with a disk, first make sure that it has plenty of available space. If it does-n't, get rid of files until it does. If it does have plenty of free space, use Disk Utility to check or repair it, as in the following steps:

1. **Launch Disk Utility.**

2. **Select a disk or partition you want to check or repair.** In most cases, you should select a disk so that the entire disk is checked or repaired, rather than just one of its partitions.

3. **Check the bottom of the Disk Utility window for information about the disk, volume, disc, or image you selected.** If you select a hard drive, you see the disk type, connection bus (such as ATA for internal drives or FireWire for an external drive), connection type (internal or external), capacity, write status, S.M.A.R.T. status, and partition map scheme. If you select a partition on a disk, you see various data about the volume, such as its mount point (the path to it), format, whether owners are enabled, the number of folders it contains, its capacity, the amount of space available, the amount of space used, and the number of files it contains.

> **Note**
> For most disks, the S.M.A.R.T. (Self-Monitoring, Analysis, and Reporting Technology) status provides an indication of the disk's health. This is Verified if the disk is in good working condition, or About to Fail if the disk has problems. If a disk doesn't support S.M.A.R.T., the status will be Not Supported. Your MacBook Pro internal drive supports S.M.A.R.T., but many external disks do not.

4. **Click the First Aid tab to see some information explaining how Disk Utility works.**

5. **Click Repair Disk.** The application checks the selected disk for problems and repairs any it finds. When the process is complete, a report of the results appears (see figure 16.5).

16.5 Disk Utility has checked this disk, which seems to be okay.

You can choose to verify a disk by clicking the Verify Disk button, rather than to repair it by clicking the Repair Disk button. When you do so, the application finds problems with the disk and reports back to you. You then have to tell the application to repair those problems.

Erasing an external hard disk with Disk Utility

You can use Disk Utility to quickly erase and reformat partitions or erasable disks (such as CD-RW discs) by performing the following steps:

1. **Launch Disk Utility.**

2. **Select a partition you want to erase.**

3. **Click the Erase tab.**

4. **Choose the format you want to use for the volume on the Volume Format pop-up menu.** The format options are Mac OS Extended (Journaled), Mac OS Extended, Mac OS Extended (Case-sensitive, Journaled), Mac OS Extended (Case-sensitive), or MS-DOS (FAT).

Genius You can use the Erase Free Space button to remove files that you have deleted from a disk or partition to make them harder or impossible to recover using data recovery tools.

5. **Click the Security Options button.** The Secure Erase Options sheet appears.

6. **Select one of the options as shown in figure 16.6.**

16.6 Use this sheet to select how you want data you are erasing to be handled.

7. **Click OK.** The option you selected is set and the sheet closes.

8. **Click Erase.** The confirmation sheet appears.

9. **If you are sure you want to erase the disk, click Erase in the sheet.** The drive's or partition's data is erased and is formatted with the options you selected.

Installing Mac OS X on an External Hard Drive

You can install Mac OS X on an external hard drive and then start up under that drive; this is very useful for troubleshooting. To install Mac OS X on an external hard drive, perform the following steps:

1. **Configure a partition or disk on which you want to install Mac OS X.**

2. **Insert the System Software disc included with your MacBook Pro.**

3. **Double-click the Install Mac OS X application.**

4. **Click Restart to restart your MacBook Pro from the DVD.**

5. **When the MacBook Pro restarts, follow the on-screen instructions to start the installation process.**

6. **When you reach the Select a Destination screen, select the partition or hard disk you configured in step 1.**

7. **Follow the on-screen prompts to complete the Mac OS X installation.**

8. **When the process is complete, run the Software Update application to update the system to the current version (see Chapter 17 for information about Software Update).** The system on the external drive is ready for you to start up from.

Using Disk Utility to check or repair the internal drive

Because you can't use Disk Utility to repair a disk with open files and your startup disk always has open files, you can't use Disk Utility to repair the internal hard drive while you are started up from it.

Genius

While you can't repair the current startup disk, you can verify it. Although this won't fix any problems, it does identify that there is a problem.

If it appears that your internal hard drive has problems, you need to start up from a different disk to repair them. You can use one of the following options to accomplish this:

- **Start up from an alternate disk and run Disk Utility from there.** If you have installed Mac OS X on an external disk, you can then start up from that disk and run Disk Utility to repair the internal disk. (See Chapter 19 to learn how to start up from an alternate startup disk.) Once you're booted up, use the steps in the section "Using Disk Utility to check or repair an external drive," earlier in this chapter, to select and repair the internal hard disk.

- **Start up from the system software disc.** Insert the system software disc that came with your MacBook Pro. Restart the computer and hold the C key down while it restarts. When it does, the Mac OS X Installation application launches. On the Utilities menu, choose Disk Utility. The Disk Utility application launches; use the steps in the section "Using Disk Utility to check or repair an external drive," earlier in this chapter, to select and repair the internal hard disk.

Defragmenting and optimizing hard disks

As files are opened and closed, data from different files is laid down in the next available space so that, instead of all the data from one file being in a continuous block, it can be stored in blocks located in various spots around the disk. In this state, the data is fragmented. Although fragmentation is a normal part of the way disk drives function, excessive fragmentation can slow down the disk. As blocks of data become more numerous and spread out around the disk, it takes longer and longer to read all the data for that file.

You use a process called defragmentation to correct this condition. You need a disk maintenance program to do this. What the defragmentation process does is pick up all the data blocks for each particular file and write them in a continuous block. It does this for every file on the disk. After the data is laid out nice and neat, the drive performs faster because it doesn't have to move as far to read and write the data for a particular file.

Because a hard drive is made up of a round disk that spins at a constant speed, data near the center is read more quickly than data out near the rim. Data can be written to the disk in such a way that the access speed of the drive is optimized. Thus, the data is read and written in an optimized (for speed) fashion. You also need a disk maintenance tool to optimize a disk.

Usually, defragmentation and optimization are done at the same time using the same tool. The steps to perform these tasks depend on the particular software you use. Generally, this is not complicated and is a matter of choosing the drives you want to defragment and optimize, and clicking Start.

Using an iPod as an External Drive

In addition to being a fantastic digital media device, your iPod can also be used as a portable, external drive on which you can store files, just like a hard drive connected to your MacBook Pro.

Configuring an iPod Classic as a hard drive

With an 80GB or 160GB hard drive, an iPod Classic packs a lot of data storage in a small package. To configure an iPod Classic to be used as an external hard drive, perform the following steps:

1. **Connect the iPod to the MacBook Pro.** If it isn't open already, iTunes launches and connects to the iPod.

2. **Select the iPod on the Source list.**

3. **Click the Summary tab if it isn't selected already.**

4. **Check the Enable disk use check box.** You see a warning prompt that explains that because the iPod will be acting as a hard disk, you must manually eject it before disconnecting it from the computer.

5. **Click OK at the prompt.**

6. **Click Apply.** The iPod is ready to be used as a disk.

Configuring an iPod shuffle as a drive

iPod shuffles don't actually have hard drives; their memory is flash memory, which means that it doesn't require any moving parts. This is why iPod shuffles can be so small, and also why they have limited memory. Still, the 1GB they offer provides space for documents and other small files. To set up an iPod shuffle for disk use, do the following:

1. **Connect the iPod shuffle to your MacBook Pro.** If it isn't open already, iTunes launches and connects to the iPod shuffle.

2. **Select the iPod shuffle on the Source list.**

3. **Click the Settings tab if it isn't selected already.**

4. **Check the Enable disk use check box.** You see a warning prompt that explains that because the iPod shuffle will be acting as a hard disk, you must manually eject it before disconnecting it from the computer.

5. **Click OK at the prompt.**

6. **Drag the slider to the right to allocate more space for data, or to the left to allocate less space for data (see figure 16.7).** Because you are limited to the total memory in the iPod shuffle, you have to trade off memory for music versus that for data. The number of songs you set on the slider determines the number that iTunes places on the iPod shuffle when you use the AutoFill tool.

7. **Click Apply.** The iPod shuffle is ready to be used as a disk.

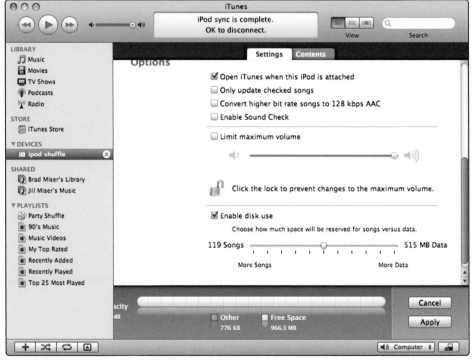

16.7 This iPod shuffle will have 515MB dedicated to data storage, which means it can hold about 119 songs.

Working with an iPod as a hard drive

Once configured, using an iPod as a drive is like using other kinds of drives. When you select an iPod on the DEVICES list, you see the folders and files it contains (see Figure 16.8).

When you select an iPod Classic, you see four folders that are used for content that is synced: Calendars, Contacts, Notes, and Photos. You should leave these folders as they are, but you can create new folders and store files within them on the iPod, just as you can other kinds of hard disks. Of course, any storage space you use for data won't be available for content in your iTunes Library.

Because there is no data synced for iPod shuffles, they don't have default folders. You can store as much data on the iPod shuffle as you've allocated on the slider. However, this setting only impacts the amount of music that is moved onto the iPod shuffle using the AutoFill tool. If you move more data onto the iPod shuffle than the slider setting implies, but you have moved less music onto it, you can store more data than the slider shows. If you manually manage music on the iPod shuffle, the slider setting has no effect. It only limits you when you use the AutoFill tool.

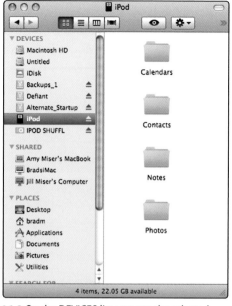

16.8 On the DEVICES list, you see the selected iPod and an iPod shuffle; both can be used for data storage.

Caution Make sure you eject iPods before disconnecting them or you risk damaging their data. You can eject iPods from the desktop or within iTunes.

Working with Flash Drives

Flash drives are a popular way to move files around. Because they have flash memory, they are very small and easy to carry. They are also quite limited; common sizes are less than 4GB. Still, a flash drive can be a good way to transfer files between computers or to back up small amounts of data when you are on the move.

Connecting a flash drive

To connect a flash drive to your MacBook Pro, simply plug it into one of the USB ports. The drive is mounted on your MacBook Pro and you can work with it. However, for best results, you should prepare the drive for use by reformatting it.

Genius

If you also want to use the drive on Windows computers, select the MS-DOS (FAT) format. This makes it easy to move files between Macs and Windows PCs.

Preparing a flash drive

To format a flash drive for your MacBook Pro, use the following steps:

1. **Launch the Disk Utility application.**

2. **Select the flash drive you want to format.**

3. **Click the Erase tab.**

4. **Select the format for the drive on the Format pop-up menu.** In most cases, you should choose Mac OS Extended (Case-sensitive, Journaled) to take advantage of the most sophisticated format option.

5. **Enter a name for the drive in the Name field.** Avoid spaces in the name, especially if you're going to use the drive on Windows computers.

6. **Click the Security Options button.** The Secure Erase Options sheet appears.

7. **Select one of the following options:**

   ● The Don't Erase Data option makes the data unviewable from the Finder but leaves the data physically on the drive.

   ● The Zero Out Data option writes zeros in all sectors on the drive. This is secure because it overwrites the entire drive, which makes the data harder to recover.

- The 7-Pass Erase option writes data over the entire drive seven times. This makes the data virtually impossible to recover. (Hey, if it's good enough for the U.S. Department of Defense, it should be good enough for you.)

- The 35-Pass Erase option overwrites the drive 35 times, making the data more than virtually impossible to recover.

Because the drive's memory is relatively small, none of these options require that much time.

8. **Click OK.** The option you selected is set and the sheet closes.

9. **Click Erase.** The confirmation sheet appears.

10. **If you are sure you want to erase the drive, click Erase in the sheet.** The drive's data is erased and is formatted with the option you selected. The drive is then ready to use.

303

How Can I Protect MacBook Pro?

Software Update

New software is available for your computer.

Installing this software may take some time. If you're not ready to install now, you can choose Software Update from the Apple menu later.

Install	Name	Version	Size
☑	iPhoto Update	7.1.3	16.9 MB

This update addresses issues with wire-bound books and cards.

Note: Use of this software is subject to the original Software License Agreement(s) that accompanied the software being updated. A list of Apple SLAs may be found here: http://www.apple.com/legal/sla/.

Security

Show All

General   FileVault   Firewall

- ○ Allow all incoming connections
- ⦿ Allow only essential services
- ○ Set access for specific services and applications

Mac OS X normally determines which programs are allowed incoming connections. Select this option if you want to allow or block incoming connections for specific programs.

File Sharing (AFP)
Screen Sharing

iChat   Allow incoming connections

Advanced...

Time Machine

Show All

Name: Valiant
Available: 87.3 GB of 465.8 GB
Oldest Backup: October 12, 2007

Change Disk...   Latest Backup: Today, 7:56 AM

Options...   Backing up: ▓▓▓▓
1.2 GB of 5.4 GB

Time Machine

OFF ◉ ON

Time Machine keeps
- Hourly backups for the past 24 hours
- Daily backups for the past month
- Weekly backups until your backup disk is full

☑ Show Time Machine status in the menu bar

🔒 Click the lock to prevent further changes.

Your MacBook Pro is valuable; protecting it is important, but this chapter is about protecting the data on your MacBook Pro, which is much more valuable. If you've purchased music, movies, or other content from the iTunes Store, you've invested hard-earned dollars in that content. If you use iPhoto, you can't replace those photos stored there at any price. Then there's personal data such as financial information that you need to safeguard. For all these reasons, you should take precautions to secure your MacBook Pro and its data.

Keeping Software Current

There are two good reasons why you should keep the software that you use current. One is that software developers frequently develop revisions to improve the features of their applications and to remove bugs. The other, and the reason this topic is included in this chapter, is that many applications, and most definitely Mac OS X itself, have a large role in how secure your MacBook Pro and its data are.

There are two basic categories of software that you need to keep current. The first is Apple software, which includes Mac OS X along with all the Apple applications you might use. The second category is the third-party software you have installed.

Keeping Apple software current

Because it is the largest factor in how secure your MacBook Pro and its data are, Mac OS X is the most important software you need to keep current. The good news is that Mac OS X includes the Software Update tool that makes it easy to keep Mac OS X and your Apple applications current. You can update software manually, and you can also configure Software Update so that it checks for and downloads updates automatically.

Updating Apple software manually

You can update your Apple software manually by performing the following steps:

1. **Choose Apple menu ⇨ Software Update.** The Software Update application launches, connects to the Internet, and compares the versions of Apple software installed on your MacBook Pro to the current versions. If it finds that newer versions are available, they appear on the list at the top of the window (see figure 17.1).

2. **To install an update, check its check box.** To prevent an update from being installed, uncheck its check box.

3. **Click Install** *numberofupdates***, where** *numberofupdates* **is the number of updates you've selected to install.**

4. **Enter your Administrator username and password (if required).**

5. **Click OK.** Your MacBook Pro downloads and installs the selected updates.

6. **Click Restart if prompted to do so.** Your MacBook Pro restarts and the software installation begins.

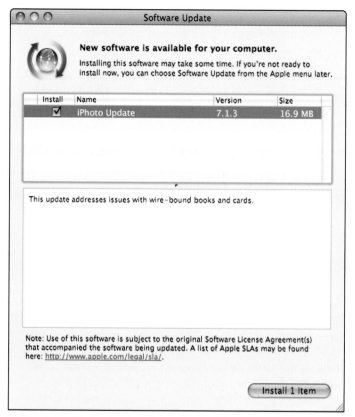

17.1 Software Update has found an update to iPhoto.

Updating Apple software current automatically

Checking for software updates is easy enough, but why not have your MacBook Pro handle this for you automatically? Here's how:

1. **Open the System Preferences application.**

2. **Click Software Update.** The Software Update pane appears.

3. **Click the Scheduled Check tab if it isn't selected already.**

4. **Check the Check for updates check box.**

5. **On the Check for updates pop-up menu, choose the frequency with which your MacBook Pro checks for updates.**

6. **If you want important updates to be downloaded automatically, check the Download important updates automatically check box.** Important updates are those that affect your system and have the most impact on its security.

7. **Quit the System Preferences application.** When the specified amount of time passes, Software Update checks for new software. When it finds new versions, it downloads them automatically and then prompts you to allow them to be installed, or to be downloaded and then installed.

Viewing installed updates

You can use the Software Update pane to view information about updates you've installed by doing the following:

1. **Open the System Preferences application.**

2. **Click Software Update.** The Software Update pane appears (see figure 17.2).

3. **Click the Installed Updates tab.** You see a list of all updates you've downloaded and installed on your MacBook Pro.

4. **Sort the list by clicking any of the column headings.**

5. **To view the updates in a log file, click Open as Log File.** The Console application opens, and you see more detailed information about the updates.

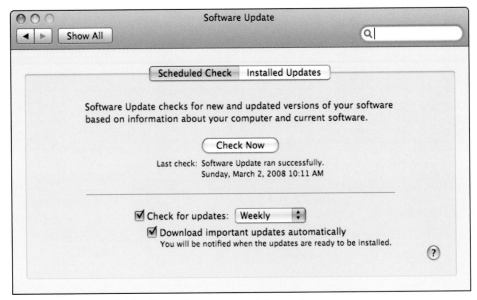

17.2 You can see from this list that updates are not an infrequent occurrence.

Keeping non-Apple software current

Support for updates to non-Apple software isn't built into Mac OS X. Instead, each application provides its own tools to download and install updates. Most of these support both manual and automatic updates. The following sections show how to update Microsoft Office applications manually and Snapz Pro X from Ambrosia Software automatically; other third-party applications are updated similarly.

Updating Microsoft Office applications manually

Most Mac users are also Office users; to update an Office application manually, do the following:

1. **Launch the Office application.**

2. **Choose Help ⇨ Check for Updates.** The Microsoft AutoUpdate application opens and checks for updates (see figure 17.3).

3. **Select the update you want to install.**

4. **Click Install.**

5. **Follow the on-screen instructions to complete the update.**

Microsoft AutoUpdate

The following updates are available for your Microsoft software. Use the check boxes to select the updates you want to install:

| ☑ Office 2004 for Mac 11.3.8 Update | 10/9/07 | 9.0 MB |

This update fixes a vulnerability in Word 2004 that an attacker can use to overwrite the contents of your computer's memory with malicious code.

(Help)   (Cancel)   (Learn More...)   (Install)

17.3 Here, an update to Microsoft Office has been found.

Genius You can configure Microsoft Office applications to check for updates automatically by selecting Help ⇨ Check for Updates. In the Microsoft AutoUpdate window, click the Automatically radio.

Updating Snapz Pro X automatically

Snapz Pro X from Ambrosia Software (www.ambrosiasw.com) is the best screen capture application for the Mac (almost all the figures in this book were captured with it). To configure it to check for updates automatically, perform the following steps:

1. **Launch Snapz Pro X.**

2. **Click the Preferences tab.**

3. **Check the Check for new versions at launch check box.** Each time you launch the application, it checks for newer versions. When one is found, you are prompted to download and install it.

Protecting MacBook Pro from Internet Attacks

When you are using your home network, you should shield your MacBook Pro from Internet attacks through an AirPort Base Station. When you are using networks outside of your control, such as one available in public places, you should use the Mac OS X firewall to prevent unauthorized access to your computer.

Caution   Never connect your MacBook Pro directly to a cable or DSL modem without first enabling the Mac OS X firewall.

Using a base station to shield your MacBook Pro

One of the easiest and best ways to protect machines on a local network from attack and simultaneously to share an Internet connection is to install an AirPort Base Station. These devices provide NAT protection for any computers that obtain Internet service through them, and for most users, this is an adequate level of protection from hacking.

To learn how to configure a base station to protect your network and the computers on it, see Chapter 3.

Using the Mac OS X firewall to shield your MacBook Pro

Whenever your MacBook Pro isn't protected by a base station, make sure you configure its firewall to protect it from Internet attacks. Common situations are when you travel and connect to various networks, such as in public places and hotel rooms. In most cases, these networks are configured to limit access to your computer (similar to how a base station shields it), but you shouldn't count on this. Instead, protect your MacBook Pro with its firewall by performing the following steps:

1. **Open the System Preferences application.**

2. **Click the Security icon.** The Security pane opens.

3. **Click the Firewall tab (see figure 17.4).**

4. **Select one of the following radio buttons to configure the protection the firewall provides:**

   - *Allow all incoming connections* disables the firewall.

   - *Allow only essential services* activates the firewall and blocks all but essential services. Essential services are those that are required for features that you've enabled by configuring your computer, such as File Sharing.

   - *Set access for specific services and applications* allows you to manually configure the services that are allowed through the firewall. To allow a service, click the Add button (+) at the bottom of the service list. Use the resulting sheet to move to and select the application or service you want to allow.

5. **Click the Advanced button.** The Advanced sheet appears.

6. **Check the Enable Firewall Logging check box.** This causes a log entry to be created each time the firewall blocks a connection attempt.

Genius

Click the Open Log button to use the Console application to view the attempts to connect to your MacBook Pro that have been blocked by the firewall.

7. **Check the Enable Stealth Mode check box.** This further protects your MacBook Pro by making sure that uninvited connection requests aren't acknowledged in any form so that the existence of your computer is hidden.

8. **Click OK.** Your settings are saved and the sheet closes.

17.4 Use the Mac OS X firewall to protect your computer from Internet attacks.

Protecting MacBook Pro with General Security

Mac OS X includes a number of general security settings that are particularly useful if you use your MacBook Pro in a variety of locations, some of which might allow you to be accessed by someone else. To configure these settings, do the following:

1. **Open the System Preferences application.**

2. **Click the Security icon.** The Security pane opens.

3. **Click the General tab (see figure 17.5).**

4. **Check the Require password to wake this computer from sleep or screen saver check box to require that a user enter their account's login password to stop the screen saver or wake up the MacBook Pro from sleep.** This setting impacts only the account that is currently active; if you want this to be required for each user account, you need to log in to each one and set this option for that account.

```
○ ○ ○                          Security
◀ ▶    Show All                                    🔍

                    General   FileVault   Firewall

        ☐ Require password to wake this computer from sleep or screen saver

        For all accounts on this computer:
        ☑ Disable automatic login
        ☐ Require password to unlock each System Preferences pane
        ☐ Log out after    60 ⬍  minutes of inactivity
        ☐ Use secure virtual memory

        ☐ Disable remote control infrared receiver
          This computer will work with any available          Pair...
          remote.


    🔓  Click the lock to prevent further changes.                    ⑦
```

17.5 The General tab helps you to protect your MacBook Pro from unauthorized access.

5. **To prevent someone from being able to use your computer just by starting it, check the Disable automatic login check box.**

6. **To restrict a user's ability to change system settings, check the Require password to unlock each System Preferences pane check box.**

7. **To cause user accounts to be automatically logged out after periods of inactivity, check the Log out after check box and set the amount of inactive time using the time box.**

8. **To protect the contents of your MacBook Pro virtual memory, check the Use secure virtual memory check box.** When this feature is active, data written to disk is stored securely when virtual memory is required.

9. **To prevent your MacBook Pro from being controlled through an infrared remote control, check the Disable remote control infrared receiver check box.**

10. **Quit the System Preferences application.** Your security settings take effect.

Genius

When you allow access to your MacBook Pro through a remote control, you can click the Pair button and follow the on-screen instructions to pair your MacBook Pro with a remote.

Protecting Data with Time Machine

The most important thing you can do to protect your MacBook Pro and its data is to back it up. Backing up simply means having at least one copy of all the data on your computer in case something should happen to that data.

To drive this point home, think about how much money you've spent on content from the iTunes Store. You can only download this content once. After that, if you need to download it again, you have to pay for it again. Going beyond money, consider photos that you manage in iPhoto. Many of those are irreplaceable; without a backup in place, you could lose them and never be able to get them back. Then there are documents you've created, financial records, and so on.

The good news is that with an external hard drive, you can use the Mac OS X Time Machine to back up with minimal effort on your part; in fact, once you set it up, the process is automatic. Time Machine makes recovering files you've lost easy and intuitive.

Time Machine backs up your data for as long as it can until the backup hard drive is full. It stores hourly backups for the past 24 hours. It stores daily backups for the past month. It stores weekly backups until the backup disk is full. Once the disk is full, it deletes the oldest backups to make room for new backups. To protect yourself as long as possible, use the largest hard drive you can, and exclude files that you don't need to back up (such as system files if you have the Mac OS X installation disc) to save space on the backup drive.

To use Time Machine, you need to gain access to an external hard disk and then configure Time Machine. And, you should know how to use Time Machine to restore files, should you need to.

Preparing a backup disk

To use Time Machine, you need to be able to store data on an external disk. To accomplish this, you have the following options:

- **Time Capsule.** This Apple device is a combination AirPort Extreme Base Station and hard drive (see figure 17.6). With capacity options of 500GB and 1TB, you can gain a lot of backup storage space. Additionally, a Time Capsule is also a fully featured AirPort Base Station, so it makes an ideal backup drive for any computer connected to the AirPort network it provides. The downside of Time Capsule is that it is more expensive than a standard hard drive, but if you don't already have an AirPort Base Station, it is slightly less expensive than buying a base station and hard drive separately.

17.6 The Apple Time Capsule is useful as a backup disk for your MacBook Pro, and it is also an AirPort Base Station.

⦿ **Hard drive connected through USB, FireWire, or FireWire 800.** You can use a hard drive directly connected to your MacBook Pro as a backup drive. This provides the fastest performance of any option, and hard drives are inexpensive and easy to configure.

Note Presently, Time Machine doesn't support backing up to a hard drive connected to an AirPort Extreme Base Station. This is unfortunate because that would be a very convenient option. Hopefully, a future software update will provide this capability. You can't use Time Machine to back up to an iPod, either.

⦿ **Shared hard drive.** You can back up to a hard drive that you can access through File Sharing over a local network.

Backing up with Time Machine

Once you've gained access to a backup hard drive, you can configure Time Machine to back up your data.

To configure Time Machine, perform the following steps:

1. **Choose Apple menu ⇨ System Preferences.**

2. **Click the Time Machine icon.** The Time Machine pane opens.

3. **Drag the slider to the ON position.** Time Machine activates and the select drive sheet appears.

4. **Select the drive on which you want to store the backed up information.**

5. **Click Use for Backup.** The sheet closes and you return to the Time Machine page. The drive you selected is shown at the top of the pane, and the timer starts the backup process, which you see next to the text "Next Backup."

6. **Click the Stop button next to the text "Next Backup."** This stops the backup process so that you can configure it more specifically.

7. **Click Options.** The Do not back up sheet appears. This sheet enables you to exclude files from the backup process.

8. **Click the Add button (+).** The select sheet appears.

9. **Move to and select the folders or files you want to exclude from the backup.**

10. **Click Exclude.**

11. **If you selected system files, click Exclude System Folder Only to exclude only files in the System folder, or Exclude All System Files to exclude system files no matter where they are stored.**

12. **If you want to be warned as old backups are removed from the backup disk, check the Warn when old backups are deleted check box.** This is a good idea, as it lets you know when your backup drive fills up.

13. **Click Done.** You return to the Time Machine pane, which displays information about your backup (see figure 17.7). The timer starts and when it expires, the first backup is created. From then on, Time Machine automatically backs up your data to the selected hard drive. New backups are created every hour.

17.7 The progress of the current backup is shown in the Backing up progress bar.

14. **Check the Show Time Machine status in the menu bar check box.**

15. **Quit the System Preferences application.**

Restoring files with Time Machine

The reason this function is called Time Machine is that you can use it to "go back in time" to restore files that are included in your backups. You can restore files and folders from the Finder, and you can recover individual items from within some applications (such as photos from within iPhoto).

Restoring files in the Finder

If the folders or files you want to restore are included in your backups and are available in the Finder, you can restore them by performing the following steps:

1. **Open a Finder window showing the location where the files you want to recover were stored.** This can be the location where files that have been deleted were placed, or it may be where the current versions of files are stored (in the event you want to go back to a previous version of a file).

2. **Launch the Time Machine application by double-clicking its icon in the Applications folder.** The desktop disappears and the Time Machine window fills the entire space (see figure 17.8). In the center of the window, you see the Finder window that you opened in step 1. Behind it, you see all the versions of that window that are stored in your backup, from the current version to as far back in time as the backups go.

   Along the right side of the window, you see the timeline for your backups, starting with today and moving back in time as you move up the screen. At the bottom of the screen, you see the Time Machine toolbar. In the center of the toolbar, you see the time of the window that is currently in the foreground. At each end, you see controls that you use to exit Time Machine (Cancel) and the Restore button (which is active only when you have selected a file or folder that can be restored).

3. **Move back in time by:**
   - Clicking the time on the timeline when the files you want to restore were available.
   - Click the back arrow (pointing away from you) located just to the left of the timeline.
   - Click a Finder window behind the foremost one.

4. **When you reach the files you want to restore, select them.**

5. **Click Restore.** The files and folders you selected are returned to their locations in the condition they were in the version of the backup you selected, and Time Machine quits. You move back to the Finder's location where the restored files were saved, and can resume using them as if you'd never lost them.

17.8 You can use Time Machine to travel back in time to when files you want to restore were available.

Restoring files in applications

Some applications that work with individual files, such as iPhoto and iTunes, provide Time Machine support so that you can restore files from within the application instead of by selecting the files in the Finder.

The following steps show you how to restore photos in iPhoto (restoring files in other compatible applications is done similarly):

1. **Open iPhoto.**

2. **Launch the Time Machine application by double-clicking its icon in the Applications folder.** The desktop disappears and the Time Machine window fills the entire space. In the center of the screen, you see the iPhoto window. Behind it, you see all the versions of that window that are stored in your backup, from the current version to as far back in time as the backups go.

3. **Move back in time by:**

    - Clicking the time on the timeline when the photos you want to restore were available. The higher on the timeline you click, the farther back in time you go.

- Click the back arrow (pointing away from you) located just to the left of the timeline.

- Click an iPhoto window behind the foremost one.

As you move back in time, you see the versions of the window that are saved in the backup you are viewing, and the date and time of the backup in the center of the toolbar.

4. **Use the iPhoto controls to move to the photos you want to restore.**

5. **Select the photos you want to restore.**

6. **Click Restore.** The files are returned to the application, and you can use them as if they'd never been lost.

Protecting Data with Backup from Apple

If you have a MobileMe account, you can download and use the Backup application from Apple. This application enables you to have more control over your backups, and you can store them in different formats, most importantly on your iDisk (which takes the concept of off-site storage to an extreme) or DVD/CD.

Backup uses the concept of plans to back up information. A plan is a definition of the specific data you want to back up, where that data will be stored, and how the backups will be performed. Backup includes a number of useful plans, and you can also create your own custom plans. You can create and use multiple plans at the same time, and plans can be scheduled so that they run automatically. For example, you might want to create one plan to save one set of files onto DVD and another to save a different set of files on your iDisk.

Before you can use it, you need to download and install the Backup application, which requires that you have a MobileMe account.

Downloading and installing Backup

To download and install Backup on your MacBook Pro, perform the following steps:

1. **Connect to your iDisk (see Chapter 5).**

2. **Open the Software folder and then the Backup for Mac OS X folder.**

3. **Drag the Backup disk image onto your hard drive.**

4. **Open the disk image.** The installer volume mounts on the desktop (see figure 17.9).

17.9 Run the installer to be able to use Backup.

5. **Launch the Backup.pkg installer application.**

6. **Follow the on-screen instructions to complete the installation.**

Backing up with Backup

One of the most useful things you can do with Backup is to back up files to a DVD. This enables you to store the backups in a different location and provides a long-term, reliable way to store data. To create a backup, perform the following steps:

1. **Launch Backup.** You see the Welcome to Backup screen that shows a list of default plans. For example, you can use the Home Folder plan to save all of the files in your Home folder to a hard disk or DVD, or the iTunes Library plan to save the contents you manage in iTunes.

2. **Click Continue.** The empty Backup window appears. (If you selected a default plan, you see that plan in the window.)

3. **Click the New Plan button located at the bottom-left corner of the window.** The plan create/select sheet appears.

Genius

To use a default plan, check its check box and click Continue. You can then configure the plan to make changes to it. The following steps describe how to create a custom plan. Once you know how to do that, using a default plan is even easier.

4. **Click Custom.**

5. **Click Choose Plan.** At the top of the New Plan dialog, you see the name field, which is Untitled before you enter a name. The dialog has three tabs. The Back Up tab enables you to configure the backup. The History tab shows you when the backup has run. You use the Restore tab to restore files from the backup.

6. **Enter the name of the plan you are creating and press Return.**

7. **To add folders or files to the backup, click the Add button (+) at the bottom of the Backup Items pane.** You see the Choose Items to Back Up sheet.

8. **Use any of the following options to select files and folders to include in the plan:**

   - Use the QuickPicks tab to select specific kinds of data to include; options include Address Book, Application preferences, and iCal. To include data of a specific kind, check its check box.

   - Use the Files & Folders tab to move to and select files and folders using a standard Finder interface (see figure 17.10).

   - Use the Spotlight tab to search for files and folders to include in the plan. To include a file or folder in the plan, select it and click the relative Include radio button.

17.10 Use this sheet to select the files and folders you want to include in a backup.

9. **When you're done selecting files and folders to include in the plan, click Done.** The sheet closes and you move back to the Backup window.

10. **Click the Add button (+) located at the bottom of the Destination and Schedule list.** The Choose a Destination and Schedule sheet appears.

11. **On the Destination pop-up menu, choose the location where your backup will be saved.**

12. **To have the plan run automatically, check the Automatically back up at the following times check box.**

13. **On the Every pop-up menu, choose how often the plan will be run.** For example, choose Day to have the plan run daily.

14. **Use the time controls to set the specific time at which the plan will run.**

15. **Click OK.** The sheet closes and you see the destination and schedule you created on the Destination and Schedule list (see figure 17.11).

17.11 This plan backs up the files shown on the Backup Items list, weekly to my iDisk and monthly to DVD.

16. **To run the plan, click Back Up Now.**

Managing backups in Backup

Following are some pointers for managing your backups in Backup:

- After you've configured backups, they run according to the schedules you've set. If a backup is stored on a CD or DVD, when it runs, you're prompted to insert the appropriate kind of disc. If a backup is stored to hard drive or your iDisk, it works without any input from you.

- You can manually run a backup by launching the Backup application, selecting the backup you want to run, and clicking Back Up. If the backup has more than one location, choose the destination you want to run on the Choose a Destination to Back Up sheet.

- If a backup fails, it's marked with an exclamation point icon in the Backup window. Double-click it, and you move to the plan's History tab where you see the backup that failed. Select it and click View Details to open a log file.

Restoring files with Backup

The whole point of using any backup application is to be able to recover lost data. Here's how you can use Backup to recover files:

1. **Launch Backup.**

2. **Select the plan from which you want to restore files.**

3. **Click Restore.**

4. **Select what you want to restore on the Previous Backups list.**

5. **Check the check box for each item you want to restore (see figure 17.12).**

6. **To prevent something from being restored, uncheck its check box.**

7. **If you want to restore the files to a location other than the one from which they were copied, check the Restore to an alternate location check box and choose the location to which you want the files restored.**

8. **Click Restore Selection.** The selected files are restored from the backup to their previous location or to the location you selected.

Genius

If your Backup installation is lost (such as when a hard drive fails and you have to use a new one) such that you no longer see the plans in Backup, you can still restore files. Re-install Backup and launch it. Choose Plan, Restore from Backup. Then move to and select the backup from which you want to restore files.

17.12 The items with check boxes checked will be restored from my iDisk.

Protecting Data with Encryption

If you travel with your MacBook Pro, the data it contains is vulnerable because your computer can be carried away by other people. If you store important data on your computer, you can encrypt the data in your Home folder so that it can't be used without an appropriate password. Even if someone is able to mount the hard disk in your MacBook Pro, they must have the password to be able to access data in your Home folder.

The Mac OS X FileVault feature encrypts your Home folder using a password that you create so that this data can't be accessed without the appropriate password. To do this, Mac OS X has to create a copy of your Home folder during the encryption process, which means that you need to have free space that is at least the size of the information in your Home folder before you can enable FileVault.

Caution To use FileVault, the associated user account must have a password. If you didn't configure a password for your user account, or for any other user account, you need to do so before you can activate FileVault. Also, only one user account can be logged in to activate FileVault.

To activate FileVault, perform the following steps:

1. **Open the System Preferences application.**

2. **Click the Security icon.**

3. **Click the FileVault tab (see figure 17.13).**

```
⬤ ⬤ ⬤                          Security
◀  ▶    Show All                                    Q|

                    General   FileVault   Firewall

        FileVault secures your home folder by encrypting its contents. It automatically
        encrypts and decrypts your files while you're using them.
        WARNING: Your files will be encrypted using your login password. If you forget your login
        password and you don't know the master password, your data will be lost.

        A master password is not set for this computer.      ( Set Master Password... )
        This is a "safety net" password. It lets you unlock any
        FileVault account on this computer.

        FileVault protection is off for this account.        ( Turn On FileVault... )
        Turning on FileVault may take a while.


   🔒  Click the lock to prevent further changes.                              (?)
```

17.13 FileVault encrypts the data in your Home folder to prevent unauthorized access to it.

4. **Click the Set Master Password button.** The master password sheet opens. The master password enables you to decrypt encrypted files for all users. And you don't really have a choice because you must create a master password before you can activate FileVault.

5. **Enter the master password in the Master Password field and the Verify field.**

6. **Click OK to set the master password.** The sheet closes and the Set Master Password button becomes the Change button.

Caution   FileVault can interfere with backup applications, including Time Machine. You must be logged out of your user account for Time Machine to be able to back up your Home folder. I recommend that you disable FileVault when you are using your MacBook Pro in a secure location so that your backups aren't disrupted.

7. **Click the Turn On FileVault button.** The FileVault service starts up, and you are prompted to enter your password.

325

8. **Enter your user account's login password.**

9. **Click OK.** You see a warning sheet that explains what you are doing and that activating this service can take a while (you can't log out of your account until the service has been turned on).

10. **If you also want the data that is being encrypted to be erased securely when the encrypted version is created, check the Use secure erase check box (which overwrites deleted data so that it can't be recovered as easily).**

11. **Click the Turn On FileVault button.** The FileVault window appears; you can't do anything else on your MacBook Pro until FileVault has started up. When the process is complete, you see the Login window.

Caution FileVault must be activated for each user account to secure each user's Home folder. Also, it only protects data stored in the encrypted Home folder. Any data stored outside of an encrypted Home folder is vulnerable.

12. **Log back into your account.** You shouldn't notice any difference, except that your Home folder's icon is now marked with the secure icon (a lock). All your Home folder files are encrypted and aren't accessible unless a valid encryption password has been entered.

When you log in to your account (or any other user whose account is protected by FileVault), the files in your Home folder are decrypted automatically, so you won't need to do anything else to access them. The value of FileVault is for those times when you aren't logged into your account and someone else has access to your computer. For example, suppose someone steals your MacBook Pro. Although they can't access your user account without your login password, they could connect the computer to a FireWire drive with Mac OS X installed and start up from that volume. Because the files on your MacBook startup volume are not protected anymore (the OS on the computer to which the MacBook is connected is running the show), they are accessible. If FileVault is not on, these files are not encrypted and can be used, but if FileVault is on, these files are encrypted and are useless unless the password is known.

Protecting Information with Keychains

Many times, you can check a check box that causes Mac OS X to remember the passwords you enter. These passwords are remembered in the keychain associated with your account. Just by using the remember check box, you get a lot of value from the keychain because it stores the various usernames and passwords for you. All you have to remember is the password for your user account that unlocks the keychain, which in turn applies the appropriate usernames and passwords so you don't have to enter them manually.

When you have applications, such as Safari, remember usernames and passwords (such as those for Web sites you visit), they are also stored in your keychain so that you don't have to enter this information each time you need to log in. Each kind of username and password is stored as a specific type in your keychain.

Before you can use a keychain, it has to be created; a keychain is created automatically for each user account you create. However, you can create additional keychains for specific purposes if you need to.

To use a keychain, it must be unlocked. To unlock a keychain, enter its password when you are prompted to do so. When you log in to your user account, the default keychain for that account is unlocked automatically because its password is the password for the user account with which it is associated.

While entering a keychain's password can become annoying because it is a fairly common requirement, you should remember that at least you only have to remember the keychain's password instead of remembering a separate password for each resource.

Many types of resources can be added to your keychain to enable you to access them, including the following:

- **AirPort network passwords.**
- **File sharing passwords.**
- **Internet passwords.**
- **MobileMe password.**
- **Secure notes.** You can store information that you want to protect using secure notes. For example, if you want to store your credit card information so that it can't be accessed unless you are logged into your user account, you can add it to your keychain. When you need that information, you can open the secured note containing your credit card information in your keychain.

Viewing and configuring your keychains

You can view and configure your keychain with the following steps:

1. **Open the Keychain Access application located in the Utilities folder within the Applications folder (see figure 17.14).** In the top-left pane is a list of all keychains that your account can access. In the lower-left pane is a list of categories for all the keychains that are installed under your user account.

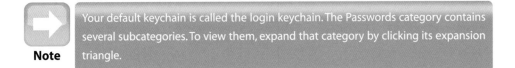

17.14 Here you can see that a number of items have been stored in my keychain.

Note Your default keychain is called the login keychain. The Passwords category contains several subcategories. To view them, expand that category by clicking its expansion triangle.

2. **To see what items are included in your default keychain, select login.**

3. **Select the All Items category.** Each item in your keychain appears in the list.

4. **To get summary information about a keychain item, select it.** A summary of the item appears at the top of the window, including the kind of item it is, the user account with which it is associated, where the location to which it relates is, and the modification date.

5. **Double-click a keychain item.** Its window appears. This window has two tabs: Attributes and Access Control. The Attributes tab presents information about the item, such as its name, its kind, the account, the location of the resource with which it is associated, comments you have entered, and the password (which is hidden when you first view an item). The Access Control tab enables you to configure how the item is used.

6. **To see the item's password, check the Show password check box.** You are then prompted to confirm the keychain's password.

7. **Confirm the password by entering it at the prompt and choosing to allow access to the item.** When you return to the Attributes tab, you see the item's password.

8. **Click the Access Control tab.** Use the access controls in the pane to control which applications can access this keychain item and how they can access it.

9. **To allow access to the item by all applications, check the Allow all applications to access this item radio button.** If you want to configure access for specific applications, continue with the rest of these steps.

10. **To allow access by specific applications but require confirmation, click the Confirm before allowing access radio button, and check the Ask for Keychain password check box if you want to be prompted for your keychain's password before access is allowed.**

11. **To enable an application not currently on the list to access the keychain item, click the Add button (+) located at the bottom of the list and select the application to which you want to provide access.**

12. **Click Save Changes.** Your changes are saved, and you return to the Keychain Access window.

Adding items to a keychain

You can add items to a keychain in several ways, including the following:

- When you access a resource that can provide access to a keychain, such as a file server, look for the Add to Keychain check box.

- Drag a network server onto the Keychain Access window.

- Drag the Internet Resource Locator file for a Web page onto the Keychain Access window.

- Manually create a keychain item.

Genius

If a particular application or resource doesn't support keychains, you won't be able to access that resource automatically. However, you can still use Keychain Access to store such an item's username and password for you, thus enabling you to recall that information easily.

One useful thing you can add to a keychain is a secure note. This protects the information you enter with a password so that it can only be viewed if the appropriate password is provided. To add a secure note to a keychain, use the following steps:

1. **Open Keychain Access.**

2. **Select the keychain to which you want to add the note.**

3. **Choose File ⇨ New Secure Note Item.** The New Secured Note sheet appears (see figure 17.15).

Keychain Item Name:

My Credit Card Number

Enter a name for this note.

Note:

12345678910

Yeah right!

Cancel   Add

17.15 Here's a secure note containing vital information.

4. **Enter a name for the note in the Keychain Item Name box.**

5. **Enter the information you want to store in the Note box.**

6. **Click Add.** The note is added to your keychain and you return to the Keychain Access window where you see the new note you added.

To view a secure note, do the following:

1. **Select the Secure Notes category.** Your secure notes appear.

2. **Double-click the note you want to read.** The note opens.

3. **Click the Show note check box.** You see the note in the window.

Working with keychains

When an application needs to access a keychain item and it is not configured to always allow access, you see the Confirm Access to Keychain dialog that prompts you to enter a keychain's password and choose an access option (see figure 17.16). When prompted, you have the following three options:

- **Deny.**
- **Allow.** A single access to the item is allowed.
- **Always Allow.** Access to the item is always allowed, and you don't see the prompt the next time it is used.

If you want to become a keychain master, check out the following information:

● Your keychains are stored in the Library/Keychains folder in your Home directory. You can add a keychain from one account to another account by moving the keychain file to a location that can be accessed by the second account. (For example, you can copy your keychain into the Public folder of your Home directory to enable other users to add that keychain to their own accounts.) To add a keychain to a user account, open Keychain Access under that account and choose File ⇨ Import Items. This is useful if you want to use the same keychain from several accounts.

● If you choose Edit ⇨ Change Settings for Keychain *keychainname*, where *keychainname* is the name of the keychain, you can set a keychain to lock after a specified period of time or lock when the MacBook Pro is asleep.

● You can synchronize keychains on different computers by using .Mac.

● If you choose Edit ⇨ Change Password for Keychain *keychainname*, where *keychainname* is the name of the keychain, you can change a keychain's password.

● Choose Keychain Access ⇨ Preferences. On the General tab, check the Show Status in Menu Bar check box. This adds the Keychain Access menu to the menu bar.

● If you choose Edit ⇨ Keychain List, you see the Configure Keychain sheet. You can use this sheet to configure keychains for a user account or the system. For example, you can check the Shared check box to share a keychain between user accounts.

● If you choose Keychain Access ⇨ Keychain First Aid, you see the Keychain First Aid dialog. You can use this dialog to verify keychains or repair a damaged keychain.

17.16 At a prompt, you can choose the kind of access you allow to an item.

How Can I Run
Windows Applications?

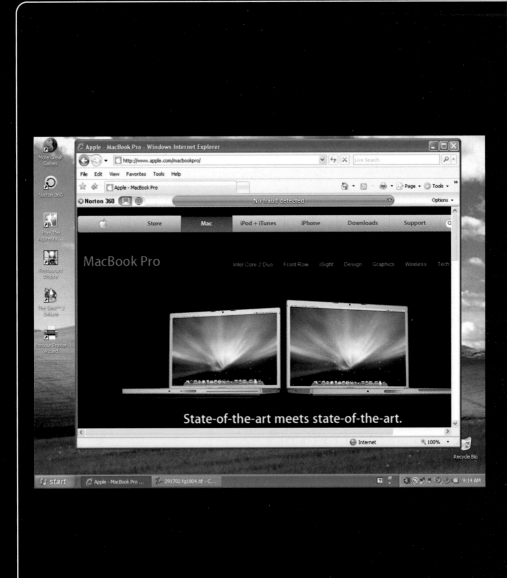

Some of us live in two worlds. One is the Mac world we know and love. The other world is that of Windows computers. For Mac fans, Windows isn't the operating system of choice for many reasons. However, Windows computers do dominate certain areas, particularly mid-size and large organizations, and there are a number of applications that run on Windows only. The good news is that with your MacBook Pro, you can run the Mac OS and Windows on the same computer, which means you really do have the best of both worlds.

Choosing a Windows Option

When the Mac platform switched to Intel processors, two basic options for running Windows on Macs became available: Boot Camp and virtualization. Each method has its advantages and disadvantages. More good news is that you can use both of these methods when you need to.

- **Boot Camp.** Boot Camp is the Apple technology that transforms Mac hardware into a fully capable Windows PC. You can choose to boot up your MacBook Pro in the Mac OS or in Windows. When you boot up in Windows, you have a fully functional Windows PC on your hands.

  The strengths of Boot Camp include great performance (your MacBook Pro can outperform many laptops designed to run Windows only), maximum compatibility for hardware and software, and a lower cost because your only expense is a copy of Windows. A minor downside is that it can be a bit more complicated to share data between the two operating systems because they can't be running at the same time.

- **Virtualization.** Under virtualization, an application provides a virtual environment (also called a virtual machine) in which you install and run Windows. You install the virtualization application and then install a version of Windows in a virtual machine. When you want to run Windows, you launch the virtualization application, and within its windows, you can run Windows and Windows applications.

  Using a virtual approach has a number of benefits, including being able to run Windows and the Mac OS at the same time because the virtualization software is just another application running on your MacBook Pro, good performance (it isn't noticeably slower than running it under Boot Camp), and easy data sharing because the Mac OS and Windows are running at the same time.

  Virtualization does have two points against it. One is the cost of the virtualization software (the Parallels Desktop for Mac application that I recommend for this is currently about $80). The other is that a virtual approach might not be compatible with all the hardware and software you want to run.

While I've explained Boot Camp and virtualization as two distinct options, if you chose the virtualization application I recommend (Parallels Desktop for Mac), you can use both options and switch between them easily.

Obtaining Windows

To run Windows on a Mac, you do have to purchase a full copy of Windows to install, whether you use Boot Camp or a virtualization application (or both). The cost for this varies, depending on the version of Windows you purchase and how you purchase it. When you purchase Windows, try to get a version that is designed for builders, also called the Original Equipment Manufacturers (OEM) version. This version is significantly less expensive than the full retail version and is ideal for installing on a MacBook Pro.

If you are getting Windows only to run specific applications, see if the applications you need are supported on Windows XP SP2. If so, you might be able to save a few dollars using this older version of Windows. At press time, Microsoft Windows XP Home Edition SP2B for System Builders was selling for about $90. If you want the most current version of Windows, a full version of Windows Vista Home Basic Edition costs only slightly more than the older XP at $110. If you're only going to be using Windows to run Windows applications, the basic edition should be sufficient. Make sure you get a full version; an upgrade version won't work.

Within each version of Windows are various sub-types, such as Home, Professional, and other categories between which the differences are difficult to understand. For most MacBook Pro users running Windows as a second operating system, the Home or Basic versions are likely to be sufficient.

Using Boot Camp to Run Windows

To get Windows running under Boot Camp, use the Boot Camp Assistant, which creates a partition on your hard disk for your Windows installation. Once the Assistant is done with its work, you install Windows in the partition it creates. Finally, use the Mac OS X Installation DVD to add drivers for your MacBook Pro hardware.

Once the installation is complete, you can run Windows at any time.

Configuring Boot Camp and installing Windows

Running the Boot Camp Assistant is mostly a matter of following the on-screen steps to work through the assistant and then using the Windows installer. The next set of steps demonstrates how to install Windows XP; if you install Windows Vista, the details might be slightly different, but the overall process is the same.

1. **Launch the Boot Camp Assistant application located in the Utilities folder in the Applications folder.** You see the first screen of the assistant.

2. **Click Continue.** You see the Create a Partition for Windows screen. On the left, you see the partition for Mac OS X, while on the right you see the partition for Windows, which is a minimum of 5GB.

3. **Set the size of the Windows partition by doing one of the following:**

   - Dragging the Resize handle between the two partitions to the left to increase the size of the Windows partition (see figure 18.1). You can set the partition to be any size you want. I recommend that you allocate at least 10GB to Windows.

Boot Camp Assistant

Create a Partition for Windows

Each operating system requires its own partition on the disk. Drag the divider to set the size of the partitions, or click one of the buttons.

"amys_drive" will be partitioned as:

Mac OS X		Windows
58 GB		16 GB
21 GB free		

Divide Equally   Use 32 GB

Go Back   Partition

18.1 Use the Create a Partition screen to set the size of your Windows environment.

● Clicking the Divide Equally button to divide the disk into two equally sized partitions. I don't recommend this option, as it significantly reduces the amount of disk space available to you under Mac OS X.

● Clicking the Use 32 GB button to set the Windows partition at 32GB. The 32GB option is a reasonable size for many Windows environments, and this option is a good choice if your MacBook Pro has plenty of free space.

4. **Click the Partition button.** When the process is complete, you're prompted to insert your Windows installation disc.

5. **Insert the Windows installation disc.**

6. **After it is mounted on your MacBook Pro, click Start Installation.** The Mac restarts and boots from the Windows installation disc. The installation application starts installing files; you see the progress at the bottom of the blue Windows Setup screen.

7. **When the Welcome To Setup screen appears, press the Return key (which is equivalent to the Enter key in Windows).**

8. **Press F8 to agree to the Windows license information.**

9. **Select the BOOTCAMP partition and press the Return key.**

Caution Make sure you select the correct partition to install Windows on. If you don't, you might overwrite a partition with Mac OS X or your data on it, in which case that data is lost.

10. **Select either the FAT (Quick) or NTFS (Quick) format option.** Choose NTFS if you want Windows to be more secure and reliable. Choose FAT if you want to be able to save files to the Windows partition while using Mac OS X.

11. **Double-check to make sure you have the BOOTCAMP partition selected and press the F8 key.** When the format process is complete, the MacBook Pro restarts running Windows instead of Mac OS X. The Windows Setup Wizard runs.

12. **Work through the various screens of the Setup Wizard to configure Windows.** For example, you need to enter the Windows product key, set time and date, name the computer, and configure how you'll connect to the Internet. You can expect this process to take about 30 or 40 minutes. When the process is complete, the Mac restarts again. This time, it starts up in Windows and you see the Windows Setup application.

13. **Follow the on-screen prompts to do some basic configuration, including selecting security settings and creating one or more user accounts.**

14. **When you complete the Setup application, click Finish.** The Windows desktop appears.

15. **Eject the Windows installation disc.**

16. **Insert the Mac OS X installation disc.**

17. **Follow the on-screen instructions to complete the installation of various drivers that Windows needs to work with the MacBook Pro hardware.**

18. **At the prompt, restart your MacBook Pro.** It starts up in Windows.

19. **If you're prompted by New Hardware Wizards, follow the onscreen prompts to work through them.** Most of the time, the default selections work, so just approve all the suggested actions.

20. **To return to the Mac OS, choose Start menu ⇨ Shut Down ⇨ Turn Off Computer (see figure 18.2).**

21. **Click Turn Off.**

22. **Restart the MacBook Pro and hold the Option key down while it starts up.**

23. **Select the Mac OS X startup volume and press the Return key.** The Mac starts up under Mac OS X again.

Running Windows using Boot Camp

Before you get started, it is important to know that running Windows on a MacBook Pro doesn't protect you from virus threats when you are using the Windows environment; it's as susceptible to the same attacks as

18.2 To shut Windows down, use the Turn Off Computer command on the Start menu.

Windows when running on PC hardware. You should install and use security software under Windows as soon as you get your Windows environment running.

Once you installed Windows, you can transform your MacBook Pro into a Windows PC by performing the following steps:

1. **Open the System Preferences application.**

2. **Click the Startup Disk icon.** The Startup Disk pane appears (see figure 18.3).

3. **Select the Windows startup disk.**

4. **Click Restart.**

Genius

As you saw in the previous section, you can choose the startup disk and operating system by holding the Option key down while your MacBook Pro is starting up.

18.3 Use the Startup Disk pane of the System Preferences application to choose a default operating system.

Genius

Right-clicking is a fundamental part of using Windows. To right-click with your MacBook Pro when you are running Windows, hold two fingers on the trackpad and click the trackpad button.

5. **At the prompt, click Restart again.** The Mac restarts and the Windows desktop or Login screen appears.

6. **When you're ready to switch back to the Mac OS, choose Start menu ⇨ Control Panel.**

7. **Click the Switch to Classic View link.** The Control Panel folder is reorganized so that the control panels are shown together in one window instead of being organized by categories.

8. **Double-click the Boot Camp control panel.**

9. **Select the Mac startup volume.**

10. **Click Restart.**

11. **Click OK at the prompt.** Your MacBook Pro starts up under Mac OS X.

Windows Activation

You must activate a copy of Windows to keep it running for more than 30 days. When you do this, the copy of Windows you run is registered to the specific computer on which you activate it as a means to limit illegal copies of Windows. Don't activate your copy of Windows until you've used it for long enough to ensure that you've got it configured the way you want and can run it under Boot Camp, in a virtual environment, or both.

Running Windows Virtually

As you learned earlier, running Windows under a virtual environment has the significant advantage that you can run Windows and the Mac OS at the same time, making it fast and easy to switch between the two environments. The general steps to get Windows running under a virtual environment are as follows:

1. **Purchase, download, and install the virtualization software.**
2. **Configure a virtual environment and install Windows.**
3. **Run Windows in the virtual environment.**

There are several virtualization applications available, but the one that works best for me is Parallels Desktop for Mac. This application is simple to install and configure, and it performs very well. It has a lot of great features, including the ability to easily share data and files between the Mac OS and Windows. You can download and try it before you purchase the application; at press time, it cost about $80 to continue using the application beyond the 15-day trial period. It also has the benefit of being able to use Windows installed under Boot Camp, in which case you don't need to install Windows again, and you retain the option of running Windows under Boot Camp any time you want to. The remainder of this section focuses on using Parallels Desktop for Mac using a Boot Camp installation of Windows; if you choose a different application or install a version of Windows directly under Parallels Desktop for Mac, your details may vary.

Installing Parallels Desktop for Mac

To download and install Parallels Desktop for Mac, perform the following steps:

1. **Move to www.parallels.com.**
2. **Click the Parallels Desktop for Mac link.**
3. **Click the Download Trial link.** You move to the My Account page.

4. **Create a Parallels user account by following the on-screen instructions.**

5. **Download Parallels Desktop for Mac.**

6. **While you're waiting for the download to complete, click the Get trial key link.**

7. **When the download process is complete, move back to the desktop and run the Install Parallels Desktop application (see figure 18.4).**

18.4 The Parallels Desktop for Mac Installer leads you through each step of installing the application.

8. **Follow the on-screen instructions to complete the installation.** When the process is done, you see the completion screen.

9. **Click Close to quit the installer.** You're ready to launch Parallels and configure a virtual environment.

Configuring Parallels Desktop for Mac

The first time you start Parallels, you configure the Windows environment you want to run. Because you've already installed Windows under Boot Camp, all you have to do is select that version of Windows to create a virtual Windows environment. Here's how:

1. **Launch Parallels Desktop (by default, it is installed in the Applications folder).** You're prompted to enter an activation code.

2. **Click Enter Activation Key.** The Enter Activation Key sheet appears.

3. **Enter the activation key and your name, and click Activate.** You see the OS Installation Assistant window. This Assistant leads you through the creation of the virtual environment.

4. **Select Custom.**

5. **Click Next.**

6. **Leave Windows selected on the OS Type pop-up menu.**

7. **Leave Windows XP selected on the OS Version pop-up menu.**

8. **Click Next.**

9. **Choose the amount of RAM you want to allocate to the virtual machine.** In most cases, the default should work. Use the slider to increase or decrease the amount of RAM available to the virtual machine.

10. **Click Next.** You see the Select a virtual hard disk option screen (see figure 18.5).

18.5 Choose Boot Camp to use your Boot Camp installation for the virtual Windows environment.

11. **Select Use Boot Camp.**

12. **Click Next.**

13. **Select Shared Networking.**

14. **Click Next.**

15. **Name your virtual environment.**

16. **Check the Enable file sharing check box.**

17. **Expand the More Options section.**

Note One of the great things about Parallels Desktop is that the Windows environment gets its network settings from the Mac. So if the Mac on which you install Parallels is connected to a network and the Internet, the Windows environment is also connected without any additional configuration by you.

18. **Check the Share virtual machine with other Mac users check box.**

19. **Click Next.**

20. **Select the Virtual machine (recommended).**

21. **Click Next.**

22. **Click Finish.** Windows starts up in the virtual environment.

Caution The first time Windows starts up, you see a warning in the window not to do anything while Parallels completes the configuration. Wait until the warning disappears before you take any action, or your data and configuration might be damaged.

23. **When the warning prompt disappears, log into Windows.** If your Windows environment has only one user account, you log in automatically.

24. **Choose Actions ⇨ Install Parallels Tools.**

25. **Click OK in the prompt.** The installer begins to install Parallels Tools, and you see a warning on the screen. When the process is complete, Windows restarts.

26. **After Windows restarts, turn it off by clicking the Turn Off Computer link.**

27. **At the prompt, click Turn Off; Windows shuts down.** You then see the Parallels Desktop Configuration screen (see figure 18.6).

28. **Quit Parallels Desktop.**

18.6 This screen provides information about, and controls for, your virtual Windows environment.

Running Windows under Parallels Desktop for Mac

After you've installed Parallels Desktop for Mac and configured a virtual environment, running Windows is a snap:

1. **Launch Parallels Desktop.** The application launches and you see information about the virtual machine in the window.

2. **Click the Start button (the green right-pointing arrow).**

3. **If prompted to, enter your Mac OS X username and password and click OK.** Windows starts up in the Parallels window.

4. **Run Windows.**

There isn't much difference between running Windows in a virtual machine and running it on a Windows PC (see figure 18.7).

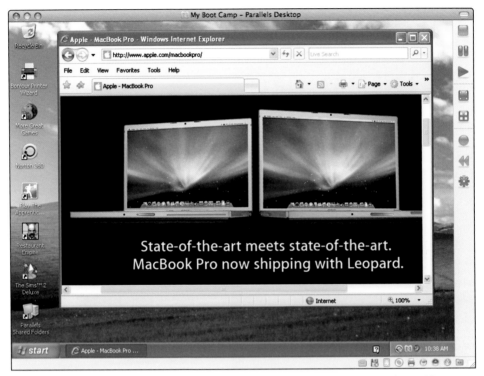

18.7 Running Windows virtually makes it just another application that you can use along with your Mac applications.

How Do I Solve MacBook Pro Problems?

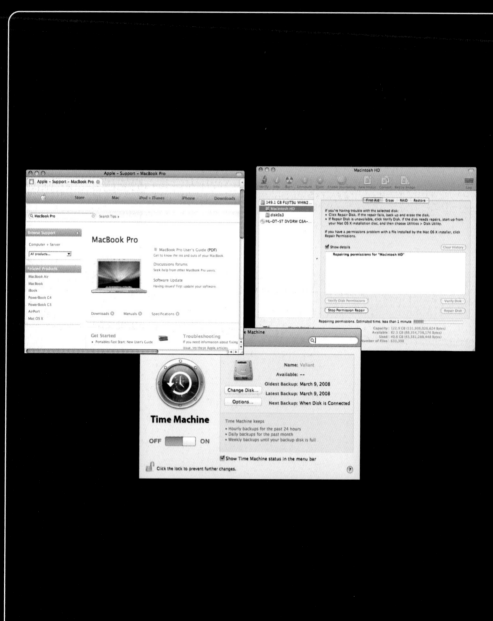

While MacBook Pros are among the most reliable and easiest-to-use computers available, they are still complex systems that involve advanced technology, complex software, and connections to networks, the Internet, and other devices. To put it in analog terms, there are a lot of moving parts. You can expect that every once in a while, something is going to go wrong. With a bit of preparation and some basic troubleshooting, you should be able to recover from most common problems relatively easily.

Looking for Trouble

You should build a MacBook Pro toolkit that you can use to troubleshoot and solve problems. This way, you aren't wasting a lot of time and energy trying to locate or create them when you need them but instead can simply put them into action.

Here are a few of the important tools you should have in your own toolkit in case of an emergency.

- **Current backups.** Backups are a critical part of your toolkit because restoring your data is the most important task that you need to be able to do. Having a good way to restore your data limits the impact of drastic problems (such as your MacBook Pro not working anymore) and makes less significant problems (such as the accidental deletion of a file you need) trivial to solve.

  Once you have an automated backup system that updates your backups frequently and stores them in at least two ways (such as on an external hard disk and on DVD or iDisk), you are protected against loss of your data (see Figure 19.1). Test your backup system periodically by restoring some files to make sure your backed-up data is ready when you need it.

- **Alternate startup disks.** Your MacBook Pro startup disk is all-important because that is where the OS is stored. If your startup disk or the system software it contains has a problem, you might not be able to start up, which reduces your MacBook Pro to being a very cool-looking piece of technology art.

  Your toolkit should include an alternate startup disk that you can use to troubleshoot and solve problems that prevent your MacBook Pro from starting up on its normal startup disk. Several possibilities exist for alternate startup volumes; you should maintain at least one, and preferably two, of the following options:

  - **A Mac OS X installation on an external hard drive.** You should install Mac OS X on an external hard drive so that you can start up your MacBook Pro from that drive when you need to.

  - **Your Mac OS X installation disc.** You can use the software installation/recovery disc that contains the Mac OS X installer as a startup disk. It contains the basic software you need to start up your MacBook Pro and accomplish a limited number of activities. Any updates you have applied to your primary system are not included in the version on the installation disc, so you have to use the version of Mac OS X that was current when the disk was produced.

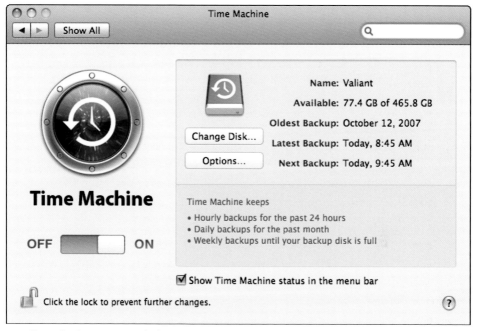

19.1 If your backup system includes Time Machine (which it should), the only data at risk is that which has changed since the last backup, which shouldn't be more than one hour ago.

- **Third-party application discs.** Some third-party applications, such as disk maintenance, antivirus, and backup software, include discs that contain system software that you can use to start up your MacBook Pro.

- **Alternate user accounts.** Because some problems can be related to preferences and other files that are specific to a user account, having an alternate user account is important during the troubleshooting process (see figure 19.2). If you haven't created an alternate test user account, you should do so now before you need it.

- **Mac OS X and application installers.** You can start up from the Mac OS X software disc that was provided with your MacBook Pro. You also need this disc to re-install Mac OS X, so you should keep it in a place where you are able to find it when you need it. If you purchase an application on disc, keep the original discs where you can access them when needed. If you purchase applications by downloading them from the Internet, burn the installer files that you download to a DVD or CD.

○ ○ ○   Accounts

◄ ►   Show All   Q

My Account

🔲 **Brad Miser**
    Admin

▼ Other Accounts

🔲 **Troubleshooting**
    Admin

👤 **Guest Account**
    Sharing only

                         (Reset Password...)

                User Name: | Troubleshooting |

         .Mac User Name: | sorebruiser |

         ☑ Allow user to administer this computer

         ☐ Enable Parental Controls (Open Parental Controls...)

🏠 Login Options

[+ | −]

🔓 Click the lock to prevent further changes.   (?)

19.2 A troubleshooting user account can help you identify a problem that is related to your primary user account.

Caution If you lose a downloaded application because of a hardware or software problem, you might have to purchase it again or even purchase an upgrade again to be able to download it. Store any application installers that you download from the Internet on a DVD or CD so that you can always return to them sometime in the future.

● **System Profiler and Apple Disk Utility.** There are a few more tools that you should consider adding to your arsenal: the System Profiler application (in the Applications ⇨
Utilities folder), which generates a report on your system (see figure 19.3), and the Apple
Disk Utility, a disk maintenance application that is part of the standard Mac OS X installation and is included on the Mac OS X software disc.

```
000              Preview of "Untitled".pdf (page 1 of 291)
 Previous  Next          Zoom        Move  Text  Select              Sidebar

   Hardware:

      Hardware Overview:

         Model Name:            MacBook Pro
         Model Identifier:      MacBookPro3.1
         Processor Name:        Intel Core 2 Duo
         Processor Speed:       2.2 GHz
         Number Of Processors:  1
         Total Number Of Cores: 2
         L2 Cache:              4 MB
         Memory:                2 GB
         Bus Speed:             800 MHz
         Boot ROM Version:      MBP31.0070.B05
         SMC Version:           1.16f10
         Serial Number:         W87510DDXAH
         Sudden Motion Sensor:
            State: Enabled

   Network:

      Ethernet:

         Type:                Ethernet
         Hardware:            Ethernet
         BSD Device Name: en0
         IPv4:
            Configuration Method: DHCP
         IPv6:
            Configuration Method: Automatic
         Proxies:
            Exceptions List:    *.local, 169.254/16
            FTP Passive Mode: Yes
         Ethernet:
            MAC Address:   00:1e:c2:06:44:45
            Media Options:
            Media Subtype: Auto Select

      AirPort:

         Type:                AirPort
         Hardware:            AirPort
         BSD Device Name:     en1
         IPv4 Addresses:      10.0.1.4

 SoftProof          Cancel        Print
```

19.3 A detailed system profile can be useful when you are troubleshooting a problem.

Understanding and Describing Problems

When you start to troubleshoot, the most important thing you can do is to understand a problem in as much detail as possible. This understanding usually enables you to know what you need to do to correct the problem, or at least it gives you ideas of things you can try. As you gain insight into your problem, you should be able to describe it in detail, so you can get help from others if you are not able to solve it yourself.

351

Being able to recognize the symptoms of various kinds of problems helps you to identify what the problem likely is, which, in turn, puts you in a position to try solutions.

Recognizing user errors

Recognizing a problem that you've caused is a bit tough, because user errors can have many consequences. The most common one is software or hardware not doing something as you expect it to; in such cases, a common cause is a failure to do things in the recommended way.

Some common user errors include the following:

- **Not following instructions.**

- **Not doing proper maintenance on your system.** The Mac OS X Software Update feature can help you to automatically keep your operating system and all your Apple applications current.

- **Not keeping enough free space on your hard drives.** If a drive is full, or very close to being full, you might have problems as you try to store more data on it.

Recognizing software problems

Software problems can manifest themselves in a number of ways, but the most common symptoms are hangs, unexpected quits, and unexpected behavior.

Hangs

A hung application is one that has stopped responding to your commands and appears to be locked up. Hangs are usually accompanied by the spinning color wheel icon, which indicates that a lot of processor activity is happening, but the process being attempted isn't moving ahead. Fortunately, because Mac OS X has protected memory, a hung application usually affects only the application itself, and your other applications continue to work normally. You are likely to lose unsaved data in the hung application, but at least your losses are limited to a single application.

Caution When you force an application to quit, you lose any unsaved data with which you are working, and so you shouldn't do it until you're pretty sure the application is actually hung.

The only immediate solution to a hung application is to force it to quit.

Unexpected quits

Sometimes, the application you are using suddenly quits. The windows that were open simply disappear. That's bad enough, but the worst part is that you lose any unsaved data with which you were working, and there's nothing you can do about it.

Likely causes of unexpected quits are software bugs, conflicts between applications, or conflicts between applications and hardware. You should always restart your MacBook Pro after an unexpected quit, and, like a hang, you should check to see if an update to the application is available.

Unexpected behavior

This one's also easy to recognize because an application starts not doing what you are telling it to, or doing things you aren't telling it to. Likely causes of this problem are bugs, or you not using the application as it was intended. Internet attacks or viruses can also be the cause of unexpected behavior. When an application starts acting oddly, quit it and perform a restart of your MacBook Pro. Then check for updates to the application that is misbehaving (see figure 19.4).

19.4 If you have a problem with an Apple application, run the Software Update application; an update might easily and immediately solve the problem.

Describing problems

Being able to accurately describe a problem is one of the most fundamental skills for effective troubleshooting. In order to describe a problem accurately, you must take an in-depth look at the various aspects of the problem, which puts you in a better position to solve it. And, if you need to get help, effectively describing your problem is critical to being able to help someone help you.

Following are some questions you need to answer:

- Which specific applications and processes were running (not only the particular one with which you were working)?
- What specifically were you trying to do (for example, print, save, or format)?
- What specifically happened? Did an application unexpectedly quit or hang? Did you see an error message?
- Have you made any changes to the computer recently (for example, installed software or changed settings)?

Identifying the trigger goes a long way toward identifying the cause.

When a problem occurs, you should recover the best you can and then immediately try to make the problem happen again. Try to recreate everything that was happening when the problem appeared the first time. Have the same applications open and follow your trail the best you can, exactly as you were doing when the problem inserted itself into your life (see figure 19.5).

19.5 You can use the Activity Monitor application to see what processes are running at any point in time, such as when you are trying to recreate a problem.

If you can re-create a problem, it is much easier to describe and it is also more likely that you'll be able to get help with it if you can't solve it on your own.

Fast and Easy Solutions

For each of the solutions described in the following sections, you learn when to think about trying it and the steps you need to follow.

Forcing applications to quit

When to try: An application isn't responding to commands, and the spinning color wheel appears on the screen and remains there (the application is hung).

What it does: The command causes the OS to forcibly stop the application and its processes.

Cautions: You lose any unsaved data in the application that you force to quit.

1. **To activate the command, do one of the following:**

   - Choose Apple menu ⇨ Force Quit.

   - Press ⌘+Option+Power key.

   - Press ⌘+Option+Esc.

   - Ctrl+click the Dock icon of the hung application and select Force Quit.

   The Force Quit Applications dialog appears. In this dialog, you see the applications that are running. An application that is hung appears with red text and the text "(Not Responding)" next to it, so that you can easily identify the hung application.

2. **Select the hung application.**

3. **Click Force Quit.** The warning sheet appears.

4. **Click Force Quit.** The application is forced to quit and closes. Forcing an application to quit leaves it unstable. Restart your MacBook Pro before you continue working to minimize the chances of additional problems.

Forcing the Finder to relaunch

When to try: The Finder isn't responding to commands, and the spinning color wheel appears whenever you try to select or work with something on your desktop, such as a Finder window.

What it does: The command stops the Finder and starts it up again.

Cautions: Relaunching the Finder is a hit-or-miss proposition, so don't be too surprised if it doesn't work.

1. **To activate the command, do one of the following:**

   - Choose Apple menu ➪ Force Quit.

   - Press ⌘+Option+Power key.

   - Press ⌘+Option+Esc.

   - Ctrl+click the Dock icon of the hung application and select Force Quit.

   The Force Quit Applications dialog appears.

2. **Select the Finder.** If the Finder is hung, its name appears in red and the text "Not Responding" appears next to it. If it isn't in red, you don't need to relaunch it.

3. **Click Relaunch.** A warning sheet appears.

4. **Click Relaunch.** Your MacBook Pro attempts to relaunch the Finder. If successful, you are able to work on the desktop again. If not, you'll need to perform the steps in "Shutting down hard," later in this section. Forcing the Finder to relaunch leaves it in an unstable condition. Restart your MacBook Pro before continuing to work.

Restarting

When to try: When your MacBook Pro or an application isn't working the way you expect, or whenever you've forced an application to quit or the Finder to relaunch.

What it does: Shuts down all applications and processes on your MacBook Pro, shuts the MacBook Pro down, and restarts it.

1. **Perform one of the following:**

   - Choose Apple menu ➪ Restart.

   - Press the Power key once and click Restart.

2. **If the Restart dialog appears, click the Restart button (see figure 19.6).** The MacBook Pro shuts down and then restarts, and you can get back to work.

Are you sure you want to restart your computer now?

If you do nothing, the system will restart automatically in 56 seconds.

Cancel   Restart

19.6 Restart your MacBook Pro when applications aren't behaving themselves.

Shutting down soft

When to try: When your MacBook Pro or an application isn't working the way you expect, or whenever you've forced an application to quit or the Finder to relaunch and normal behavior isn't restored with a Restart.

What it does: Shuts down all applications and processes on your MacBook Pro and shuts the MacBook Pro down.

1. **Perform one of the following:**

   - Choose Apple menu ⇨ Shut Down.

   - Press the Power key once and click Shut Down.

   - Press the Power key once and press the Return key.

2. **If the Shut Down dialog appears, click the Shut Down button.** The MacBook Pro shuts down.

Shutting down hard

When to try: When your MacBook Pro appears to be locked up and doesn't respond to any of your commands.

What it does: Shuts down the MacBook Pro, regardless of any running processes.

Cautions: You lose all unsaved data in all open applications.

1. **Press and hold down the Power key until the MacBook Pro screen goes dark.** The MacBook Pro turns off.

2. **Press the Power key again.** Your MacBook Pro starts up.

Logging in under a troubleshooting user account

When to try: When an application isn't performing as you expect, and restarting your MacBook Pro doesn't solve the problem.

What it does: Determines whether the problem is related to your specific user account or is more general.

Cautions: If you remove an application's preferences files, you have to recreate any preferences for the application. Make sure you have important information, such as registration information, backed up elsewhere.

1. Perform one of the following:

- Choose Apple menu ⇨ Log Out *accountname*, where *accountname* is the currently logged-in account.

- Press Shift+⌘+Q.

The Log Out dialog appears, and a 60-second countdown starts (the logout happens automatically when the timer counts down to zero).

2. Click Log Out. The Login window appears.

3. Log into your troubleshooting account.

4. Repeat what you were doing when you experienced the problem. If the problem goes away, it is most likely related to the previous user account, which means, in most cases, that a preferences file has become corrupted.

5. Log out of the troubleshooting account.

6. Log into the previous account.

7. Quit the application that is having a problem.

8. Open the Preferences folder (Home ⇨ Library ⇨ Preferences).

9. Locate the preferences files for the application that has the problem. Preferences files have the extension .plist and include the application's name somewhere in the filename (see figure 19.7). Some preferences files are stored within the company's or application's folder within the Preferences folder.

19.7 Removing a preferences file can sometimes restore an application to normal behavior.

Caution

Deleting a preferences file can remove any personalized information that is stored in it, such as registration information. Make sure you have this information stored in another location before deleting an application's preferences files.

10. **Delete the preferences files for the application.**

11. **Restart the application.**

12. **Reconfigure its preferences.** If the problem doesn't recur, you are good to go. If it does, you'll need to try one of the more drastic steps, such as reinstalling the application.

Repairing external hard drives

When to try: You see error messages relating to a hard drive, or you are unable to store data on it (and the disk isn't full).

What it does: Attempts to verify the disk's structure and repair any data problems.

1. **Quit all applications.**

2. **Launch Disk Utility (Applications ⇨ Utilities).**

3. **Select the disk you want to check or repair.**

4. **Check the bottom of the Disk Utility window for information about the disk you selected.**

5. **Click the First Aid tab to see some information explaining how Disk Utility works.**

6. **Click Repair Disk.** The application checks the selected disk for problems and repairs any it finds. When the process is complete, a report of the results appears.

If Disk Utility is able to repair any problems it found, you're done and the disk should work normally. If the problems can't be fixed, you can try a different disk maintenance application. In some cases, you might need to reformat the drive, which erases all its data.

Repairing the internal hard drive

When to try: You see error messages relating to the internal hard drive, or you are unable to store data on it (and the disk isn't full).

What it does: Attempts to verify the disk's structure and repair any data problems.

1. **Start your MacBook Pro from an alternate startup disk (see "Starting up from an alternate startup external drive on the fly" later in this section).**

2. **Select the MacBook Pro internal hard disk in the Disk Utility application.**

3. **Follow the steps in the previous task to repair the disk.**

Repairing permissions

When to try: When you are getting error messages stating that you don't have permission to do something for which you should have permission.

What it does: Repairs the security permissions associated with the files on a selected disk.

1. **Quit all applications.**

2. **Launch Disk Utility (Applications ⇨ Utilities).**

3. **Select the disk on which you want to repair permissions.**

4. **Click Repair Disk Permissions.** The application starts searching for permission problems and repairing those it finds. When the process is complete, you see the results in the information window on the First Aid tab (see figure 19.8).

19.8 If you see odd security errors, try repairing a disk's permissions.

Reinstalling applications

When to try: An application isn't working correctly, you're sure you are using the current version (all patches and updates have been applied), and you've tried restarting and shutting down soft.

What it does: Restores the application to like-new condition.

Cautions: You lose any updates or patches that were released after the installer you have was produced; you may lose all your preferences for that application, including registration information, so make sure you have that information stored elsewhere.

1. **Delete the application by doing one of the following:**

   - Run the uninstallation application for the application you want to remove if one was provided.

   - Drag the application's files and its preferences files to the Trash; then empty the Trash.

Genius
You can re-install many applications using the receipt that was created when you first installed it. To do this, open the following folder: *startupdisk*/Library/Receipts, where *startupdisk* is the name of your startup disk. To re-install an application, double-click its .pkg file in this folder.

2. **Run the application's installer (see figure 19.9).**

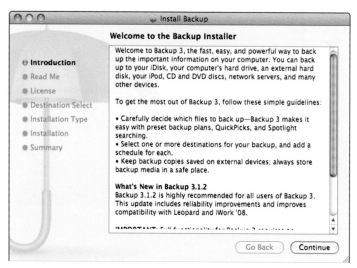

19.9 Re-installing an application can restore it to its proper behavior.

3. **Update the application to its latest version.**

4. **Reset your preferences.** If the application still doesn't work normally, the cause is likely a conflict between the application and the version of Mac OS X you are using or some other part of your system. In most cases, you'll need to get help to figure out exactly what the conflict is.

Starting up from an alternate startup external drive

When to try: When you try to start up your MacBook Pro, the normal startup sequence stops with a flashing folder icon on the screen, or when your MacBook Pro is behaving oddly and you want to isolate the problem to your current startup disk.

What it does: Starts up your MacBook Pro from the software installed on the external disk.

Cautions: You must have created an alternate startup disk (see Chapter 16); you'll use the version of the OS installed on the external disk, which might not be the latest version if you haven't kept it updated.

1. **Connect the external disk to your MacBook Pro.**

2. **Restart your MacBook Pro.**

3. **As it restarts, hold the Option key down.** After a few moments, each valid startup disk appears.

4. **Select the external hard drive from which you want to start up.**

5. **Click the arrow pointing to the disk you selected.** Your MacBook Pro starts up, using the OS installed on the external disk.

6. **Use the MacBook Pro.** If things work as expected, you know the problem is related to the previous startup disk, in which case, you'll have to take more drastic action, such as re-installing Mac OS X on that disk. If the problem recurs, you know that it is related to a specific application, to a hardware device, or to the MacBook Pro itself, in which case the solution is to re-install the application or to get help with the problem.

Starting up from the Mac OS X installation disc

When to try: When you try to start up your MacBook Pro, but the normal startup sequence stops with a flashing folder icon on the screen; when your MacBook Pro is behaving oddly and you want to isolate the problem to your current startup disk; or when you want to re-install Mac OS X.

What it does: Starts up your MacBook Pro from the software installed on the installation disc.

Cautions: Only limited functionality is available, and the version of Mac OS X and its software is the one that was current when the disc was produced.

1. **Insert the Mac OS X installation or System restore disc.**

2. **Restart your MacBook Pro.**

3. **As it restarts, hold down the C key.** The MacBook Pro starts up from the software on the disc.

4. **When you see the language selection screen, select your language.**

5. **Press Return.** You move to the Welcome screen, where you have limited access to the computer, mostly through the Mac OS X Installer menus.

Getting Help with MacBook Pro Problems

We all need a little help once in a while. When it comes to your MacBook Pro, there's a wealth of assistance available to you.

Getting help from the Mac Help system

Mac OS X includes a sophisticated Help system that you can use to find solutions to problems you are experiencing, or to get help with a specific task. In addition to Mac OS X, other applications also use the same Help system. To search for help, follow these steps:

1. **Choose Help.** The Help menu opens.

2. **Enter the term for which you want to search in the Search box.** As you type, matches are shown on the menu. These are organized into two sections (see figure 19.10). In the Menu Items section, you see menu items related to your search. In the Help Topics section, you see links to articles about the topic.

3. **To see where a menu item is located, select it.** The menu opens and the item is highlighted (figure 19.10 shows the Empty Trash menu item being selected).

4. **To read an article, click its link.** The Help window opens, and you see the article in the window (figure 19.10 shows an article about removing files and folders from the Trash in the background).

363

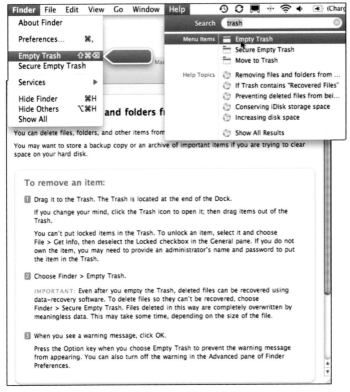

19.10 The Mac OS X Help system is, well, helpful.

Describing a problem in detail

If none of the fast and easy solutions presented earlier result in a problem being solved, you may have to create a more detailed description so that when you ask for help, you increase the odds that someone will be able to help you. In this section, you learn about some tools that can help you increase the level of details in your problem descriptions.

Profiling a MacBook Pro

You can use the System Profiler application to capture all the details about your system so that they are available to you when you need them, such as when you need to get help.

To create a profile for your MacBook Pro, perform the following steps:

1. **Choose Apple menu ⇨ About This Mac.** The About This Mac window appears.

2. **Click More Info.** The System Profiler application appears. In the left pane, you see various categories of information about your MacBook Pro, such as hardware components, network information, and software information.

3. **Select an area about which you want detailed information.** The details appear in the right pane of the window.

4. **When you see information you need, choose File ⇨ Print.** System Profiler builds a printable version of the profile.

Genius

The full profile is very long, sometimes 300 pages or so. You can create smaller versions of the profile to print by choosing View ⇨ Mini Profile, or View ⇨ Basic Profile.

5. **When the Print dialog appears, click PDF to open the PDF menu.**

6. **Choose Save as PDF.**

7. **Name the profile.**

8. **Choose a save location.**

9. **Click Save.** The profile is saved with the name and at the location you selected.

Monitoring MacBook Pro activity

When a problem occurs, the Mac OS doesn't provide a lot of feedback directly. However, you can use the Activity Monitor application to get a closer look at what's happening in the background. Here's how:

1. **Open Activity Monitor (Utilities folder within the Applications folder).**

2. **Click the CPU tab.** In the upper part of the window, you see a list of all the processes running on the MacBook Pro. For each process, you see a variety of information, such as how many CPU resources it is using and the amount of memory. At the bottom of the window, you see a graphical representation of the current thread and process activity in the processor (see figure 19.11).

3. **Click the CPU column heading to sort the list of processes by the amount of processor activity.** When a process is consuming a large amount of CPU resources or a lot of disk activity over a long period of time, it can indicate that the process is having a problem or is the cause of problems you are experiencing.

4. **On the pop-up menu at the top of the window, select Windowed Processes.** The list is reduced so that it includes only processes associated with applications.

5. **Use the other tabs at the bottom of the window to explore other areas of the system.** You can use the Disk Usage tab to assess how much free space your disks have. You can use the System Memory tab to assess the status of your MacBook Pro RAM and its virtual memory.

PID	Process Name	User	CPU	Thr	RSIZE	VSIZE	Kind
477	Activity Monitor	bradm	3.1	5	12.89 MB	846.18 MB	Intel
486	Address Book	bradm	0.0	7	9.83 MB	803.23 MB	Intel
179	AppleVNCServer	bradm	0.0	2	2.17 MB	721.66 MB	Intel
186	ATSServer	bradm	1.8	2	4.80 MB	650.57 MB	Intel
183	Dock	bradm	0.0	3	12.25 MB	781.36 MB	Intel
185	Finder	bradm	0.4	13	26.97 MB	853.97 MB	Intel
484	Firefox	bradm	15.8	11	27.93 MB	837.14 MB	Intel
253	helpdatad	bradm	0.0	2	17.42 MB	612.48 MB	Intel
194	iTunes Helper	bradm	0.0	2	2.42 MB	730.95 MB	Intel
84	launchd	bradm	0.0	3	532.00 KB	585.73 MB	Intel
161	loginwindow	bradm	2.1	3	7.01 MB	800.23 MB	Intel
476	mdworker	bradm	2.1	4	2.32 MB	598.99 MB	Intel
195	Microsoft AU Dae...	bradm	0.0	2	9.76 MB	796.12 MB	PowerPC
187	pboard	bradm	0.0	1	584.00 KB	586.63 MB	Intel
488	PubSubAgent	bradm	1.2	2	2.84 MB	587.62 MB	Intel
485	Safari	bradm	1.5	5	25.84 MB	815.78 MB	Intel

CPU | System Memory | Disk Activity | Disk Usage | Network

% User: 6.96
% System: 5.47
% Nice: 0.00
% Idle: 87.57

Threads: 253
Processes: 62

CPU Usage

19.11 If CPU activity is maxed out for a long period of time, then a process is hung and you'll probably need to restart your MacBook Pro.

Capturing screenshots

When you experience a problem, being able to capture a screenshot is a great way to describe and document the problem. There are two built-in ways to capture a screenshot in Mac OS X. You can use keyboard shortcuts or the Grab application. To use a keyboard shortcut to capture the screen, perform the following steps:

1. **When something appears on the screen that you want to capture and you want to capture the entire screen, press ⌘+Shift+3.** An image file is created on the desktop and you can skip to step 4.

2. **When something appears on the screen that you want to capture and you want to capture part of the screen, press ⌘+Shift+4.**

3. **Drag over the area of the screen you want to capture; release the trackpad button when the area you want to capture is highlighted.** An image file is created on the desktop.

4. **Open the image file you created.** It is named Picture *X*, where *X* is a sequential number. The file opens in Preview and is ready for you to use for your own purposes, or to provide to someone else when you ask for help.

Mac OS X includes the Grab application, which enables you to capture screenshots in a slightly more sophisticated manner. Here's how:

1. **Launch the Grab application by double-clicking its icon in the Utilities folder within the Applications folder.** The application opens, but you don't see any windows until you capture a screenshot. You do see the Grab menu.

2. **Choose Capture ➪ Timed Screen.** The Timed Screen Grab dialog appears.

Genius

In addition to the Timed Screen option on the Capture menu in Grab, you can use Selection to capture part of the desktop that you select by drawing a box around it; Window to capture the active window; or Screen to capture the entire desktop.

3. **Click Start Timer (see figure 19.12).** Grab's timer starts. After ten seconds, the capture is taken.

4. **Save the image file.** The screen capture is ready for you to use for your own purposes, or to provide to someone else when you ask for help.

19.12 Using the Timed Screen option lets you configure the screen as you want it captured.

Getting help from others

After you've tried the fast and easy solutions and the various Help systems on your MacBook Pro, your next stop should be the Internet. Here are some places to try:

- **www.apple.com/support.** The Apple support pages are a great source of information, and you can also download updates to system and other software. Check out the Tech Info Library, which can search for specific problems. You can also read manuals and have discussions about problems in the forums that are available here. If the problem you are having seems to be related to the OS, Apple hardware, or an Apple application, this should be your first stop.

- **www.macfixit.com.** This is a good source of information related to solving Mac problems, because you can get help on just about every aspect of using a Mac. Most of the information comes from Mac users, and you can ask specific questions, although the answer to your question is probably already available.

- **www.macintouch.com.** This site offers a lot of news that can help you solve problems, especially if those problems are solved by a software update of which you might be unaware.

- **www.versiontracker.com.** You can quickly find out whether updates have been released for applications with which you are having trouble.

Note

If you do ask for help without doing the basics yourself, you might get the response RTFM. The "R" stands for "Read." The "T" stands for "The." The "M" is for "Manual. I won't describe what the "F" stands for, but you can probably guess. If a quick search on the Apple Web site would find the help you need and it's clear you didn't even bother to do it, an RTFM might be in your near future.

Genius

You can e-mail me at bradmacosx@mac.com to ask for help, and I will do my best to provide a solution for you, or at least point you to a more helpful source if I can't help you directly.

Trying Harder or More Expensive Solutions

Hopefully, you'll never need to do any of the tasks described in this section, because they apply only when you have a significant problem. And they either take a lot of time and effort or can be expensive. Still, you have to do what you have to do.

Reinstalling Mac OS X

If you discover that your system has major problems, such as when your internal drive is no longer recognized as a valid startup drive, you might need to reinstall Mac OS X. Because it takes a while, and you might lose some of the installation and configuration you've done, you shouldn't do this lightly. If you determine that you do need to reinstall Mac OS X, here's how to go about it:

1. **Back up your data.**

2. **Make sure your data is backed up.**

3. **Start up from the Mac OS X Installation disc.** After you've selected a language, you see the Welcome screen.

4. **Click Continue.**

5. **Agree to the license.** You move to the Select a Destination screen. In most cases, the version of the OS you have installed is newer than the one on the disc, and so you have to configure the installation option you want to use.

6. **Select your internal hard drive.**

7. **Click Options.**

8. **Click the Archive and Install radio button.**

9. **Check the Preserve Users and Network Settings check box.** This preserves the settings of your user accounts and applications.

10. **Click OK.**

11. **Click Continue.**

12. **Follow the on-screen instructions to complete the installation.** When the process is complete, your MacBook Pro restarts.

13. **Update your software (see Chapter 17).**

14. **Reinstall any applications that don't work correctly.** Mostly, these are applications that install software into the system; these need to be re-installed because the software they installed was removed when Mac OS X was re-installed.

Hopefully, your MacBook Pro has returned to prime condition and is working like you expect. If so, the last thing to do is to remove the archived system to free up disk space. Do this by moving to the Finder and selecting the startup disk on the Sidebar. Delete the Previous Systems folder. This removes the previous version of your system software.

Melting and repouring

Sometimes, things get so bad that you just need to start over; this is commonly called a melt-and-repour. This goes even farther than simply re-installing Mac OS X because you erase the internal hard drive, which means that all the data on it is deleted, including the system and all the files stored on it. This is drastic action, and should be taken only if you really need to do it. Also expect the initial process to take a long time.

1. **Back up your data.**

2. **Start up from the Mac OS X Installation disc.** After you've selected a language, you see the Welcome screen.

3. **Click Continue.**

4. **Agree to the license.** You move to the Select a Destination screen.

5. **Select your internal hard drive.**

6. **Click Options.**

7. **Click the Erase and Install radio button.**

8. **Click OK.**

9. **Click Continue.**

10. **Follow the on-screen instructions to complete the installation.** When the process is complete, your MacBook Pro restarts. When it does, your MacBook Pro is in the same condition as when you first took it out of its box and turned it on.

11. **Follow the on-screen instructions to perform the initial configuration. Again, this is just like the first time you started your MacBook Pro.**

12. **Create the user accounts you need (see Chapter 2).**

Genius

If you use Time Machine for your backups, you can restore your data into the appropriate user accounts.

13. **Update your software (see Chapter 17).**

14. **Re-install your applications.** The iLife applications should have been installed through the Mac OS X installer, but you'll have to manually install all your third-party applications.

15. **Restore your data from your backups.** Your MacBook Pro should be back to its old self, but without the problems you were having.

Professional Repairs by Apple

If your MacBook Pro has hardware problems, you'll probably need to have it repaired by Apple or by a third-party service center. You can do this by taking it to a local Apple Store or using the Web site to arrange technical support. To get started with the Web approach, do the following:

1. Move to www.apple.com/support.

2. Search for "repair."

3. Click the Online Service Assistant link. You move to the Online Service Assistant Web page.

4. Enter you MacBook Pro serial number. This number is on the MacBook Pro case and in your profile document. You can also get your serial number by opening the About This Mac window and clicking the Mac OS X version information twice.

5. Select your country and click Continue. On the resulting screen, you see warranty information about your MacBook Pro, along with links to various resources you can use to have Apple repair it for you.

Index